S0-BWW-735

UNIVERSITY OF ILLINOIS STUDIES IN THE SOCIAL SCIENCES

Vol. XVII MARCH–JUNE, 1929 Nos. 1–2

BOARD OF EDITORS

ERNEST L. BOGART
JOHN A. FAIRLIE
ALBERT H. LYBYER

PUBLISHED BY THE UNIVERSITY OF ILLINOIS
UNDER THE AUSPICES OF THE GRADUATE SCHOOL
URBANA, ILLINOIS

series:
Illinois. University.
Illinois studies in the social sciences.

ANGLO-CHINESE RELATIONS DURING THE SEVENTEENTH AND EIGHTEENTH CENTURIES

By

EARL H. PRITCHARD

PUBLISHED BY THE UNIVERSITY OF ILLINOIS
URBANA

H
31
.I4
v. 17
no. 1-2

600 9 30 9027

UNIVERSITY
OF ILLINOIS
PRESS

Library
UNIVERSITY OF MIAMI

12/1/70 JRR

PREFACE

The historian, in his careful account of important events and developments in world affairs, has touched very lightly upon the origin and early centuries of Anglo-Chinese relations. A. J. Sargent in his admirable study, *Anglo-Chinese Commerce and Diplomacy*, dismisses the first century and a half of relations between the English East India Company and China in two short chapters. H. B. Morse devotes but two chapters of his well known three volumes, *The International Relations of the Chinese Empire*, to facts which, at the time of its writing, were considered the essentials of early Anglo-Chinese relations. Most other books dealing with the subject cover the formative centuries in two or three pages. *The English in China* (1600-1843) by J. B. Eames, the one book which proposes to treat solely and completely the relations between the trader-diplomats of the East India Company and the Chinese, devotes the greater part of its content to tracing diplomatic disputes which occurred during the last ten years of the period. The earlier chapters are devoted to a survey of the causes of English interest in China, and to a very hurried treatment of the most spectacular political and diplomatic events. They neglect almost entirely analysis of the commercial intercourse which lay at the basis of the whole relationship, and devote too little space to the story of the growth and evolution of commercial and diplomatic institutions, practices, and attitudes which later became of the utmost importance in the misunderstanding between foreign nations and China.

Such inadequate treatment of exceedingly important early relations between Englishmen and Chinese is much to be regretted. Another factor makes the present study even more advisable. Until the last few years the records of the East India Company's factory in China have remained little used in the files of the India Office. Recently, however, has appeared H. B. Morse's five volume *Chronicles of the East India Company Trading to China*. These volumes, in the main, are documentary material of a statistical and diplomatic nature gathered from a careful examination of the collections in the India Office. They reveal many facts heretofore inaccessible to most students, which justify a revision of some earlier conclusions and make worth while a more complete study and interpretation of Anglo-Chinese relations prior to the nineteenth century. The present account attempts to remedy the inadequacy above pointed out, and looks forward ultimately to a comprehensive study of Anglo-Chinese relations from the cultural as well as the economic and political viewpoint.

With great pleasure I express my gratitude to all the kind and thoughtful people who have helped in the preparation of this work. With especial satisfaction I record my sincere appreciation for the helpful advice and aid given me by Professor Lybyer of the University of Illinois and Professor Treat of Stanford University. Valuable suggestions have also been given by Professors Bossenbrook and Deutsch of Washington State College, both of whom have carefully examined parts of the manuscript. Miss Naomi Walker and Miss Nita Fitschen of Washington State College, and Mr. Robert W. Green of Oriel College, Oxford, have given me especially valuable aid in revising the manuscript and reading the proofs.

Pullman, Washington **E. H. P.**
March 27, 1930

TABLE OF CONTENTS

LIST OF FIGURES

LIST OF TABLES

CHAPTER I

INTRODUCTION

The "Opium War," it is generally said, marked the beginning of official relations between China and Western powers. Strictly speaking this is true if the word "official" be used to designate only recognized relations between equal states. From a practical point of view nothing could be farther from the truth. Almost everyone is dimly acquainted with the fact that for nearly two centuries before the Opium War foreigners had traded with the Chinese at Canton. Few people, however, understand the character and organization of this early intercourse, and realize that in its development certain movements were started which made inevitable the first war between the East and the West.[1]

Between the years 1839 and 1842 England, the most important nation trading with China, waged a war to free British and foreign trade from the shackles of a very unprogressive commercial system, and to force the very arrogant and aloof Chinese government to recognize England upon a parity with itself.[2]

Several questions at once present themselves. Why should England at this time take it upon herself to force a modification of the existing relationships with China? How did the peculiarly unsatisfactory commercial and diplomatic system originate, and what were its main characteristics? Finally, why did the Chinese government adopt an attitude of exclusive superiority toward foreign powers?

In answer to the first question it may be said that for some time the British government had been displeased with

[1]For a good short discussion of the character of this early intercourse see H. B. Morse, *International Relations of the Chinese Empire* (New York, 1910), v. 1, chaps. 2-4, pp. 40-118. Also, Payson J. Treat, *The Far East* (New York, 1928), chaps. 5, 6, pp. 45-69.

[2]For an account of this war, its causes, and its results, see Morse, *op. cit.*, chaps. 6-11, pp. 118-318; Treat, *op. cit.*, chap. 7, pp. 69-82; Edward T. Williams, *A Short History of China* (New York, 1928), chap. 10, pp. 251-78; and David E. Owen, *Imperialism and Nationalism in the Far East* (New York, 1929), pp. 23-38. For treaties following the war see Godfrey E. P. Hertslet, *China Treaties* (London, 1908), v. 1, pp. 7-12.

the confining of all trade between China and England to the single port of Canton under severe and humiliating regulations.[3] The events, however, which brought the trouble to a crisis were the abolition of the East India Company's monopoly of English trade with China,[4] and the seizure and destruction of a large quantity of British owned opium by the Chinese.[5] The termination of the East India Company's monopoly made it necessary for the British government to send official representatives to oversee the Canton trade.[6] When these dignitaries were disregarded and buffeted about by the Chinese, as had been their commercial predecessors, Great Britain felt its honor impaired. Relations between the two countries were steadily approaching a crisis over this question of equality when the British opium was seized and destroyed.[7] Injury had now been added to insult so far as England was concerned, while China felt much the same. A clash of arms was the only possible result.

After considering the above, there still remain two unanswered questions relative to the character of the Canton System and the cause of the Chinese attitude of superiority, and at the same time two new ones arise, namely, how did it happen that all relations between England and China were so long confined to the monopolistic East India Company, and why did the opium trade exist?

An answer to these four questions will lay the groundwork for an understanding of the real causes of the Opium War, and disclose the basis of a large part of the difficulties which have

[3]Trade was confined to Canton in 1757 under rather severe regulations which tended to increase in troublesomeness as time progressed. For a discussion of this subject by a man who was an actual participant in some of the events with which he deals see John F. Davis, *China* (London, 1857), v. 1, pp. 48-49 ff. See also Peter Auber, *China* (London, 1834), pp. 170-71 ff.

[4]The East India Company had possessed a monopoly of the English trade to China since 1600. See *Charters Granted to the East India Company* (London, 1774), pp. 4-26. For statute abolishing the Company's monopoly of the China trade see 3 and 4 William 4, cap. 85, sec. 3, and 3 and 4 William 4, cap. 93.

[5]For a discussion of the opium problem see Morse, *op. cit.*, chaps. 8-9, pp. 171-255; Harold M. Vinacke, *A History of the Far East in Modern Times* (New York, 1928), pp. 33-41; and Tyler Dennett, *Americans in Eastern Asia* (New York, 1922), pp. 115-28.

[6]*British and Foreign State Papers*, v. 22, pp. 1228, 1232.

[7]The note of Lord Palmerston to the Minister of the Emperor of China, Feb. 20, 1840 in Morse, *op. cit.*, p. 621, sums up the British official view upon the whole problem.

arisen between foreigners and Chinese since that time. A complete answer requires that we go back some two centuries to the beginning of English trade with the Far East, and trace historically from that time the various threads of development which led to the first war between Orient and Occident. To do this one must deal with such problems as the origin of the East India Company and of British trade to the East, the beginning of Anglo-Chinese trade, the development of anti-foreign attitudes in China, the growth of commercial and diplomatic institutions and practices which made up the Canton System, and finally the expansion of commerce and its effect upon the Canton System. In these things we find a basis for the whole misunderstanding between China and the West during the first half of the 19th century, and only through a realization of this can the later events be estimated adequately.

Before attacking the general problem of the origin of British trade to the Far East it seems advisable to devote some space to an analysis of those elements of Chinese culture which tended to complicate relations between Orientals and Occidentals. A thorough knowledge of these cultural differences will aid materially in understanding why there arose many of the difficulties which are to be discussed in the following pages.

CHAPTER II

FEATURES OF CHINESE CULTURE WHICH HAVE COMPLICATED RELATIONS WITH THE WEST

1. *The Problem of the Relationship with China is Primarily One of Cultural Contacts and Conflicts*

Oswald Spengler would probably say that it is useless for a person belonging to one culture or *kultur* to attempt to discuss elements of another. If, however, the modern student, surrounded by all the available historical materials, is still unable to understand a foreign culture, how much more so were our English ancestors of four centuries ago when they first came into contact with the strange land of Cathay.

As one reviews the story of foreign intercourse with China, and especially that of England, one becomes impressed with the fact that the primary difficulty between the two peoples has been a cultural one. It is true that the specific points of conflict have been first over trade; next over the treatment of foreigners, especially the official representatives of other nations; and finally over religious doctrines. But what are all of these things if not certain aspects of culture? Trade disputes arose because the Chinese had different trade conceptions and usages from those practiced by the West. These problems were enhanced by difficulties over the treatment of foreigners—diplomatic officials in particular. Here again the trouble developed because China had a code of treatment for foreigners different from that practiced in Western Europe. What was it but a difference in culture, if the Chinese officials considered themselves superior to the Westerners, and elected to close the doors of the "Celestial Empire" to the cannon-shooting, meddling European rather than go to war with him as a Western nation would have done? If the missionary were persecuted and driven out it was because he preached a doctrine contrary to the sacred maxims of the Chinese and especially objectionable to the literati, the natural defenders of Oriental culture. If the Westerners objected to Chinese judicial methods it was not because they were treated unjustly, according to Chinese maxims, but rather because the two groups had different standards of justice. So one might go on displaying further evidence to show that the trouble between China and the West did not originate because China deliberately decided to maltreat the foreigners, but because the two peoples had a different standard of conduct, because the two peoples reacted differently to the same situation, and because each was equally unable to see the other's viewpoint.[1] All of the contact was not conflict, of course, but where conflict arose it was traceable in its last analysis to the fundamental and age-old problem of the impact of culture upon culture. The aim of this chapter is to point out some of the most obvious features of Chinese civilization which in their very nature or through their operation conflicted with the West. Had these differences not existed the problem would have taken some other turn—the conflict would have been of another character.

2. *Difference in Attitude and Viewpoint*

The backward and passive character of Chinese culture in contrast with the more active and aggressive Western culture is the first feature to be noted. Generally speaking the Chinese, especially if of the official class, were opposed to change, satisfied with things as they were, and desirous of sliding quietly along with the least amount of effort. The officials, chosen from among the literati and admiring the classics as their ideal, served as a guide to the rest of the Chinese.[2] Injustice in the courts was even encouraged in order to keep their dockets clear and so to help preserve the tranquil immobility.[3]

[1]No better illustration of this fundamental cultural difference, which makes two groups unable to understand each other, could be furnished than is found in Sherard Osborn's *Past and Future of British Relations with China* (Edinburgh, 1860). Mr. Osborn spends the first eleven pages of his book expatiating on the characteristics of Chinese reasoning which always makes them answer, "Me no thinke so" to the conclusions of the European. He never once considers that his own actions seem just as absurd to the Chinese as the latter's appear to him. It is this ever present condition which makes the man of one culture unable to understand the man of another unless one is willing to give up his preconceptions. A good discussion of this matter is to be found in James Bromley Eames, *The English in China* (London, 1909), pp. 103-05.

[2]S. Wells Williams, *The Middle Kingdom* (New York, 1883), v. 1, pp. 381-84; James W. Bashford, *China, an Interpretation* (New York, 1919), p. 306; Treat, *op. cit.*, pp. 27-28.

[3]Frank J. Goodnow, *China, an Analysis* (Baltimore, 1926), pp. 87-90. To avoid the use of an excessive number of footnotes, authors once cited will

Against this passive and slow moving culture came the more dynamic and active spirit of the West. The persons who led the movement to China were ambitious, grasping adventurers and business men, and they clashed with Chinese conservatism. They overstepped barriers and trampled on sacred traditions and customs. All of this created trouble and caused the Chinese to look with dislike upon the foreigner. In concluding these remarks, nothing is more appropriate than a quotation from King-Hall, which although applying to a later period is apropos in a considerable degree to the period under discussion.

Deep down at the bottom of this thing is the impact of West on East; the dynamic thrust of Western philosophy, with its insistence on forward movement, its harnessed science, its active spirit, impinging upon the self-satisfied contemplative calm of the East.[4]

The exalted position of the classical scholar also contributed to the difficulties with the West. In the ancient social classification he ranked first, and because of the respect rendered him he served as guide and model for the masses.[5] We have previously noted how he contributed to conservatism and backwardness. His narrow classical training made him totally unfit to meet the administrative problems which grew out of contact with the West.[6] Further, his training in the classics and Confucian doctrine caused him to venerate the ancient Chinese system and to resist encroachment by Western missionaries upon ancestor worship and other traditional doctrines.[7]

The submissiveness of the Chinese to higher authority was another feature which complicated relations with the West. Until recently at least, it would seem that the Chinese as a people were indifferent to the ruling power so long as comparative order and prosperity were preserved. During the last six hundred and fifty years the Chinese have twice been governed by alien dynasties whose régimes comprised some three hundred and fifty-five years, while the north of China has been under

not again be referred to except for special information. It should be understood, however, that all authorities mentioned in this chapter have been studied and their information and viewpoint carefully considered.

[4]Stephen King-Hall, *Western Civilization and the Far East* (London, 1925), p. 314.

[5]H. H. Gowen and J. W. Hall, *An Outline History of China* (New York, 1929), p. 58.

[6]See Bashford, *op. cit.*, pp. 103-109.

[7]Chong Su See, *Foreign Trade of China* (New York, 1919), pp. 105-06; Treat, *op. cit.*, pp. 24-31.

foreign rulers even longer.[8] The masses were content to plod along, submitting quietly to any ruler until conditions became unbearable, and then to rise with the cry, "They have exhausted the mandate of heaven," and drive them from power.[9] Not only was this general indifference to government evident in the attitude toward the central power, but it applied to local government as well. The Chinese generally submitted quietly to all forms of local exaction and oppression, and tried to avoid, as much as possible, relations with the imperial officials.[10] Under such a system the mandarin practiced his extortion and domination at will, each act of submission on the part of the people increasing his arrogance and conceit. However, when he tried the same tactics on the haughty and independent Europeans serious conflict arose.

Business was regarded as subordinate to most other occupations in China, and the merchant ranked near the bottom of the social scale.[11] The Manchus were "disposed to view trading emigrants in the light of pirates and traitors."[12] The government

> consider[ed] agriculture the only source of permanent riches, and trade often hostile to the pursuit of such a laborious profession, [consequently] various laws [were] issued to check its growth . . . The supreme government pretended to look upon all trade with utter contempt, and hence never burdened it with heavy duties, leaving its minions to oppress it by exactions, fees and grinding.[13]
>
> From the very first the trader seemed to have taken rank with our conventional usurer, and to have been regarded as a small-minded person whose main object in life was, not to increase the public wealth, but to corner supplies; nor does the abstract idea of more legitimate trade appear ever to have been conceived in the sense of 'mutual exchange for the fur-

8Morse, *International Relations*, v. 1, p. 2; Treat, *op. cit.*, p. 20.

9Stanley K. Hornbeck, *Contemporary Politics in the Far East* (New York, 1916), pp. 1-5; Pao Chao Hsieh, *The Government of China (1644-1911)* (Baltimore, 1925), pp. 5-11.

10E. H. Parker, *China, her History, Diplomacy, and Commerce* (London, 1917), pp. 207-09; Alexis Krausse, *China in Decay* (London, 1900, 3d ed.), pp. 57-69; Bashford, *op. cit.*, pp. 276-82. No better example of this submission to gross extortion is to be found than in the story of the relations between the Hong Merchants and the official. This will be dealt with in more detail in chap. 7, sec. 2 and chap. 8, sec. 3.

11Williams, *Middle Kingdom*, v. 1, p. 411. This same idea was very forcefully expressed by Dr. T. T. Lew, in a lecture delivered at Washington State College in the fall of 1927.

12Parker, *China History*, p. 37.

13R. Montgomery Martin, *China, Political, Commercial and Social* (London, 1847), v. 2, p. 103.

therance of comfort and luxury,' but rather in that of 'steps to keep the needy from starving, and the armies supplied with food and weapons.' With this attitude toward business, it is easy to understand why foreign traders were looked down upon and oppressed by both the local officials and the central government. The ancient adage of the *Book of History*, "Do not overvalue strange commodities, and then foreigners will be only too glad to bring them,"[14] was followed in every way.

Custom was the greatest binding force in China. The Empire was literally held together by habit and practice, and convention served as the greatest limitation upon the Emperor and his officials.[15] The force of age-old practice made change difficult, and caused an unfavorable reaction to foreigners who by their very presence tended to upset the existing system. The scant courtesy shown foreigners was but a grudging modification of existing procedure, while each new imposition upon the traders became a custom tenaciously upheld by the native officials. Precedent could be found for everything which the Chinese did, and no toleration was granted the newcomer who wanted to change it.[16]

The doctrine of mutual responsibility which pervaded the whole Chinese system was perhaps the most potent source of trouble between the foreigners and the natives. In its final analysis this doctrine held each Chinese responsible for occurrences near him or in any way related to him. "In every situation under the government, both of a public and of a private nature, the master of a family [was] responsible for the inmates of that family, the father [for] his children, the magistrate [for] the inhabitants of his district,"[17] the governor for his province and

[14]Parker, *China History*, p. 42, for the last two quotations.

[15]T. R. Jernigan, *China in Law and Commerce* (New York, 1905), p. 33; Charles Gutzlaff, *A Sketch of Chinese History* (London, 1834), v. 1, pp. 47-50; Morse, *International Relations*, v. 1, p. 5; Bashford, *op. cit.*, pp. 293-97.

[16]The finest example of this appeal to precedent is in the Emperor's letter to the King of England in reply to the demands of Lord Macartney; in H. B. Morse, *Chronicles of the East India Company Trading to China* (Cambridge, 1926), v. 2, p. 251. "To Conclude, as the Requests made by your Ambassador militate against the Laws and Usages of Our Empire . . . I cannot acquiesce in them."

[17]G. T. Staunton, *Miscellaneous Notices Relating to China* (London, 1850), v. 2, p. 169. This statement was made by the author, who was a supercargo at Canton for many years, before an examining committee of the House of Lords. He was the son of George Staunton, secretary to the Macartney Mission.

the Emperor to heaven for his empire. More than this the farmer was responsible for his neighbor, and the merchant for his fellow merchants.[18] Everywhere this system of personal responsibility for actions of relatives and neighbors, and for conditions or events within areas under one's control was followed. It culminated in the cruel practice of holding responsible all male relatives of a person convicted of treason.[19] This onerous doctrine held the Hong Merchants and linguists at Canton liable for the actions of foreigners, it also held the Company's supercargoes responsible for all Englishmen, and caused officials to demand a life for a life whenever a Chinese was killed as a result of contact with the Westerners.[20]

The "code of face" was very much like "polite lying" in Western Europe, multiplied tenfold and made a recognized practice by society. Writers generally agree that an Oriental would do anything to preserve his good outward appearance; in other words, to save his face. This "code of face" tended to make bribery common, and to make lying on the part of officials and merchants prevalent. It encouraged administrators to issue preposterous edicts and threats of impending punishment when trouble arose until some means could be devised to save face.[21] Such conduct was not well understood by the European and was a source of vexation to him.

The Chinese possessed a highly developed idea of their own superiority. This was especially true of the officials who were chosen from among the literati, and who considered the civilization of the "Middle Kingdom" to be the last word in perfection.[22]

[18] Williams, *Middle Kingdom*, v. 1, pp. 436-38; Morse, *International Relations*, v. 1, pp. 114-15; Jernigan, *op. cit.*, pp. 75-76.

[19] M. Huc, *The Chinese Empire* (London, 1855), v. 2, pp. 258-60. Quoted from the first chapter of the second volume of the Penal Code. All persons who shall have been convicted of treason "or of having intended to commit it, shall suffer death by a slow painful method, whether they be principals or accessories. All male relatives in the first degree of the person convicted of the above mentioned crimes—the father, grandfather, and paternal uncles, as well as their sons, grandsons, and sons of their uncles, without any regard being had to their place of abode, or to any natural or accidental infirmities, shall be indiscriminately beheaded."

[20] Williams, *Middle Kingdom*, v. 1, pp. 481-82; Morse, *International Relations*, v. 1, pp. 115-16.

[21] Rodney Gilbert, *What's Wrong in China* (New York, 1926), pp. 168-200. This is a complete but prejudiced discussion. See also Williams, *Middle Kingdom*, v. 1, pp. 834-36; Parker, *China History*, pp. 275-81.

[22] *Cambridge Modern History*, v. 11, p. 803; Treat, *op. cit.*, p. 28.

This egocentric attitude rose largely out of the system of education, China's domination of the Eastern world, and her great isolation.[23] This conceit and superiority was best displayed in the titles which the Chinese attached to themselves,[24] the relations between the East India Company's supercargoes and the officials, and in the various edicts. The following excerpt from a letter sent by the Emperor to the ruler of Persia in 1412 fairly reeks with vanity: "As we consider that the most high God has created all things in heaven and earth, to the end that all his creatures may be happy, and that it is in consequence of his sovereign decree, that we are become lord of the face of the earth."[25] This exalted notion bred contempt and jealousy, and caused considerable trouble when it came into conflict with the equally egotistical and self-important attitude of the European. Peculiarly self-satisfied was the Manchu official, representing the conquering and domineering element in China.[26]

Jealousy, distrust, and exclusiveness are given by a score of writers as characteristics of 17th and 18th century Chinese.[27] An examination of the facts, however, shows that this is not entirely true. It seems rather that the attitude of superiority encouraged the above tendencies, and as conflict with the Westerners developed these natural predispositions obtained the upper hand. During the late 18th, and the 19th century these characteristics certainly were revealed in an ever increasing measure and complicated severely relations between Europe and China.

The bad conduct of the early Westerners served to accentuate many of the differences afore mentioned. When the Portugese and Dutch proceeded to seize junks, maltreat the natives, and act in a buccaneering fashion,[28] the Chinese scholar-admin-

[23]Charles F. Remer, *The Foreign Trade of China* (Shanghai, 1926), pp. 2-3; Kenneth Scott Latourette, *History of the Early Relations between the United States and China* (New Haven, 1917), pp. 18-19; M. J. Bau, *Foreign Relations of China* (New York, 1921), pp. 3-4.

[24]Such as "the Middle Kingdom" and "The Celestial Empire."

[25]The letter is quoted in detail in Martin, *op. cit.*, v. 1, pp. 253-54.

[26]Parker, *China History*, pp. 272-74.

[27]For examples see Auber, *op. cit.*, pp. 56-68.

[28]Norman D. Harris, *Europe and the East* (Boston, 1926), p. 377; John W. Foster, *American Diplomacy in the Orient* (New York, 1903), pp. 6-8; William Milburn, *Oriental Commerce* (London, 1813), v. 2, pp. 462-63; Richard Cocks, *Diary* (London, 1883), v. 1, pp. 259-60, v. 2, pp. 4-43, 302-03; E. Lavisse and A. Rambaud, *Histoire générale* (Paris, 1895), v. 5, pp. 904-09.

istrators were all the more convinced of their own superiority, and felt that the "Middle Kingdom" should close its doors to the profaning European. When the Dutch and English came seeking trade at all cost, contempt for the money-seeking merchant increased.[29] When the Spanish massacred and maltreated the Chinese at Manila,[30] the latter became more determined to apply their doctrine of responsibility to foreigners. And finally, when the missionaries came demanding the abolition of ancestor worship and images, the scholars held more firmly to tradition and prepared to drive out the intruders.[31]

3. *The Political Organization*[32]

Theoretically the Chinese government was a patriarchal absolutism. "The vital and universally operating principle in China, [was] the duty of submission to parental authority," and since "the Emperor [was] looked upon as the father of the empire" complete respect and subordination were rendered to his absolute power.[33] The Emperor's

> word [was] law; his very actions, how trivial soever, the pattern of conduct; he [could] slay and respite at pleasure; the lives and whole property of all his subjects [were] at his disposal, he [was] under no responsibility to a watchful parliament, or a powerful nobility. Sole master and lord, under the endearing title of a father, he [did] what seeme[d] good to him.[34]

He was the head of the constitution, the source of law, the granter of all privileges and rights, the fountain of honor, the highest legislative and executive authority.[35] The appointment of all officials was also in his hands.[36]

[29] S. Wells Williams, *A History of China* (New York, 1897), pp. 54-55.

[30] Krausse, *op. cit.*, p. 73; Chong Su See, *op. cit.*, pp. 43-45.

[31] Vinacke, *op. cit.*, pp. 28-31; See, *op. cit.*, pp. 105-06. For a more complete discussion of this see *postea*, chap. 6, sec. 4.

[32] The great source of material for the study of the central government is the 48 volumes published by the Chinese government. In these volumes details of the duties and responsibilities of the various departments and offices are prescribed. The titles of the individual books and the subjects are briefly summarized by Jernigan, *op. cit.*, pp. 64-69. Also H. B. Morse, *Trade and Administration of China* (New York, 1921), chap. 2, gives a very complete and lucid analysis of the government of China under the Manchus, as does chap. 3 in H. A. Giles, *China and the Chinese* (New York, 1912), pp. 73-107.

[33] Auber, *op. cit.*, pp. 51-53; Williams, *Middle Kingdom*, v. 1, p. 380.

[34] Charles Gutzlaff, *The Life of Taou-Kwang* (London, 1852), p. 2.

[35] The best treatment of Chinese government under the Manchus is to be found in Hsieh, *op. cit.*, especially note chaps. 1 and 2. See also *Universal History, Modern* (London, 1781), v. 7, pp. 128-30, and Lavisse and Rambaud, *op. cit.*, v. 5, pp. 897-900.

[36] Jernigan, *op. cit.*, p. 43. As a parallel statement of the complete political

The Emperor was more than this; he was the high priest of the Empire and

> regard[ed] himself as the interpreter of the decrees of Heaven, and he [was] recognized by the people over whom he rule[d] as the connecting link between the gods and themselves. He [was] designated by such titles as the Son of Heaven, the Lord of Ten Thousand Years, the Imperial Supreme; and he [was] supposed to hold communion with the deities at his pleasure, and to obtain from them the blessings of which he, personally, or the nation [might] stand in need.[37]

This position as Vice-gerent of heaven, a virtual god upon earth, gave him a religious sanctity and veneration which greatly increased his power and importance. The government was, therefore, a sort of patriarchal theocratic absolutism representing the most unlimited authority possible. This tremendous power could, if the Emperor chose, be turned without limitations against the foreigners. In practice he did not often do this, but occasionally, as we shall see, he did; and then the foreigners had to suffer in silence or appeal to their home governments for aid.

The very nature of this Oriental despotism, however, served as the first check upon its own authority, and at the same time made its activity more tyrannous if the Emperor chose to exercise it. Like other Oriental despots, the Emperor was surrounded by a large court with its attendant ceremonies and practices.[38] Furthermore, his duty as a priest devolved upon him the performance of many solemn and important rites and sacrifices, and

power of the Emperor the following quotation from Jernigan, pp. 33-34 is apropos. "According to the theory of the government of China the Emperor is an absolute ruler. His power over the lives and property of his subjects is unlimited. He disposes of all places in the Empire, and punishes as he may decree. He can appoint to, or remove from, office, impose taxes at will, confiscate or appropriate property without compensation, and there is no appeal against his decision. No other ruler possesses as despotic power over as many people, . . .

"Politically the government of China turns on the reciprocal duty of parents and children. The Emperor is the head of the government, but the family is its base."

[37]Tcheng, Ki Tong and J. H. Gray, *The Chinese Empire* (New York, 1900), p. 77; Martin, *op. cit.*, v. 1, p. 108.

[38]Gutzlaff, *Taou-Kwang*, pp. 3-6, has a good discussion on this subject. A few extracts are worth quoting. The Emperor "must be himself a slave to custom"; "he has to attend to the most trivial demands of etiquette"; "he may break through them . . . but he will not hold long his high rank"; "he may be a tyrant" if he chooses but he must "be attentive to the sacrifices of his ancestors." "On the other hand, let him neglect the behests of the Board of Rites, withdraw from the frequent audiences that are regularly given, dress or deport himself differently from what is prescribed by immemorial usage, and a hundred voices will exclaim against the unworthy ruler."

necessitated his following prescribed lines of conduct. Any deviation from the customary practice would bring down the vengeance of heaven upon the Empire, and so his strict observance of these duties was demanded by the people.[39] The fact that he had to devote so much time to ceremonial duties; that he was constantly cut off from the real world by custom and by the court; that he was always surrounded by the mystery, licentiousness, and impersonality of an Oriental system, prevented him from traveling about the Empire and devoting himself wholeheartedly to the problem of enlightened government.[40] Under such circumstances he was forced to lean heavily upon the bureaucracy, and to depend upon advisers who might exercise tremendous influence.

The character of the bureaucracy was a further factor in complicating relationships with the West. As we know, the Emporer was forced to rely upon it for advice, and he was by necessity forced to follow most of its suggestions. He was entirely dependent upon it for his knowledge of outside conditions.[41] The central administration was rather complex and gave employment to a large number of officials and hangers-on. During the first century of the Manchu rule the Emperor relied heavily upon the Cabinet or Imperial Chancery. This body was composed of from four to six persons who advised the ruler, presented all business to him together with their opinions, and took down his decrees, which usually followed their recommendations.[42] After 1732 another body generally known as the Council of State became the most important organ of government. It was composed of heads of the administrative boards, and other persons chosen by the Emperor. It conferred with him on all important matters, took down his edicts, and had them published. Its meetings were rather informal and its

[39]Williams, *Middle Kingdom*, v. 2, pp. 191-205; Julia Corner, *History of China and India* (London, 1846), pp. 76-77; see also Chinese proverbs, in Bashford, *op. cit.*, pp. 167-68.

[40]Edward T. Williams, *China*, pp. 230-31.

[41]Morse, *International Relations*, v. 1, p. 2; Krausse, *op. cit.*, pp. 52-53; Williams, *Middle Kingdom*, v. 1, p. 415.

[42]Gutzlaff, *Chinese History*, v. 1, pp. 38-46; Williams, *Middle Kingdom*, v. 1, pp. 416-21; Jernigan, *op. cit.*, pp. 43-49; Morse, *International Relations*, v. 1, pp. 6-9. The best discussion of the central bureaucracy is to be found in Hsieh, *op. cit.*, chap. 4; see also Lavisse and Rambaud, *op. cit.*, v. 5, pp. 898-99.

power tremendous.[43] Only through these two bodies could the Emperor be reached, which fact placed enormous power in the hands of these men. All appeals or memorials from the provinces had to be directed to a Board of Transmission, which gave them to the Cabinet for transference to the Emperor.[44] The execution of imperial decrees depended upon the provincial governments and the six administrative boards at Peking. These latter boards dealt with appointments, finance, rites, military affairs, punishments, and public works.[45] The most important feature of this system was the great influence which a few men in the central administration could wield over the Emperor. A bureaucracy, seldom noted for its incorruptibility, was especially dangerous in China where "squeeze" and bribery were recognized institutions. For a consideration metropolitan officials could influence the issue of decrees through their control of information and their intimate relations with the Emperor.

The provincial government was the agency for enforcing the imperial will. It was more than that; it was virtually a separate and independent unit. "The main idea that [ran] throughout the entire provincial organization [was] that each province exist[ed] as an independent unit and [was] sufficient unto itself."[46] Except for appointing the viceroy or governor and other officials, the central government interfered very little with the conduct of the province so long as it sent its annual tribute and maintained order. The most important provincial officials were the governor and the viceroy, the latter controlling several provinces. Theoretically these men were directly responsible to the Emperor, and had the same absolute power over the province which he held over the Empire.[47] This peculiar system of absolutism in which the local province was practically autonomous

[43] Martin, *op. cit.*, v. 1, pp. 109-10; Treat, *op. cit.*, pp. 36-39.

[44] Williams, *Middle Kingdom*, v. 1, p. 433.

[45] Krausse, *op. cit.*, pp. 53-57; Williams, *Middle Kingdom*, v. 1, pp. 421-27; and Harold E. Gorst, *China* (London, 1899), chap. 13. There were also other boards and offices, among which were the Censorate, which by its freedom of criticism, served as a check upon the central and provincial administration; the Imperial Astronomical College; the Hanlin (or classical) College; the Colonial Office, and others.

[46] Jernigan, *op. cit.*, p. 42. See also Morse, *International Relations*, v. 1, pp. 9-16; Parker, *China History*, pp. 177-82.

[47] Putnam Weale, *The Fight for the Republic in China* (New York, 1917), chap. 1; Jernigan, *op. cit.*, pp. 39-43; Krausse, *op. cit.*, pp. 57-60; Martin, *op. cit.*, v. 1, pp. 121-22; Williams, *Middle Kingdom*, v. 1, p. 395; Lavisse and Rambaud, *op. cit.*, v. 5, p. 899.

was not well understood by the European, and such decentralization left the provincial government free to practice extortion upon the foreign traders. In fact, the central government insisted that the provinces settle by themselves all affairs with Western merchants.[48]

The Hsien or District, however, was the vital unit in Chinese government. It was ruled by a magistrate who served as the "father and mother" of his people.[49] He was appointed by the Emperor, but was responsible to the governor who virtually controlled his appointment. So long as the magistrate kept order and turned over sufficient revenue to higher officials his position was secure.[50] The district magistrate exercised power over foreigners only in the enforcement of local regulations, the preservation of order, and criminal cases.[51] He did, however, constitute one more governmental agent with which the foreigner had to contend.

Duplication of official function and lack of political responsibility were plainly the defects of this system so far as the Westerner was concerned. There were at least six officials besides the Hong Merchants to whom the Europeans were more or less responsible. These were, in addition to the viceroy, governor, and district magistrate which have been mentioned, the Hoppo, who had charge of the collection of customs; the Tartar General, commander of the Manchu garrison in the province and the equal in power of the viceroy and governor; and the provincial judge who had charge of all capital criminal offenses.[52] When trouble arose the foreigners might appeal to any one or to all of these persons, each one of whom in turn would shift the responsibility to another and so avoid action. On the other hand they

[48]Morse, *International Relations*, v. 1, p. 9. For a good account of the entire provincial organization see the following authorities: Treat, *op. cit.*, pp. 39-40; Williams, *Middle Kingdom*, v. 1, pp. 438-47; Gutzlaff, *Chinese History*, v. 1, pp. 44-47; Gray, *op. cit.*, pp. 85-87; Hsieh, *op. cit.*, chap. 11; Charles Denby, *China and Her People* (Boston, 1906), v. 2, chap. 1.

[49]Jernigan, *op. cit.*, pp. 35-37; Morse, *International Relations*, v. 1, pp. 16-20; Treat, *op. cit.*, pp. 40-41.

[50]Williams, *Middle Kingdom*, v. 1, pp. 440-43; Martin, *op. cit.*, v. 1, pp. 123-24; V. K. Leong and L. K. Tao, *Village and Town Life in China* (New York), pp. 3-22 and 45-66.

[51]Most of the direct control over foreigners was exercised by the Hoppo and the provincial officials, through the Hong Merchants. Treat, *op. cit.*, pp. 60-63. The district magistrate did, however, have local police power.

[52]Morse, *International Relations*, v. 1, pp. 15-16; Jernigan, *op. cit.*, pp. 42-43; Williams, *Middle Kingdom*, v. 1, pp. 438-40.

might all descend upon the Europeans with demands. Thus, in spite of the direct personal responsibility which every Chinese bore, there was a hopeless lack of any political responsibility upon which the Europeans could rely. The multiplicity of offices further increased the number of pockets which had to be filled from local taxation and exactions on foreign trade.[53] Finally, this plurality of offices, and the refusal of officials to deal directly with the foreigners, made it very difficult to bring complaints before the proper authorities. Direct appeal to Peking was rendered practically impossible unless each of the long line of officials through whom it had to go was favorably inclined.[54]

4. *Religious and Educational System*

The Chinese religious outlook was entirely different from that of the foreigners who came to the Orient. In the 17th century there were three main religious groups in China—Buddhism, Taoism, and Confucianism.[55] The first was an alien religion brought by Buddhist missionaries from India. Its ideal stage represented lofty moral principles, but its practical usage had degraded into base mysticism and ceremonialism. Taoism as it then existed was a degeneration of the rationalistic teaching of Laotze into fetish worship. Confucianism, which was the state religion, and to which the majority of Chinese lent at least a partial allegiance, developed from the teaching of the philosophical moralist, Confucius.[56]

While distinctly not a religion, the Confucian teachings, with their emphasis upon the worship of the supreme and lesser gods, the holy men, sages and heroes of the past, as well as the ancestors of the family, served to meet, in part, the religious needs of the people. His teachings were concerned primarily with human conduct,

and constituted an ethical code rather than a religion.[57] There

[53]See section five of this chapter for a full discussion.

[54]Morse, *International Relations*, v. 1, pp. 67-71; Robert K. Douglas, *Europe and the Far East* (Cambridge, 1904), pp. 43-45.

[55]Williams, *Middle Kingdom*, v. 2, chap. 18, gives an excellent account of the religious life and organization of China, as does Bashford, *op. cit.*, chap. 10, and Treat, *op. cit.*, chap. 3. See also Emile Bard, *Chinese Life in Town and Country* (New York, 1905), chap. 7, pp. 44-58, and Lavisse and Rambaud, *op. cit.*, v. 5, pp. 900-902.

[56]Williams, *Middle Kingdom*, v. 2, pp. 193-95; Bashford, *op. cit.*, pp. 244-46 and chaps. 8, 9.

[57]Treat, *op. cit.*, p. 30 and p. 32 for mention of other religions.

were a few other groups of which Mohammedanism was the most important. All of these beliefs lent to China a religious viewpoint which was out of harmony with that of the West, and this very fact led to misunderstanding, disharmony, and eventually to conflict.

Filial piety was the dominant feature of Chinese religious life. It was the keynote of Confucian teachings and represented itself in ancestor worship and extreme respect for elders. Confucian principles formed the cornerstone of Sinic culture, and his name and command of filial piety were respected by all Chinese. His teachings, as the basis of the state religion, were officially respected.[58] They were expressed in the following manner in the Sacred Edict of Kanghi:

> Pay just regard to filial and fraternal duties, in order to give due importance to the relations of life.
>
> Respect kindred, in order to display the excellence of harmony . . .
>
> Degrade all strange religions, in order to exalt the Orthodox doctrines.[59]

With such universally accepted canons supported by the state power it was little wonder that the missionaries encountered difficulties when they opposed rites in veneration of ancestors.

Education was largely a state function in China. The system had a two-fold object: training officials, and instilling the canons of Confucianism. Scholarship was especially venerated, and the aim of every youth was to become one of the literati.[60] The preparation of the scholar consisted of an intensive study of the Chinese Classics, which included the teachings of Confucius and the other sages. It was of a very literary and impracticable nature and tended to breed conservatism, veneration for the past, and filial respect. One of the classics was known as the *Canon of Filial Piety*, and the others breathed of the same dogmatic character, as a study of extracts from them will show.[61] Passing the first of the four literary examinations was necessary for eligibility to minor offices. The first examination was held in the district and prefectural cities twice every three years.

[58] Williams, *Middle Kingdom*, v. 2, pp. 236-37; Treat, *op. cit.*, pp. 30-31; Bashford, *op. cit.*, pp. 252-53, 257-58.

[59] *Chinese Repository*, v. 1, pp. 297-315; Martin, *op. cit.*, v. 1, pp. 163-84, also quotes this edict in brief.

[60] Williams, *Middle Kingdom*, v. 1, pp. 519-26; Treat, *op. cit.*, pp. 23-24; Bard, *op. cit.*, chap. 12, pp. 97-121.

[61] Treat, *op. cit.*, pp. 24, 27-28; Bashford, *op. cit.*, pp. 98-99, 105-08 and proverbs, p. 166; Williams, *Middle Kingdom*, v. 1, pp. 526-41.

The second was held in the provincial capital once in every three years, and success in this was necessary to become a fully-fledged literatus, and to become eligible for the Metropolitan examination. Successful completion of the Metropolitan examination at Peking made one eligible for the highest offices in the land. The Palace examination which followed was not eliminative, but designed to classify students who had passed the Metropolitan.[62]

The results of this educational system, in so far as we are concerned, were three. First, it raised up a group of conservative officials who were to a large extent unfit for problems of enlightened administration. Second, a literary and ruling class was created which profoundly admired existing Chinese civilization, and which resented the teachings of missionaries, that seemed to endanger its position and attack its cultural standards. Third, the system fostered corruption. Extreme severity in examinations led influential men to purchase degrees and positions, in return for which they expected to get rich by extortion while in office. Competition among scholars stimulated corruption before getting into office and extortion afterwards, to make up for the long years of privation and financial loss.[63]

Officials were chosen from among the literati, the apostles and supporters of the canons of Confucius. Confucianism was the religion of the Empire of which the sovereign was high priest. This provided a close alliance between the Emperor, officialdom, the literati, and Confucianism. Their interests were identified, and anything which struck at one was considered dangerous to the others. The officials and the literati, therefore, always worked together to preserve the Confucian system, and the Emperor was easily influenced to follow them.

5. *Administrative Peculiarities*

We have already sketched in some detail the features of the Chinese political system which caused trouble with the Westerners. In this section a few of the more distinctively adminis-

[62]Treat, *op. cit.*, pp. 25-27; Williams, *Middle Kingdom*, v. 1, pp. 545-62.

[63]Bashford, *op. cit.*, pp. 104-05; Williams, *Middle Kingdom*, v. 1, pp. 566-70. According to Treat, *op. cit.*, p. 26, about 1,810 candidates were given the degree during each year of the provincial examinations, while Williams, *Middle Kingdom*, v. 1, p. 438, says that the total number of provincial offices did not exceed 2000. The Chinese *Red Book* or list of those eligible for office showed 20,327 names in 1852, indicating that many of the literati had to wait a long time for office or, perhaps, never attain it.

trative characteristics which further complicated the situation will be mentioned.

The method of choosing officials in China has already been dealt with to some extent. It has been noted that they were chosen by literary examinations, and appointed by the Emperor with the advice of a special board, and that they were not particularly competent for the work given them. These appointments, however, involved considerable fraud and bribery, and to make matters worse the Manchus, in 1635, adopted the sale of offices as a revenue measure.[64] As a result of this system, positions to a large extent went to the highest bidders, and a large group of office seekers was constantly to be found at Peking. Chinese law provided that an official must be sent to a strange province, which meant that he could know little of its needs when he arrived.[65] The net result of this system was the creation of an official class resembling more a group of hungry wolves than honest administrators, persons who went to their provinces with the purpose of self-enrichment.

The position of the Chinese official was comparatively insecure. The Hoppo was appointed for from one to three years only, during which time he tried to milk the trade as much as possible. He was the imperial representative and the link through which Peking obtained its share of the Canton spoils. The average term for an ordinary civil official was three years in the same province.[66] Not only was the term short but the official was subject to sudden and summary dismissal. If he should fail to perform his duty in a satisfactory way, to preserve order, or to make his regular revenue returns, he was likely to be turned out of office and disgraced. The story of Duke Ho or of Commissioner Keshen [67] afford good examples of this, while that of Commissioner Lin is perhaps the most famous. He rose from humble position to great heights, but his failure to arrange a successful conclusion to the opium question caused his degradation and banishment. After a time he was pardoned and returned to

[64]Martin, *op. cit.*, v. 1, pp. 132-36, 149-51; Hsieh, *op. cit.*, pp. 105-113. The date is given as 1637 by Martin, but Hsieh is more reliable.

[65]E. H. Parker, *China Past and Present* (London, 1903), pp. 230-32; Williams, *Middle Kingdom*, v. 1, pp. 448-49.

[66]Morse, *Chronicle*, v. 1, p. 139; Krausse, *op. cit.*, pp. 57-64; Morse, *International Relations*, v. 1, pp. 15, 34; Martin, *op. cit.*, v. 1, p. 130.

[67]Williams, *Middle Kingdom*, v. 1, pp. 452-53, for Duke Ho; Martin, *op. cit.*, v. 1, pp. 130-31 for Commissioner Keshen.

favor.[68] Men whose tenure was so insecure generally tried to make hay while the sun shone.

As a whole Chinese officials were underpaid. Their salaries were at all times far below their office expenses. These salaries were to be padded by a legal allowance from the funds collected, but such practice naturally did not encourage honesty. For example; a viceroy received a regular salary of from T. 180 to T. 200, while in allowances or anti-extortion pay he was permitted T. 15,000-25,000. Martin reports the salary of a governor as T. 15,000 (this included his anti-extortion money), while his actual expenses were ten times as much.[69] Under such circumstances one readily sees why exaction was a recognized practice among officials.

That extortion and corruption were almost universal in China is testified by most contemporary writers.[70] Practically all officials resorted to such expedients; tax collectors charged all that the traffic would bear; offices went to the highest bidder; out of every public deal each official got his "squeeze"; and justice was dealt out to the clink of silver.[71] This account is not intended to portray the Chinese as a moral degenerate, and it may be well to remember that in contemporary England Sir Francis Bacon was found guilty of accepting bribes.[72] On the other hand it does seem that "squeeze" was more highly developed in China; in fact, it was reduced to a recognized system—a sort of extra-legal institution.[73] The main causes of this condition have been mentioned in the two previous paragraphs and to them may be added, (1) the excessive number of minor offices; and (2) the general irresponsibility of the whole system of government. With an administration dominated by this viewpoint the European

[68]Williams, *Middle Kingdom*, v. 1, pp. 457-59.

[69]Morse, *International Relations*, v. 1, pp. 25-30; Williams, *Middle Kingdom*, v. 1, pp. 294-95; Martin, *op. cit.*, v. 1, pp. 129-30.

[70]See statement of Magaillans, a man who lived forty years in China, writing in 1688, quoted in Williams, *Middle Kingdom*, v. 1, p. 473. See also Parker, *China History*, pp. 205-09, another contemporary observer writing toward the close of the 19th century.

[71]This statement is based upon the memorial of a Censor in 1829, which is quoted on p. 480 of Williams, *Middle Kingdom*, v. 1; see also Gray, *op. cit.*, pp. 101-07; Krausse, *op. cit.*, pp. 60-64.

[72]T. P. Taswell-Langmead, *English Constitutional History* (London, 1881), p. 520.

[73]Morse, *International Relations*, v. 1, pp. 39-40, gives an account of how this system of squeeze worked and why it was practically inevitable. Also Krausse, *op. cit.*, pp. 43-46.

trade served only as another fruitful source of "squeeze"; no wonder that the foreigners were constantly beset with new exactions.

The Chinese official was primarily a tax collector. His chief function in life was to get money and to transmit it to his superiors. He was not particularly interested in administrative duties, and discouraged everything which tended to increase his official work. It would appear that the chief function of the administrative system was to provide a livelihood for its members rather than to render service to the people.[74] The mandarin with this conception of his office saw in European trade an easy source of revenue.

"Words not deeds" was the favorite practice of the Chinese mandarin. Edicts were issued by the dozens but few of them were enforced. A capital example of this was the solemn order to destroy the grasshoppers, issued in 1833.[75] Threatening language and actions were constantly used to intimidate evil-doers and to impress the public, but such measures were seldom enforced. The citizens and the traders as a consequence came to pay very little attention to them, which fact led to serious difficulties when an administrator appeared who insisted upon the enforcement of his edicts.

6. *Commercial Organization*

The attitude of scorn which the government adopted toward merchants and traders has been noted, and this fact must be kept in mind constantly when dealing with the commercial relations of China.

Guilds played a tremendously important part in Chinese life.[76] In fact practically every type of industrial and commercial enterprise was so organized. There were bankers' guilds,

[74]Morse, *International Relations*, v. 1, pp. 26-30.

[75]Quoted in Williams, *Middle Kingdom*, v. 1, pp. 469-71. Practically all the edicts contained ferocious and terrible words but many of them were absurd and no attempt was ever made to enforce them honestly. The best examples of this are the edicts against opium. Its sale was prohibited in 1729 upon the pain of confiscation of property and death to the purchaser (Morse, *Chronicle*, v. 1, p. 215). It was never enforced, however, and in 1799 the prohibition was again enacted but was not enforced. See document, Morse, *Chronicle*, v. 2, pp. 344-46.

[76]For a discussion of the guilds of China see H. B. Morse, *The Guilds of China* (New York, 1909); Jernigan, *op. cit.*, pp. 205-21; and Bashford, *op. cit.*, pp. 62-71. Chapters 2 and 3 give a valuable discussion of Chinese commercial and industrial life.

tea guilds, silk guilds, and many others. The purpose of the guild was to protect and advance the interests of its particular industry and to serve the intellectual and social needs of its members. These societies were similar to the medieval European guilds, with the exception that they were less monopolistic and had special clauses in their by-laws against organizations which tended to corner a product at the expense of the public. Such monopolies were also prohibited by law, as extracts from the code show.[77] Guilds were very old and originated in a peculiar way as the following excerpt from the by-laws of one will indicate. "*Wei Kuan* (guilds) were first established at the metropolis by mandarins, among compatriots or fellow-provincials, for mutual aid and protection. Subsequently, merchants formed guilds like those of the mandarinate, and now they exist in every province."[78] These organizations developed great power, and with their virtual control over the commercial jurisprudence of the Empire they were able to present a strong front to the foreign traders.[79] With this basic organization the idea soon developed of uniting all the merchants who dealt with foreigners into a monopoly or Co-hong.

Chinese commercial ideas and methods were a peculiar hodge-podge. Despite the proverb, "Deviate an inch; lose a thousand miles,"[80] Chinese business methods were chronically inaccurate, and this difficulty was increased by the lack of a uniform currency or monetary standard. Interest as high as three per cent per month was allowed by law, but the borrowing of money from foreigners was totally prohibited. Imprisonment for debt was practiced, and the directors of a partnership or corporation were liable for the debts of the organization.[81] Despite prevailing corruption in the official world Chinese merchants, on the whole, seem to have been honest and reliable in fulfilling

[77]Jernigan, *op. cit.*, pp. 212-13.

[78]*Ibid.*, p. 206.

[79]Parker, *China History*, pp. 311-12; Frank R. Eldridge, *Trading with Asia* (New York, 1926), pp. 112-14.

[80]Chinese proverb quoted in Bashford, *op. cit.*, p. 165.

[81]For a discussion of Chinese commercial ideas and methods see Bashford, *op. cit.*, pp. 88-96; Morse, *International Relations*, v. 1, pp. 68-69; Jernigan, *op. cit.*, pp. 94-101 and chap. 10, especially pp. 233-35. As we shall see later the mandarins held the Hong Merchants individually responsible for the debts of the organization.

contracts when no interference was offered by officials.[82] The Chinese, however, was an industrious and shrewd trader, who always persisted in haggling and bargaining, which practice irritated the European. This was particularly true of the small shopkeepers, who were to be found in great numbers. "Bargain money" or an advance upon a contract was almost universally demanded, and Europeans were much opposed to paying it.[83]

The officials, theoretically, were above the petty details of business. Practically, however, they interfered a great deal in commercial enterprise, intent upon pecuniary gain. Their interference in trade was based primarily upon the following section of the Penal Code,

> Whenever a trader, after having observed the nature of his neighbor's business, stocks his shop, and puts prices on his goods in such a manner that his neighbors cannot sell theirs, and thus obtains more than the customary advantage, he shall be punished with forty strokes of the bamboo,

and upon the doctrine of mutual responsibility.[84] This official interference was practiced praticularly in commercial relations with foreigners.

7. *Chinese Law and Justice*

Chinese law has been characterized as barbarous, and in contrast with our modern idea this was undoubtedly true.[85] But to judge correctly it must be considered in the light of its time and in comparison with existing European law of the 17th and 18th centuries. Chinese law, breathing of absolutism, was fitted to the needs of an absolute monarchy. It was based largely upon the Chinese classics and therefore reflected a patriarchal character. Laws were numerous and minute, and aimed to reach every department of life, and if strictly enforced, would have been tremendously burdensome. Corporal punishments pre-

[82]Bashford, *op. cit.*, pp. 93-94; Jernigan, *op. cit.*, p. 225. We shall have occasion to note the truth of this statement in the dealings of the Hong Merchants with the foreigners.

[83]Jernigan, *op. cit.*, pp. 222-26, 259-60; Alleyne Ireland, *China and the Powers* (Boston, 1902), pp. 11-12.

[84]Huc, *op. cit.*, v. 2, pp. 258-59. From v. 1, p. 274 of the Penal Code; see also Harris, *op. cit.*, p. 378.

[85]The Chinese Penal Code exists in a translation by Sir G. T. Staunton, made in 1810. The Code, as it existed during the period in which we are dealing, had been compiled and reorganized by a judicial committee during the reign of Shunche and issued in 1647.

dominated and many of them were severe and barbarous. Strangulation, decapitation, piecemeal hacking, castration, slicing of the knee-cap, branding, beating with the bamboo, and wearing the cangue were the most important.[86] On the other hand we must remember that in England until 1870 hanging, drawing, and quartering was the punishment for treason; until 1790 women could be burnt alive; and several hundred crimes, some as petty as stealing five shillings, were punishable by death until well into the 19th century.[87] The *Edinburgh Review* (August, 1810, pp. 481-91) said that on the whole the dominant character of the Chinese Penal Code was its "great reasonableness, clearness and consistency."

The chief laws with which the foreigners came into contact may be briefly summarized as follows: (1) Premeditated murder or killing by musket fire was punishable by decapitation, the most degrading of all executions. (2) Killing in an affray, or upon suspicion of theft, or of being an accessory to a murder was punishable by strangulation. (3) Accidental wounding or killing was punishable by fines or types of corporal punishment depending upon the seriousness of the injury. (4) Killing in lawful self defense was justifiable and not punishable. (5) Fighting or wounding was punishable by exile, fines, or corporal means varying with the degree of the injury. (6) Committing outrages while intoxicated was punished by exile to a foreign country, in servitude. (7) Robbery and theft were punishable by fines or blows depending upon the damage done.[88] It is obvious that these laws were not in themselves unreasonable. No foreigner could rightfully object to their application. The method in

[86]For a discussion of Chinese law see Williams, *Middle Kingdom*, v. 1, pp. 384-393; Jernigan, *op. cit.*, pp. 70-111; Staunton, *Notes Relating to China*, v. 1, pp. 387-402, quotes a long article from the *Edinburgh Review* of August, 1810, discussing the Chinese Penal Code; Parker, *China Past and Present*, pp. 309-10, 376-87; Mr. Parker writes from personal observation.

[87]Parker, *China History*, p. 308; J. S. Schapiro, *Modern and Contemporary European History* (New York, 1923), p. 63.

[88]These statements are based upon extracts from the Chinese Penal Code and may be found in Morse, *Chronicle*, v. 2, p. 343; Gutzlaff, *China Opened or a Display* (London, 1838), v. 2, p. 78; Jernigan, *op. cit.*, pp. 76-90; Morse, *International Relations*, v. 1, p. 110; Auber, *op. cit.*, pp. 207-08. The legal amount of the fine seems to have been T. 12.42, and was payable to the parents of the injured party. See Morse, *International Relations*, v. 1, p. 110. Punishments for disorderly conduct were as follows: striking with the hand, 20 blows; tearing more than one inch of hair, 50 blows; breaking a tooth or bone, 100 blows.

which they were applied, especially to outsiders, caused the trouble.

The method of applying these laws to Europeans was established by Kien-lung about 1738. He said, "The native law alone is not to be the guide of the local government, it is incumbent to have life for life, in order to frighten and repress barbarians."[89] That this method was followed whenever possible in dealing with foreigners is supported by ample testimony and by facts in cases later to be discussed. The great dispute with the English arose because the latter contended that most cases fell under numbers three and four above, while the Chinese contended that they fell under number two and were punishable by strangulation.[90] One cause for the insistence of the Orientals upon this was the doctrine of responsibility which we have noted. In applying this doctrine the magistrates demanded a life for a life, and it made no difference to them whether it was the guilty person who suffered, so long as somebody was given up. As it was upon this point that the Chinese and English collided most seriously, further examination of the administration of Chinese justice is necessary.

The organization of Chinese law courts was comparatively simple. At the bottom of the system was the district court presided over by the district magistrate. All cases went to his court and were decided there, but appeals were allowed to the prefect (*chih-fu*), supervisor of the prefecture (*fu*), and then to the provincial court presided over by the provincial judge. The Emperor served as a final court of appeal, and all executions for capital offenses had to be approved by him.[91] This seems a relatively simple system which would insure justice; but in reality it involved a considerable amount of red tape and the actual procedure made justice in the Western sense impossible.

The administration of justice was hopelessly corrupt and brutal. Magistrates were constantly bribed and the most atrocious judicial methods were used. Juries and attorneys were

[89]Gutzlaff, *China Opened*, v. 2, p. 78.

[90]See Staunton, *Notes Relating to China*, v. 1, pp. 425-26; Martin, *op. cit.*, v. 2, p. 13; Morse, *International Relations*, v. 1, pp. 110-17.

[91]Gray, *op. cit.*, pp. 89-93; Jernigan, *op. cit.*, pp. 176-92; Hsieh, *op. cit.*, pp. 219-20; Morse, *International Relations*, v. 1, pp. 12-18. The *fu* was the largest political division within the province and consisted of from two to six districts.

unknown and the entire decision in each case was left to the magistrate. The crowning cause of injustice was the theory that confession was necessary to conviction, while the doctrine of responsibility made the conviction of someone necessary. Torture was legitimate and was used to extort confessions from the accused. It was also practiced on witnesses and some of the methods were cruel beyond measure.[92] "To this the English could not agree. Their own law of homicide was more harsh than the Chinese, but at least they expected a fair trial for the accused."[93] This the Chinese authorities, driven on by the necessity of convicting someone, could not grant. The contrast between English and Chinese administration of justice must not be carried too far, for in England as late as 1658 a man was pressed to death for refusing jury trial; in 1726 another person was pressed until he chose jury trial; in 1615 Edmund Peacham was put to the rack, and Henry VIII executed Buckingham without giving him attorney or jury trial.[94] The insistence of the Chinese that someone must suffer whether guilty or not was really the fundamental cause of the judicial trouble.

In a Chinese trial the magistrate sat

> behind a large table which [was] covered with red cloth. The prisoner [was] made to kneel in front of the table as a mark of respect to the court, by whom he [was] regarded as guilty until he was proved to be innocent . . . At the commencement of the trial the charge [was] . . . read aloud in the hearing of the prisoner, who [was] called upon to plead either guilty or not guilty.

He seldom pleaded guilty.

> During the course of a trial the prisoner [was] asked a great many leading questions which [had] a tendency to criminate him. Should his answers be evasive, torture [was] at once resorted to as the only remaining expedient.[95]

The conduct of torture is well described by Huc, an eye witness.

> At the first glance we cast into the hall, we felt a cold perspiration come

[92] For a discussion of Chinese justice see Krausse, *op. cit.*, pp. 67-69; Morse, *International Relations*, v. 1, pp. 109-17; Staunton, *Notes Relating to China*, v. 2, pp. 488-92; Jernigan, *op. cit.*, pp. 178-89; Gray, *op. cit.*, pp. 93-101; Martin, *op. cit.*, v. 1, pp. 158-59.

[93] Morse, *International Relations*, v. 1, p. 117.

[94] F. W. Maitland, *Constitutional History of England* (Cambridge, 1911), p. 212. For a discussion of this subject of forcing persons to accept jury trials see Morse, *International Relations*, v. 1, pp. 112-14; Taswell-Langmead, *op. cit.*, p. 512; Arthur D. Innes, *England under the Tudors* (London, 1926), pp. 77-78.

[95] Gray, *op. cit.*, pp. 93-94. This is a generalized account from personal observation and he also describes the most common modes of torture. See also Williams, *Middle Kingdom*, v. 1, pp. 504-05, for official report of a trial.

over us, and our limbs tottered under us; . . . The person on . . . trial . . . was suspended in the middle of the hall . . . Ropes attached to a great beam in the roof held him tied by the wrists and feet . . . Beneath him stood five or six executioners, armed with rattan rods and leather lashes . . . ; their clothes and faces spotted with blood . . . ; the unfortunate creature was uttering stifled groans, while his flesh was torn almost in tatters.

The magistrate told the observers that the man was a thief and went on to say,

He has ended by confessing all his crimes . . . , but he persists in not denouncing his companions, and I am obliged to employ these extreme methods to reach all the guilty.[96]

After all, this may be little worse than the "third degree" practices of our enlightened modern age.

8. *Lack of Proper Means of Intercourse*

The language difficulty was one of the greatest handicaps suffered by the English.[97] Until Mr. Flint learned Chinese about 1750 the English were completely devoid of all knowledge of this language. During the early years of the British trade a corrupt form of Portuguese was the only means of communication between individuals of the two peoples. Later a cross between Chinese, English, and Portuguese grew up known as "pidgin" English. The British had to rely upon the Chinese interpreter, who understood this miserable language, as the only means of communicating with the merchants and officials. Even if the linguist were honest many serious mistakes could be made which would complicate good commercial and political relations. The Chinese attempted to prevent the foreigners from learning their language, and it was not until the time of Sir G. T. Staunton and Doctor Morrison, that the Company was supplied with competent linguists.

The difficulty of communicating with officials was a further irritation. During the early years direct intercourse was not banned, but the English had no one who understood Chinese or who could translate their appeals. By the time the English produced such linguists, all communications had been confined

[96]Huc, *op. cit.*, v. 2, pp. 245-47.

[97]For a discussion of the linguistic problem see Eames, *op. cit.*, pp. 82-85; *Chinese Repository*, v. 4, p. 432; Jernigan, *op. cit.*, pp. 224-25; Williams, *Middle Kingdom*, v. 2, pp. 448-49; Morse, *Chronicle*, v. 2 and 3, *passim* and v. 1, pp. 287, 296-98.

to the Hong Merchants, and memorials direct to the officials and in Chinese were not permitted. Direct appeals to Peking were forbidden and all communications addressed to the Emperor had to go through the local officials who generally refused to forward them.[98]

9. *Inevitability of Conflict between the Two Cultures*

From the analysis previously given it would appear that conflict between the East and the West was inevitable. Each side had a highly developed culture; each considered its civilization the best, and neither was willing to make concessions. The English led the attack for the West because they were most vitally interested in securing a large share of the Chinese trade. Commerce and missionary endeavor were undoubtedly the forces which brought Chinese and Europeans together, but they were not the main causes of the trouble. The conflict came because the two peoples did not, could not, and would not understand each other. Their viewpoints were totally at variance, their methods different, and their aims divergent; their every way of doing things collided. Each was haughty and arrogant, and under these circumstances trouble arose. When the missionaries seemed to endanger Chinese culture they were driven out and the traders suffered because of it. In the end the West chose to take up arms, in large part to defend the superiority of its cultural ideas.

10. *The Racial Problem*

It would seem that the long continued struggle between the East and the West was not at first and does not now appear to be primarily of a racial character. The two races were different and their color was a mark of identification, but hatred first developed out of cultural conflict and later became identified with race. During the latter stages of the Anglo-Chinese conflict the groups undoubtedly disliked each other because of their difference in color, which fact served as a basis for classifying and intensifying group antagonism. In its origin this dislike was

[98]Morse, *International Relations*, v. 1, p. 70; Morse, *Chronicle*, v. 3, p. 288. This was very forcefully demonstrated in the case of Mr. Flint in 1757-59. See Auber, *op. cit.*, pp. 170-71.

associated with more definite and tangible cultural problems such as commercial disputes, judicial quarrels, religious differences, and linguistic misunderstandings.[99]

[99] Authors who give enlightening discussions on this problem of race are J. H. Oldham, *Christianity and the Race Problem* (New York, about 1923), especially chap. 3; A. L. Kroeber, *Anthropology* (New York, 1923), chap. 4, especially; Jean Finot, *Race Prejudice* (New York, 1906).

CHAPTER III

ORIGIN OF ENGLISH TRADE TO THE EAST AND THE FIRST ATTEMPTS TO TRADE WITH CHINA

1. *Introduction*

The trade between England and China did not develop by accident. There were specific reasons for its growth. There were also definite factors which prevented its earlier origin, and there were causes which made it a monopoly closed to all but a few British subjects. The beginning of the China trade and the peculiar course which it later took were due to a multiplicity of causes operating in England, Europe, China, the East, and the world generally during the 16th and 17th centuries. It is necessary, therefore, to deal at length with forces which were only remotely related to the China trade: the Renaissance spirit, the early English adventurers, the early chartered companies, the Dutch and the Portuguese, European wars and European trade, the attitude of kings and emperors, public prejudices, anti-foreignism; because they all help to explain in its proper historical setting the beginning and later course of trade between England and China. After the first century the action of these factors did not directly influence the China trade. They may be dropped into the background while the story of the trade in China takes the foreground.

2. *Early Interest of the English in China and the East, 1497-1590*

The Renaissance, internal economic development, and the spice trade account for early British interest in the East. The 14th to the 16th century was the age of the Renaissance in Europe; an age of awakening, expansion, and renewed endeavor. The little peninsula had become too small to satisfy the yearnings of awakened Europe, and such men as Prince Henry, Diaz, and Columbus began the movement toward world expansion. The spirit of adventure, the call to be doing things, came also to the embryonic national state in the isles of Britain. Strange stories of the wonders and riches of the East, the taste for spices, and the outward pressure of economic development—

especially that of the rising woollen industry—created the expansion movement in England.[1]

Inspired by the Renaissance spirit of adventure and the hope of glory and gain, John Cabot sailed from England in 1497 to seek a western passage to Cathay and the Indies.[2] This voyage provided a basis for England's claim to the New World, but it failed to achieve its purpose. It was not followed up because England became absorbed in the Reformation until past the middle of the 16th century. In 1553 Sebastian Cabot, son of the earlier explorer, organized the "Merchant Adventurers for the discovery of lands not yet known or frequented by any English," with a capital stock of £6000.[3] The struggle of England for a share in the Eastern trade had begun.

In 1554-55 this organization was granted its first charter and became famous in history as the Russian or Muscovy Company.[4] Under its guidance, Sir Hugh Willoughby in 1553 sailed along the coast of Norway and into the Arctic Ocean in search of a passage to Cathay; the ship commanded by Willoughby never returned, and its crew lost their lives in the frozen North.[5] The failure of this voyage did not discourage others. In 1566 Sir Humphrey Gilbert tried to persuade the Queen to give him exclusive rights to the trade of all lands which he might discover

[1]Good accounts of this development may be found in Wilbur C. Abbott, *The Expansion of Europe* (New York, 1924), v. 1, chaps. 1-16; F. C. Dietz, *Political and Social History of England* (New York, 1927), chaps. 4-9; W. Cunningham, *The Growth of English Commerce and Industry during the Middle Ages* (Cambridge, 1905), chaps. 4 and 5; L. M. Larson, *History of England and the British Commonwealth* (New York, 1924), chaps. 8-12; Eames, *op. cit.*, pp. 1-7; G. M. Trevelyan, *History of England* (London, 1926), pp. 267-375; W. H. Woodward, *The Expansion of the British Empire* (Cambridge, 1899), chap. 1, pp. 9-16; James A. Williamson, *History of British Expansion* (New York, 1922), pp. 12-81.

[2]David Macpherson, *History of European Commerce with India* (London, 1812), p. 72; Sir William W. Hunter, *History of British India* (London, 1899), v. 1, pp. 194-95.

[3]Macpherson, *India*, p. 73; *State Papers, Colonial; East Indies* (1513-1616), pp. 7-8; W. A. S. Hewins, *English Trade and Finance* (London, 1892), p. 32; Courtenay Ilbert, *The Government of India* (London, 1915), pp. 11-12. According to Hunter (*op. cit.*, v. 1, pp. 196-200), two earlier expeditions, one in 1527 and the other in 1536, attempted to find a northwest passage to the East without success.

[4]John Bruce, *Annals of the East India Company* (London, 1810), v. 1, pp. 106-07; Macpherson, *India*, p. 73 in a footnote.

[5]*State Papers, Colonial; East Indies* (1513-1616), pp. 3-4, 266; Macpherson, *India*, pp. 73-74. The remains of Willoughby's ship and his diary were found. Richard Chancellor, commander of another ship, escaped and made his way overland to the Russian Court and thence back to England.

by a northeast passage to Cathay. The Queen refused, because it would violate the privileges of the Russian Company of which he was a member.[6] In 1565 Anthony Jenckynson (Jenkinson), in a memorial to the Queen, pointed out the desirability of discovering a northeast route to Cathay.[7] Between 1576-78, Frobisher, with the aid of Michael Lock, a trader who had spent some time in Spain and who realized the wealth of the East, attempted several voyages to discover a northwest passage to China and India.[8] In 1580 the Russian Company, without success, sent Arthur Pet and Charles Jackman in two small ships to search for the northeast passage.[9]

Thus far all the attempts had been directed toward a northwest or northeast route, but in 1582, Edward Fenton, sailing for a group organized by the Earl of Leicester, attempted to reach India by a southern voyage. This expedition, reaching the coast of Brazil but failing in its main purpose,[10] showed that the point of attack was shifting in the right direction. The voyages of the Gilberts in 1583, of Richard Penkevell in 1607, of Henry Hudson in 1610, and of the "Governor and Company of the Merchants of London, discoverers of the North-West Passage" in 1612,[11] were but belated attempts, and reveal the initiative and zeal for discovery and expansion which were present in Elizabethan England.[12]

The continuity of these attempts should be noted. John Cabot was an Italian who knew the value of Oriental trade. His son organized the Russian Company, and members of it, together with men who knew the value of the Eastern trade, such as Michael Lock, carried on all the early enterprises.

3. *The Origin of English Trade to the East*

The general causes of interest in the Eastern trade, and the failure of early attempts to open such commerce have already

[6] *State Papers, Colonial; East Indies* (1513-1616), pp. 6-8.
[7] *Ibid.*, pp. 4-5; Hunter, *op. cit.*, v. 1, p. 202.
[8] *State Papers, Colonial; East Indies* (1513-1616), pp. 11-25, 35-38, 63-67.
[9] *Ibid.*, pp. 61-62.
[10] *Ibid.*, pp. 73-88.
[11] *Ibid.*, Gilberts, pp. 92-93, 287-88; Penkevell, p. 146; Henry Hudson and others, pp. 238-42.
[12] H. D. Trail, *Social England* (New York, 1898), v. 3, pp. 477-508, and Woodward, *op. cit.*, chap. 2, pp. 17-63, have good accounts of these early attempts to reach the East.

been mentioned. The desire to find a market for woollens, and the interest in the spice trade must be considered as constant factors which encouraged voyages toward China and the East.[13] More specific causes, however, establish the historical continuity of its origin. The Anglo-Portuguese treaty of 1576, by allowing the British open trade to all Portuguese ports in European waters, first brought the English into direct contact with the Eastern trade.[14] The record-breaking voyage of Drake (1577-80) for the first time directly acquainted Englishmen with the riches of the East and the seaways leading to it.[15] In 1580 the crowns of Portugal and Spain were united. This led, in 1594, to the exclusion of Holland and England from the Lisbon spice market, and subjected the Eastern Colonial Empire of Portugal to attacks by Dutch patriots and English pirates.[16] The formation of the Levant Company in 1581 also brought Englishmen into direct contact with the Eastern trade and showed them its real value.[17]

Stimulated in part by these factors, Edward Fenton (before mentioned) in 1582, made the first definite attempt to reach the East by the southern route. The most important voyage in this connection was Cavendish's journey around the world in 1586-88,[18] from which he returned with a glowing picture of the possibilities of the East. "I navigated to the island of the Philippinos hard upon the coast of China, of which country I have brought such intelligence as hath not bene heard of in these parts. The stateliness and riches of which country I feare to make report of, lest I should not be credited." He then went on to say that the natives of the Moluccas treated the English well, and there "our countrey men may have trade as freely as the Portugals if they will." The victory over the Armada opened the seas to British traders, and between 1587 and 1589 Drake captured two

[13]Henry Stevens, *Dawn of the British Trade to the East Indies (1599-1603)* (London, 1886), pp. 312-14; Auber, *op. cit.*, pp. 131-34. Document showing interest in cloth market. See also Trevelyan, *op. cit.*, p. 347.

[14]Bruce, *op. cit.*, v. 1, pp. 54-55.

[15]*Ibid.*, p. 108; Hunter, *op. cit.*, v. 1, p. 212.

[16]Bruce, *op. cit.*, v. 1, p. 22; Abbott, *op. cit.*, v. 1, pp. 317-18; Morse, *International Relations*, v. 1, p. 47.

[17]Bruce, *op. cit.*, v. 1, pp. 107-08; Florence Bowman and Esther Roper, *Traders in East and West* (London, 1924), p. 11.

[18]E. K. Chatterton, *The Old East Indiamen* (London, n. d.), p. 27; Bruce, *op. cit.*, v. 1, p. 108; *Universal History, Modern*, v. 8, pp. 264-65.

Spanish and Portuguese ships with goods and information from the East.[19]

Aroused by the unheard-of wealth (£114,000) of one of these vessels and by the stories of Cavendish, a group of London merchants petitioned the Queen for permission to send ships to the East. In 1591, their petitions were granted, and an expedition under Captain Raymond was sent. James Lancaster and some of his men were the only survivors of those who reached the East Indies. Their return in 1594 brought the secrets of the seaways to England, and marked the end of the Portuguese monopoly.[20]

The first voyage to China, fitted out by Sir Robert Dudley and others, with Elizabeth's help, consisted of three ships and sailed in 1596 under the direction of Richard Allen and Thomas Broomfield, merchants of London. These men carried with them a letter from the Queen to the Emperor of China asking that they be given free trade and protection, and promising like treatment to Chinese who should come to England.[21] This expedition captured some Portuguese ships, but sickness reduced its numbers, and the survivors were seized and murdered by the Spaniards without ever having reached China.[22]

If all of these factors were operating to create a trade with the East, it remained for the Dutch to give the impetus which produced the East India Company, the tool for expanding English trade to the Orient. After 1595 Dutch ships had sailed to Asia and were fast displacing the Portuguese in control of the spice trade. The English, whose national interest looked askance on this Dutch commercial supremacy, were stimulated to action when the latter raised the price of pepper from 3*s*. to 6*s*. and 8*s*.

[19]For quotations see, Bowman and Roper, *op. cit.*, p. 14, and also Chatterton, *op. cit.*, pp. 27-30. A letter from Cavendish to Lord Chamberlain at the Queen's Court. For Drake's exploit see John Macgregor, *Commercial Statistics* (London, 1850), v. 4, p. 296.

[20]Bruce, *op. cit.*, v. 1, p. 109; Chatterton, *op. cit.*, pp. 29-45; Macpherson, *India*, p. 76; F. P. Robinson, *The Trade of the East India Company from 1700-1813* (Cambridge, 1912), p. 5.

[21]Eames, *op. cit.*, pp. 7-8; Macgregor, *op. cit.*, v. 4, p. 297; Milburn, *op. cit.*, v. 2, p. 466; Lavisse and Rambaud, *op. cit.*, v. 5, p. 910, and Henri Cordier, *Relations de la Chine* (Paris, 1901), v. 1, p. 12. For text of this letter see Martin, *op. cit.*, v. 2, pp. 1-2; A. J. Sargent, *Anglo-Chinese Commerce and Diplomacy* (London, 1907), p. 1; Hakluyt, *Voyages, Travels and Discoveries of the English Nation* (London, 1810), v. 4, p. 372.

[22]Macpherson, *India*, pp. 76-77; *State Papers, Colonial; East Indies* (1513-1616), p. 98; Bruce, *op. cit.*, v. 1, p. 110; Morse, *Chronicle*, v. 1, p. 6.

per pound.[23] A group of merchants, many of whom belonged to the Levant Company, met in Founders Hall, London, in 1599 and organized an association to trade to the East and combat the Dutch.[24] The London Adventurers consisted of one hundred and one persons with a total capital stock of £30,133. Suit was immediately made to the Privy Council and the Queen for a charter,[25] "for the honour of [their] native country and for the advancement of the trade of merchandise with [the] realm of England."[26] The Queen at first was favorably disposed, and the company began preparations for a voyage. However, when peace negotiations were initiated with Spain the project had to be dropped.[27] These came to nothing, and on the 31st day of December, 1600, the adventurers were incorporated as, "The Governor and Company of Merchants of London, Trading into the East-Indies."[28] The Company, as finally incorporated, consisted of 215 knights, aldermen, and merchants, and was capitalized at £57,543. It was to be managed by a governor and twenty-four committeemen, and was granted a monopoly for fifteen years of all English trade eastward from the Cape of Good Hope to the Straits of Magellan. It was empowered to

[23]Abbott, *op. cit.*, v. 1, pp. 350-52; Bowman and Roper, *op. cit.*, pp. 11-12; Macpherson, *India*, p. 77; Macgregor, *op. cit.*, v. 4, p. 297; G. L. Craik, *History of British Commerce* (London, 1844), v. 2, pp. 9-11.

[24]Documentary account of the founding of the East India Company is found in Stevens, *op. cit.*, see pp. 1-11 for substance of this reference; Bruce, *op. cit.*, v. 1, pp. 110-11. "Influential members of the Levant Company, thus finding that their extended charter of 1593 availed little for an overland trade to India, led the movement in September 1599 for a voyage direct around the Cape. That movement, although it derived a patriotic impulse from the Dutch purchase of ships in London for their Indian expeditions, seems to spring out the embarrassments of our Mediterranean trade. Among its most active promoters were Richard Staper and Thomas Smythe, two of the original founders of the Levant Company." See Hunter, *op. cit.*, p. 242 ff.

[25]Stevens, *op. cit.*, pp. 1-10; *State Papers, Colonial; East Indies* (1513-1616), p. 99; Bruce, *op. cit.*, v. 1, pp. 111-26. See petition to the Queen.

[26]Stevens, *op. cit.*, p. 5. For a good account of the founding of the East India Company see Hunter, *op. cit.*, v. 1, pp. 229-250; Williamson, *op. cit.*, pp. 123-24.

[27]Stevens, *op. cit.*, pp. 10-12; Macgregor, *op. cit.*, v. 4, p. 298.

[28]*Charters of the East India Company*, pp. 3-6. The heading of this document gives the date 31st Dec., in the 43rd year of Elizabeth, *Anno Domini* 1601, as does the copied manuscript charter in the India Office. Elizabeth's 43rd year, however, ended on Nov. 17, 1601, while documents in vol. 1 of the *Court Book* show that it was issued on Dec. 31, 1600. As it was not customary to date charters by anything other than the year of the reign, and since the only date mentioned in the body of the charter is the 43rd of Elizabeth it seems probable that 1601 was erroneously added later by a copyist.

make by-laws and inflict punishments, and was allowed to export foreign bullion. It was given exemption from customs duties for four years, and severe penalties were provided for violations of its monopoly by Englishmen.[29] This charter served as the basis of later ones, and with it the great tool for opening the Eastern trade was created.

From the above analysis it appears that the English trade to the East grew out of: (1) the Renaissance spirit of adventure and expansion, (2) the economic growth of England, (3) interest in the spice trade, and (4) the desire for private gain.

4. *The First Successful Years of the Company, 1600-1620*

The stock of the Company was immediately raised to £69,091, and extensive preparations were begun for the first voyage.[30] Lancaster was made captain and in April, 1601, four ships set sail.[31] The expedition was not a complete success for two ships were lost. However, trade had been instituted with the Spice Islands and hope was aroused. In 1604, a second undertaking was sent out and proved to be very successful. The profit of the first two voyages was said to have been 95 per cent.[32] The first nine voyages (twelve according to some methods of reckoning), were each fitted out as separate undertakings; the capital for each was subscribed separately, and the profits went only to those who had contributed. The joint-stock principle of the Company was, therefore, not adhered to in this matter.[33] The total capital subscribed for the "separate voyages" according to Milburn was £464,284, or an average of £38,690

[29] *Charters of the East India Company*, pp. 3-26; Macgregor, *op. cit.*, v. 4, pp. 298-99; Bruce, *op. cit.*, v. 1, pp. 136-43; *State Papers, Colonial; East Indies* (1513-1616), p. 99; Ilbert, *op. cit.*, pp. 3-13; Macpherson, *India*, pp. 79-81; Stevens, *op. cit.*, pp. 64, 198; Bowman and Roper, *op. cit.*, pp. 14-16; Anderson, *Origin of Commerce* (London, 1787), v. 2, p. 196.

[30] Macpherson, *India*, p. 81 ff; Stevens, *op. cit.*, pp. 12-135.

[31] Stevens, *op. cit.*, pp. 57-58; Macgregor, *op. cit.*, v. 4, p. 300.

[32] Craik, *op. cit.*, v. 2, pp. 13-15: Macgregor, *op. cit.*, v. 4, pp. 300-301 ff.

[33] Macgregor, *op. cit.*, v. 4, p. 307; Ilbert, *op. cit.*, p. 13; Stevens, *op. cit.*, p. 146. Commenting upon the character of the Company's early organization Hunter (*op. cit.*, v. 1, pp. 353-54) says, "A corporation so constituted seems closely to resemble a modern joint stock company, but the resemblance is by no means complete. Its nature was rather that of a modern syndicate formed to obtain from the Crown a concession of the East India Trade for a certain number of years, and then to work the concession by means of successive new syndicates or groups of subscribers from among its own members for separate voyages, but under its corporate control."

per voyage, which gave an average profit of 138 per cent.[34] Approximately £200,000 of merchandise and bullion were exported in twenty-six ships, while at least a million pounds sterling were returned in spices and silks.[35]

In 1609, James I had granted the Company a perpetual charter and had somewhat expanded its former privileges.[36] Strengthened by this and finding the arrangement of the first voyages not wholly satisfactory, the Company organized its trade on a joint-stock basis in 1612-13. A capital of £429,000 was provided and a number of ships were equipped.[37] The next four voyages proved to be very successful, making an average profit of 87½ per cent, and in 1617 a second joint-stock amounting to £1,629,040 was eagerly subscribed.[38] Figures show that the trade continued to grow rapidly until 1620. The total exports of goods and bullion to the East from 1601-24 amounted to about £1,100,000 in one hundred and seven ships, while imports from the East totalled at least £3,260,000.[39]

The key to the trade was spices. Pepper, cloves, mace, nutmegs, and indigo, together with raw silk, were the chief articles of import.[40] Iron, tin, lead, woollens, and bullion constituted most of the export trade—bullion predominating.[41] In 1617 the Company had twelve factories in the Orient. The spice trade centered about Bantam, while other important centers were

[34]Milburn, *op. cit.*, v. 1, p. XI. Excellent accounts of these early voyages are in Milburn, pp. V-XI and Hunter, *op. cit.*, v. 1, chap. 7. For an explanation of how the number nine or twelve voyages may be obtained see appendix X.

[35]Bal Krishna, *Commercial Relations Between India and England* (London, 1924), pp. 282 and 286. See also Macgregor, *op. cit.*, v. 4, pp. 305-06, and for complete figures relating to this early trade see appendix X. Other authorities dealing with these first twelve years are: Chatterton, *op. cit.*, pp. 46-105; Traill, *op. cit.*, v. 4, pp. 51-55, 134-42; *Universal History, Modern*, v. 8, pp. 260-70; Bruce, *op. cit.*, v. 1, pp. 143-65.

[36]*Charters of the East India Company*, pp. 25-53; Chatterton, *op. cit.*, pp. 74-77; J. W. Kaye, *The Administration of the East India Company* (London, 1853), p. 112.

[37]Bruce, *op. cit.*, v. 1, pp. 165-67; Chatterton, *op. cit.*, pp. 106-07; Macgregor, *op. cit.*, v. 4, pp. 307-08; Macpherson, *India*, pp. 93-97.

[38]Macgregor, *op. cit.*, v. 4, p. 310; Hunter, *op. cit.*, v. 1, pp. 307, 364; Milburn, *op. cit.*, v. 1, p. XV.

[39]Krishna, *op. cit.*, pp. 282, 286. For more complete statistics see appendix VIII, IX, X. For a fuller discussion of the events of these years see Bruce, *op. cit.*, v. 1, pp. 165-251.

[40]Statement of Thomas Munn in Macpherson, *India*, pp. 103-04; Bruce, *op. cit.*, v. 1, p. 159.

[41]Stevens, *op. cit.*, pp. 36-37; Krishna, *op. cit.*, p.282.

Surat in India and Firando (Hirado) in Japan.[42] With the Company's financial and commercial position so favorable, and with the growing demand at home for an expanded woollen market, it seems probable that a trade would soon have been established with China had adversity not befallen the Company.[43] These misfortunes will be developed in succeeding sections.

5. *Dutch Competition and the Beginning of the Decline of the Company, 1620-1635*

The first of the forces which brought about the decline of the London Adventurers was the competition of the Dutch East India Company. This was felt from the beginning, and by 1614 the conflict between the two had assumed considerable proportion.[44] By 1619 it had become so severe that the governments of England and Holland intervened and arranged an agreement for united action between the two companies. It provided that each should

> continue to carry on the trade separately, but upon the principle of each sharing in the different branches of it in certain specific proportions, under the superintendence of what was called a Council of Defence, to be composed of four of the principal servants of each company's resident in the country.[45]

The agreement, however, was never kept, and the Dutch adopted definite means to obtain possession of the Spice Islands. This policy of engrossing the spice trade culminated in the Amboyna massacre of 1623.[46] This massacre and the continued opposition of the Dutch compelled the English to abandon Firando and most of the factories in the Spice Islands from which expeditions to China might have been made. In fact the English were virtually excluded from areas east of India, and thus all

[42]Macgregor, *op. cit.*, v. 4, pp. 305, 311-12; Bruce, *op. cit.*, v. 1, pp. 168-69, 188-90.

[43]Stevens, *op. cit.*, pp. 198-99. The hope was to find a market for woollens in a northern country.

[44]Bruce, *op. cit.*, v. 1, p. 199; Macgregor, *op. cit.*, v. 4, p. 308; Macpherson, *India*, pp. 94-111. The company encountered the opposition of the Portugese from the first, but this was soon broken and had largely disappeared by 1622. See Hunter, *op. cit.*, v. 1, chap. 8. For a discussion of the development of Portugese and Dutch power in the East see Lavisse and Rambaud, *op. cit.*, v. 5, pp. 903-10.

[45]Craik, *op. cit.*, v. 2, p. 17; Bruce, *op. cit.*, v. 1, pp. 31, 212; Macpherson, *India*, pp. 100-01; Hunter, *op. cit.*, v. 1, pp. 368-70.

[46]Bruce, *op. cit.*, v. 1, pp. 221-28, 232-33, 237-39, 345-47; Macgregor, *op. cit.*, v. 4, pp. 312-17; Hunter, *op. cit.*, v. 1, pp. 371-404; *Universal History, Modern*, v. 8, pp. 286-309.

projected intercourse with China had to be abandoned.[47] This seems to have been the most important result of the conflict with the Dutch, for the figures show no extensive immediate decline in the Company's trade, and no great advance in that of the Dutch.[48] This friction between the two rivals continued intermittently through the rest of the period, and after 1635 it became stronger than ever.[49] It was a constant menace and deterred the Company from undertaking any very ambitious moves. The piratical attacks of the Dutch upon the Chinese also served to prejudice the latter against foreigners.[50]

Lack of royal support was a second factor which contributed to the difficulties of the Company and prevented expansion of its Eastern trade. The first two Stuarts seemed unable or unwilling to offer the organization adequate protection against the Hollanders or against its enemies at home. Several times between 1618 and 1635 the Company petitioned the King for redress against the Dutch, but it never received satisfaction. The massacre of Amboyna was allowed to pass with only a feeble protest.[51] In 1628 the Company became desperate and petitioned Parliament, whose dissolution the following year prevented its taking action. Not only did the King fail to offer protection but he allowed Buckingham to extort £10,000 from the Company before its fleet was allowed to sail in 1624.[52] About the only thing that Charles I did for the organization was to talk about the renewal of its charter in 1629, issue an order in 1631

[47]Bruce, *op. cit.*, v. 1, pp. 250-51, 263-64, 268-69, 278-81; Robinson, *op. cit.*, pp. 5-6.

[48]Krishna, *op. cit.*, pp. 285-87 and especially tonnage figures pp. 323-24 for the English trade; for the Dutch trade see p. 289. The early years of the conflict did perhaps slow down the rate of the English Company's advance, but it certainly did not cause any marked decline, as figures in appendix IX will show. It was not until after 1635 that the dangerous decline of the Company began.

[49]*State Papers, Colonial; East Indies* (1630-34), p. 437; (1635-39), pp. 139, 271, 272, 273, 295, 303, 315, 334, 335, 336, 341; Bruce, *op. cit.*, v. 1, pp. 296, 312, 316-17, 327-28; Hunter, *op. cit.*, v. 1, chaps. 9-10.

[50]Eames, *op. cit.*, pp. 7-8; Cocks, *Diary*, v. 1, pp. 259-60; v. 2, pp. 40, 41, 42, 56, 70, 302, 303, 324, 327.

[51]Eames, *op. cit.*, pp. 10-12; Bruce, *op. cit.*, v. 1, for petitions delivered by the Company against the Dutch, and negotiations carried on, pp. 202, 219, 226-28, 252-54, 266, 276-78, 284-86, 318; *State Papers, Colonial; East Indies* (1622-24), pp. 193-94; Hunter, *op. cit.*, v. 1, pp. 404-34.

[52]Bruce, *op. cit.*, v. 1, pp. 282, 298-99, for petition to Parliament; Kaye, *op. cit.*, p. 112; G. Cawston and A. H. Keane, *Early Chartered Companies* (London, 1896), p. 96; Anderson, *op. cit.*, v. 2, p. 307.

restraining the private trade of its servants, and promise to secure redress from the Dutch.[53]

Popular opposition was the third difficulty encountered by the East India Traders. During the latter years of Elizabeth, public wrath had been aroused against internal monopolists, and this trouble once more came to a head in the early 1620's, with the impeachment of a number of these royal favorites.[54] Public dislike of the Company was apparent from the first, but after 1614 it became more pronounced and reached a climax in the early twenties at the time of the general attack on monopolies.[55] It is interesting to note that the years of this outbreak (1620-24) were years of crisis in the woollen trade, and that the main argument used against the East India Traders was that they exported too much bullion and not enough goods.[56] Thomas Munn ably defended the Company by pointing out that it supplied England with spices at one-half the former price, that it trained men for the navy, that it employed many persons, that it increased the total trade of the nation, and that it was generally beneficial to England.[57] The idea of monopoly, however, seemed to grate on the nerves of the liberty-loving English. In 1628 there occurred another severe attack upon the Company which was ably met and so did not prevent its receiving a new charter.[58] The nature of the attacks was in part public and in part private. The private grievances soon culminated in the formation of various "interloping" groups who continually interfered with the Eastern trade.

Decline in the Company's prestige characterized this period. Its actual trade did not decrease but remained stationary at

[53]For charter renewal see Bruce, *op. cit.*, v. 1, p. 293. For restraining order see Milburn, *op. cit.*, v. 1, p. XXIII; Bowman and Roper, *op. cit.*, pp. 29-30.

[54]*Parliamentary History* (London, 1751-71), v. 4, pp. 416, 452-82; Craik, *op. cit.*, v. 2, pp. 23-28.

[55]Krishna, *op. cit.*, p. 56. Dudley Diggs in a pamphlet, the *Trades Increase*, in 1614, ably pointed out that the export of money did not injure English trade. *New London Magazine*, June, 1786, pp. 286-87.

[56]E. Lipson, *The Woollen Trade* (London, 1921), p. 109; Kaye, *op. cit.*, pp. 110-11; Traill, *op. cit.*, v. 4, pp. 137-40; Macgregor, *op. cit.*, v. 4, pp. 314-17.

[57]See Thomas Munn, *Defense of the East India Trade;* Craik, *op. cit.*, v. 2, pp. 108-10; Macpherson, *India*, pp. 103-04.

[58]*Lords Journal*, v. 3, p. 878; Traill, *op. cit.*, v. 4, pp. 137-42; *Common Journal*, v. 1, pp. 852, 893; David Macpherson, *Annals of Commerce* (London, 1805), v. 2, p. 351; Anderson, *op. cit.*, v. 2, p. 329.

about 2000 to 3000 tons per annum. It lost a number of ships, it became indebted at home, and its shares sold at twenty per cent discount.[59] In 1631, a third joint stock of only £420,700 was subscribed, and about one-half of it went to former stockholders for their interest in the equipment.[60] All of these factors show that the Company's popularity and fortune were declining.

6. *The Appearance of the Interlopers and the First Attempt to Trade with China*

"Interlopers" were a fourth source of trouble. These men who traded in the East in defiance of the Company's charter were a constant menace, often threatening to overpower it.

The first interloper appeared in 1604, immediately after the success of the first voyage to India. The King granted a license to "Sir Edward Michelborne, with his associates to discover the countries of Cathaia, China, Japan, Corea, and Cambaia, and the islands and countries thereto adjoining, and to trade with the people there, notwithstanding any grant or charter to the contrary."[61] Michelborne sailed to the East and seized some Indian and Chinese junks, thus revealing the predatory character, typical of so many of his successors.[62] In 1618 James I granted letters of patent to a Scotch Company under the leadership of Sir James Cunningham, but the London Adventurers were able to secure its annullment in return for a certain monetary consideration.[63] Examples of the interlopers appeared sporadically until 1635 when a strong and powerful organization came into existence. Part of the trouble in 1628 was due to the petition of the Earl of Warwick for redress from the Company, which had seized two of his ships in the East Indies.[64] On the whole the interlopers, due to their bad behavior, were detrimental to English commerce, but in spite of this, it remained for them to carry the first English flag direct to China. Before deal-

[59]Krishna, *op. cit.*, p. 323 for trade figures; for other facts pp. 61-65, 282; Kaye, *op. cit.*, pp. 112-13; Macpherson, *India*, pp. 111-12; Macgregor, *op. cit.*, v. 4, pp. 313-15.

[60]Bruce, *op. cit.*, v. 1, pp. 306-07; Macgregor, *op. cit.*, v. 4, pp. 321-22.

[61]Bruce, *op. cit.*, v. 1, pp. 153-54; Cordier, *op. cit.*, v. 1, p. 12; *State Papers, Colonial; East Indies* (1513-1616), p. 141.

[62]Macpherson, *India*, p. 84; Macgregor, *op. cit.*, v. 4, p. 301; Craik, *op. cit.*, v. 2, p. 13; Eames, *op. cit.*, pp. 9-10.

[63]Bruce, *op. cit.*, v. 1, pp. 193-94; Macgregor, *op. cit.*, v. 4, pp. 312-13.

[64]*Lords Journal*, v. 4, p. 878.

ing with this, however, one must consider the early activities of the Company in the direction of China.

Silks and china-ware early appeared as articles which the traders wanted. For these, the merchants were forced to depend upon indirect trade with Chinese junks.[65] To facilitate this exchange and to establish a base for later attempts at the China trade, the English established a factory in Japan in 1613.[66] Letters from Firando, the English center in Japan, show a constant interest in commerce with China, and also that traders there had a copy of a letter from King James to the Emperor.[67] This move toward establishing a trade with Cathay culminated in the work of Richard Cocks, factor at Firando between 1615-22.[68] Cocks attempted, with the aid of a friendly Chinese merchant, Captain Dittis, to get the King's letter translated and to establish trade with the Chinese. Apparently neither of these objects was ever accomplished, and no recorded voyage was ever made to China, although it appears that in 1621 the English were granted the privilege of sending two ships a year to Foochow.[69] Misfortune descended upon the factory, as a result of Dutch and Japanese hostility, and in 1622 Cocks wrote complaining of the deplorable conditions, and calling attention to the opportunities which still existed in China except for the civil wars. In 1623 the factory was withdrawn following the Amboyna disaster, and so ended an experiment which might have opened trade with China a half-century earlier.[70]

The first English ship at Canton was sent from India under a "Truce and Free Trade" with Portugal in 1635. After 1622 the English traders and the Court of Directors maintained a con-

[65] *Factories in India* (1618-21), pp. 207-08; Martin, *op. cit.*, v. 1, p. 301; *State Papers, Colonial; East Indies* (1513-1616), p. 292.

[66] Macpherson, *India*, pp. 89-90; Martin, *op. cit.*, v. 1, pp. 295-98; Anderson, *op. cit.*, v. 2, p. 259.

[67] *State Papers, Colonial; East Indies* (1617-1621), p. 40 and (1513-1616), pp. 343, 356-57, 283; Cocks, *Diary*, v. 2, p. 298; Eames, *op. cit.*, pp. 11-12. The letter was probably sent out in 1612-13 when the factory was opened in Japan.

[68] Cocks' work is best set forth in his *Diary*, and in the letters contained therein. See v. 1, pp. 20, 23, 25, 29, 32, 58, 60, 66, 74, 83, 101, 116, 223, 296, 298, 340, 341, 342; v. 2, pp. 2-3, 21, 44, 125, 126, 139, and letters v. 2, pp. 271, 284, 309, 321, 324, 327, 333, 339.

[69] *State Papers, Colonial; East Indies* (1513-1616), p. 460, and (1517-21), pp. 105, 124-29, 132, 412.

[70] Cocks, *Diary*, v. 2, pp. 338-40; *State Papers, Colonial; East Indies* (1622-24), pp. 65, 88; Morse, *Chronicle*, v. 1, pp. 10-12.

stant interest in the China trade, as letters from the East show. They wanted to use the "Middle Kingdom" as a market for woollen goods and a purchasing place for silk, but the hostility of the Dutch and Portuguese and the financial weakness of the Company prevented any positive action.[71] In fact the Company refused to accept an offer of trade at Taiwan in Formosa made in 1624. Traders were also of the opinion that the Chinese would "admit no stranger in their country,"[72] but the facts already presented show this to be not entirely true. (See sec. 3 of chap. 6 for a fuller discussion.) It is probable that this idea was fostered by the Portuguese and the Dutch who were trading in China at the time. In 1633 the Court of Directors in London indicated its willingness to attempt trade with China, and in 1635 Mr. Smithwich read before the Court a proposal for such trade.[73] In the meantime the factors in India had patched up a "Truce and Free Trade to China" with the Portuguese. They were to be allowed to trade freely in return for carrying Portuguese treasure from Macao to Goa.[74] Under this agreement the ship *London* was sent from India to Macao in 1635. The Portuguese objected to commercial dealings but the Chinese officials indicated that trade might be had if a present were given. The *London* did little trading, paid a measuring fee of 1400 reals of eight, and returned to Goa, where the Portuguese appropriated most of the profits.[75] It would seem that Portuguese hostility rather than Chinese, caused the failure of this voyage, and the same is true of many later ones.

The first voyage direct from England to China was made by ships sent by an interloping association formed by William Courteen and others. The organization was licensed by Charles I in 1635 for financial reasons and he himself became a member. In spite of the Company's protest that such action violated its charter, the new combination was formally established with ex-

[71] *State Papers, Colonial; East Indies* (1625-29), pp. 48-49, 154-56, 312, 373, and (1630-34) p. 335; Auber, *op. cit.*, pp. 130-34; Macpherson, *India*, pp. 106-11.

[72] Morse, *Chronicle*, v. 1, pp. 29, 41.

[73] *State Papers, Colonial; East Indies and Persia* (1630-34), p. 375; *Court Minutes* (1635-39), pp. 118-19.

[74] Eames, *op. cit.*, pp. 11-12; Morse, *Chronicle*, v. 1, p. 12; Bruce, *op. cit.*, v. 1, p. 325.

[75] *Factories in India* (1634-36), pp. 211, 226-30. Report of Henry Bornford the commander of the *London*. Morse, *Chronicle*, v. 1, p. 13.

tensive privileges in 1637 and continued to harass the Company for many years.[76] The new association, taking advantage of the "Truce and Free Trade to China," sent a fleet of four ships under the command of Captain Weddell to Macao in 1637. He was refused trade by the jealous Portuguese, and upon proceeding to Canton he was stopped by the Chinese and asked to wait until permission could be obtained from the officials. Finally the British merchants were allowed to go to Canton to trade, but the ships were kept outside the Bogue forts.[77] The Portuguese in the meantime intrigued with the Chinese with the result that the latter began preparations to drive away the English. The attack seems to have been opened by the Chinese; Weddell at once opened fire, silenced and seized the Bogue forts, and proceeded to Canton. The Chinese, only too willing to cover their error, laid the blame upon the Portuguese and allowed trade to continue.[78] The Chinese merchants seemed desirous of trading, and some 10,000 reals of eight were distributed among the officials. A cargo consisting of sugars, ginger, silks, china-ware, and other articles to the amount of 62,000 reals of eight was obtained. This was loaded in one ship which was sent to England while the others cruised about the East Indies.[79] Before leaving Weddell entered into the following agreement regarding future trade: that in "leiwe of free and ample trade and residence, the English would yearly paye the King 20,000 tayes [30,000 reals of eight], fowre peece of iron ordnance and 50 musketts."[80] On the whole it would appear that the difficulties encountered were due more to the Portuguese intrigues than to innate Chinese hostility. The greed of the officials was apparent, but the terms for future trade were rather liberal and showed no exclusive tendencies.

[76] *Court Minutes* (1635-39), pp. 124-31 and 275-76; Macpherson, *India*, pp. 112-15; Morse, *Chronicle*, v. 1, pp. 14-15; Macgregor, *op. cit.*, v. 4, pp. 318-19; Cordier, *op. cit.*, v. 1, pp. 12-13.

[77] Morse, *Chronicle*, v. 1, pp. 14-25; Martin, *op. cit.*, v. 2, pp. 4-6; Lavisse and Rambaud, *op. cit.*, v. 5, p. 910 gives the date of Weddell's voyage as 1634 but this is obviously at variance with the documents. See Peter Mundy, *Travels of* (London, 1919), v. 3, ser. II of Hakluyt publications, pp. 158-316.

[78] Martin, *op. cit.*, v. 2, pp. 4-6; Eames, *op. cit.*, pp. 12-22; Morse, *Chronicle*, v. 1, pp. 25-26. See account quoted from Captain Weddell's *Journal*, in G. Staunton, *Embassy* (London, 1798), v. 1, pp. 3-12, and in Milburn, *op. cit.*, v. 2, pp. 466-68.

[79] Morse, *Chronicle*, v. 1, pp. 21-27. The best accounts other than those already mentioned are Williams, *History of China*, pp. 92-93, and *Middle Kingdom*, v. 2, pp. 444-45, and Macpherson, *India*, pp. 113-14.

[80] Morse, *Chronicle*, v. 1, p. 25.

In the years which followed the Weddell expedition the Company fell into great distress, and the interlopers seemed to be little interested in the China trade. A few ships were sent to Canton from the factories in India under the Anglo-Portuguese treaty, and an occasional interloper ship visited Macao, but little trade of importance was carried on.[81] In 1644 the *Hinde* made a trip from Surat to Macao. It was well treated by the Chinese but badly treated by the Portuguese. After paying an exceptionally high measuring fee of 3500 reals of eight, it took on a cargo and returned. The *Hinde* also reported that the *William* of the Courteen association was at Macao in 1644.[82]

The Manchu conquest of China, between 1644 and 1660, served as a fifth handicap to the development of trade. Its damage to commerce and industry was amply testified by reports from the East. The Portuguese trade at Macao was falling off and the junk trade with the Indies was interrupted.[83] This together with the other severe troubles of the Company with which we shall deal in the next section, served to prevent any extensive trade developing with China during the period.

7. *Decline of the Company 1635-1657*

Relatively little need be said regarding the history of the Company during these two decades. This was the greatest period of discouragement which it ever witnessed, and at times it appeared to be disintegrating, but it finally recovered and emerged stronger than ever.[84] Many of the causes for the decline have been noted and during this period they acted with an ever increasing vigor, bringing the Company into dire straits. The first of these causes was the interlopers. The Courteen association, above noted, harassed the Company for a number of years. Not only did it compete with the London Merchants, but it attacked native ships and committed piracies which generally discredited the English with the Orientals.[85] Negotiations were

[81] *Factories in India* (1637-40), pp. 25, 131, 281.

[82] Morse, *Chronicle*, v. 1, pp. 31-35; *Factories in India* (1642-45), pp. 179-80, 254; Martin, *op. cit.*, v. 2, p. 7; Cordier, *op. cit.*, v. 1, p. 13.

[83] *Factories in India* (1646-50), pp. 231-32, and (1651-54), pp. 88 and 121; Martin, *op. cit.*, v. 2, p. 7; Craik, *op. cit.*, v. 2, p. 60.

[84] Bruce, *op. cit.*, v. 1, pp. 329-528 gives the best account of these years. Eames, *op. cit.*, pp. 23-26 sums up the Company's troubles quite well.

[85] Macgregor, *op. cit.*, v. 4, p. 319; *Court Minutes* (1640-43), pp. 48, 74, 133, 233, 241, 242, 272.

early begun to bring it into the Company, and these were partly successful in 1649.[86] However, some of the Courteen interlopers formed a new organization called the Assada Merchants.[87] These fused in part with the Company in 1650; but a group of them split off in 1655 to form the Merchant Adventurers when Cromwell opened the East to free trade. In 1657 Cromwell decided to support the London Merchants and withdrew the license of the Merchant Adventurers.[88] This partially silenced the interlopers for a time.

The second difficulty confronting the Company was the duplicity of the rulers. Charles I granted charters to interlopers; then in 1640 he sold the Company's pepper at a loss of £31,500. He also failed to protect it from the Dutch or from attacks at home.[89] Cromwell forced the organization to lend him £50,000, declared the East India trade open, and licensed interlopers before he finally decided to confine the trade to the Company.[90] The severe competition and attack of the Dutch and Portuguese constituted a third factor.[91] A fourth obstacle was the civil war at home.[92] Financial embarrassments and sailing losses constituted a fifth obstruction to the Company.[93] A sixth complication was the high tariffs which it had to pay,[94] and a final difficulty was internal attacks upon its monopoly.[95]

The obstacles which so greatly hampered the Company were summed up a number of times in petitions to the King, to the Council of State, and in 1641 to Parliament.[96] All of these failed,

[86] *Court Minutes* (1640-43), pp. 151, 239-42, 265; Morse, *Chronicle*, v. 1, p. 27, see footnote; and Cordier, *op. cit.*, v. 1, p. 12.

[87] Bruce, *op. cit.*, v. 1, p. 568; Macgregor, *op. cit.*, v. 4, p. 322.

[88] Bruce, *op. cit.*, v. 1, pp. 433-35, 489-96, 512-27, 569-70; Macgregor, *op. cit.*, v. 4, pp. 322-25. A good account of the whole interloping question during these years is to be found in Macpherson, *India*, pp. 112-25.

[89] Macpherson, *India*, p. 116, for the pepper incident, and *Court Minutes* (1640-43), pp. 132-33 for other details.

[90] Eames, *op. cit.*, p. 24; Bruce, *op. cit.*, v. 1, pp. 487-527 especially 504, 569-70; Macgregor, *op. cit.*, v. 4, pp. 319, 324-25.

[91] Eames, *op. cit.*, p. 25; Bruce, *op. cit.*, v. 1, p. 564; *Court Minutes* (1640-43), pp. 50-52.

[92] *Court Minutes* (1640-43), introduction, p. iii; Craik, *op. cit.*, v. 2, p. 60; Eames, *op. cit.*, pp. 25-26; Auber, *op. cit.*, pp. 135-36.

[93] Eames, *op. cit.*, p. 24; Bruce, *op. cit.*, v. 1, pp. 468-69; Craik, *op. cit.*, v. 2, p. 48; *Commons Journal*, v. 4, p. 34; Macpherson, *India*, pp. 115-17.

[94] *Court Minutes* (1640-43), pp. 132-33.

[95] *Lords Journal*, v. 4, pp. 265, 271, 274; v. 9, pp. 20-24.

[96] *Petition and Remonstrance* (London, 1641). This is a masterly argument presented to Parliament calling for aid when the King failed to give it. The

however, until Cromwell finally decided to support the London Merchants.

Evidences of retrogression are to be found not only in every letter from the East and in the Court Records,[97] but also in the decreasing value of the Company's stocks and trade. Its stocks showed an appreciable decline, and even in 1661 were sold as low as 90-94, while in 1651 only £30,246 could be raised by subscriptions toward a fourth joint stock.[98] Table 1 which shows the amount of the Company's trade for five-year periods indicates conditions better than anything else.

TABLE 1.—TRADE OF THE EAST INDIA COMPANY—TOTALS FOR FIVE-YEAR PERIODS*

Years	No. of ships	Tonnage	Export £	Years	No. of ships	Tonnage	Export £
1601–05	11	3,270	40,904	1630–35	31	14,620	692,711
1605–10	6	2,170	100,780	1635–40	16	8,400	299,268
1610–15	33	13,057	127,054	1640–45	25	11,810	380,058
1615–20	44	22,799	471,318	1645–50	25	10,450	386,000
1620–25	28	11,686	326,516	1650–55	23	8,470	209,853
1625–30	30	14,050	496,410	1655–60	36	11,585	390,583

64 private ships also sailed to the East between 1635 and 1660.
*Based on Krishna, *op. cit.*, pp. 282, 323-24.

With the Company's trade in a declining condition, its position in India insecure, and its very existence threatened, it is little wonder that no serious attempts were made to open the China trade. Add to this the civil war in China, and the fact that the country at that time provided no articles of trade vital to English welfare. These factors constitute sufficient reason for the late beginning of the Canton trade. Appeal to the prosaic bogey of Chinese exclusiveness is unnecessary.

petitions to the King run over a number of years and their texts may be found in the following:

For 1637, *Court Minutes* (1635-39), pp. 270-74.
1640, *Court Minutes* (1640-43), pp. 52-54.
1641, *Ibid.*, pp. 128, 132-133.
1648, *Lords Journal*, v. 10, pp. 374, 394; Eames, *op. cit.*, pp. 28-29.
1649, Macgregor, *op. cit.*, v. 4, p. 322; Bruce, *op. cit.*, v. 1, pp. 434-35.
1651, Bruce, *op. cit.*, v. 1, p. 458.
1652, *Ibid.*, pp. 466-69—25 private petitions included.

[97]See Bruce, *op. cit.*, v. 1, pp. 329-528, *passim.*

[98]Krishna, *op. cit.*, p. 316; Bruce, *op. cit.*, v. 1, pp. 468-69.

CHAPTER IV

THE ORIGIN OF THE CHINA TRADE (1660-1700)

1. *Royal Favor and the Establishment of the East India Trade, 1657-1688*

In the period succeeding 1657, the Company flourished under royal patronage and other favorable conditions. It was enabled to establish itself firmly at home, deal with its foreign opponents, and stabilize its factories and trade in India. Then and only then was it ready to begin extensive experimentation in the China trade. The story of the Company's recovery together with its causes will be told briefly in the following pages.

First among the factors which restored the strength and prosperity of the London Merchants was official patronage and support.[1] Prior to 1657 Cromwell's policy was inconsistent. The Navigation Acts and his war on the Dutch were favorable to the Company, but he virtually repudiated all of this by throwing open the Eastern trade to all English in 1655.[2] However, in 1657 he yielded to the petitions of the Company, and, acting upon the advice of the Council of State, revoked the license to the Merchant Adventurers and decided in favor of confining the Eastern trade to an exclusive organization. In consequence of this the two groups were amalgamated.[3] A new charter was granted to the Company in 1657, and the government undertook to suppress interlopers. A new capital stock of £786,000 was immediately subscribed,[4] and in 1658 twenty-five ships were sent to the East against a total of nine for the previous five years.[5]

Charles II and James II were consistently favorable to the Company because it supported their anti-Dutch policy. Charles II granted it a new and liberal charter in 1661, and confirmed

[1] *Universal History, Modern*, v. 8, pp. 309-24.

[2] Anderson, *op. cit.*, v. 2, p. 431; Macpherson, *Annals*, v. 2, p. 460.

[3] Bruce, *op. cit.*, v. 1, pp. 512-20, 528-39; Macgregor, *op. cit.*, v. 4, pp. 324-25; Cordier, *op. cit.*, v. 1, p. 12.

[4] Robinson, *op. cit.*, pp. 6-9; Macpherson, *India*, pp. 122-24; *Commons Debates* (1660-1680), v. 1, p. 410; Craik, *op. cit.*, v. 2, pp. 61-62; Milburn, *op. cit.*, v. 1, p. XXIX.

[5] Krishna, *op. cit.*, p. 324. See appendix VIII.

this in subsequent grants made in 1677 and 1683.[6] He also accorded it numerous other privileges and in 1669 sold it the island of Bombay.[7] James II renewed the charter in 1686, and sent a frigate to India to protect its traders.[8] Parliament even took an interest in the Company and had a committee appointed in 1660 to consider its welfare.[9]

The second cause for the progress of the Company was the decline of interlopers. Most of these had merged with the London Merchants, and those who remained were suppressed with the support of the government.[10] In 1658, Skinner, a prominent interloper, was seized by the Company, and his trial involved the two houses of Parliament in a violent quarrel which was not ended until 1671.[11] Interlopers practically vanished until 1675. The London Merchants adopted a vigorous policy toward them, and in 1681 Charles II embargoed and seized some of their ships.[12] James II issued a patent especially restraining them, and this held them in check until the Glorious Revolution.[13]

The third cause for the revival of the Company was the foreign policy of the government. Cromwell forced the Dutch to pay it £85,000 compensation for damages done, while his strong foreign policy and favorable commercial treaties were beneficial to its trade.[14] Agreements with Portugal in 1654 and 1661 opened all of her eastern ports to England and thus aided the Company a great deal.[15] The various continental wars in which

[6]*Charters Granted to the East India Company*, pp. 54, 108, 116; Bowman and Roper, *op. cit.*, pp. 13-14; Macpherson, *India*, pp. 125, 136. See G. Birdwood, *Papers of the East India Company*, plate 8, a facsimile of part of the charter. Bruce, *op. cit.*, v. 1, pp. 555-61.

[7]*Charters Granted to the East India Company*, pp. 80, 96 and pp. 9-10 of a List of Charters printed in the back; for facsimile of grants of 1669 and 1677 see plates 9 and 11 of Birdwood, *op. cit.*; also note Craik, *op. cit.*, v. 2, pp. 100-102; Macgregor, *op. cit.*, v. 4, pp. 331-32; Macpherson, *India*, p. 127; Leon Levi, *History of British Commerce* (London, 1872), pp. 238-40.

[8]*Charters Granted to the East India Company*, pp. 125-41; Macpherson, *India*, pp. 141-43.

[9]*Commons Journal*, v. 8, p. 179.

[10]Bruce, *op. cit.*, v. 2, pp. 106-09 and 675.

[11]Anchitell Grey, *Debates of the House of Commons* (1667-94), v. 1, pp. 150-55, 445-62; *Lords Journal*, v. 11, pp. 20, 29; Macpherson, *India*, pp. 127-28; Milburn, *op. cit.*, v. 1, p. XXX.

[12]Macpherson, *India*, p. 138; Bruce, *op. cit.*, v. 2, pp. 351-54, 551.

[13]*Charters Granted to the East India Company*, p. 10 of the List of Charters found in the back of the book.

[14]Macpherson, *India*, pp. 122-24; Bruce, *op. cit.*, v. 1, pp. 71-75, 502-03.

[15]Auber, *op. cit.*, p. 137; Bruce, *op. cit.*, v. 1, pp. 71-72, and v. 2, pp. 101-06.

Holland was forced to participate weakened her and strengthened England commercially. The Treaty of Westminster in 1674 closed the conflict between the Dutch and the English and opened a new era of peace in the East which was followed by a great expansion of trade.[16] Dutch competition steadily declined, and the union of the crowns of England and Holland in 1689 served further to decrease this rivalry. England's foreign trade seemed generally to expand during the period, and much of this prosperity was shared by the Company.[17]

The final factor which led to the revival of the Company was the commercial policy of the government. The first Navigation Act, passed in 1651, was followed by others in 1660, 1661, and 1663. In reality these acts confined all English trade from the East Indies to the Company's ships. They were directed against the Dutch, and aided the English organization in outdistancing its old rival.[18] The fact that the Company was paying about £35,000 per year as revenue, and that its annual export was well above £300,000, accounts in part for the favorable treatment received from the government.[19]

Some difficulties, however, were encountered. The woollen and silk weavers were aroused by the importation of Indian calicoes which tended to displace their goods.[20] A series of petitions was presented to Parliament and considerable popular agitation provoked.[21] Josiah Child, in his *New Discourse on Trade* in 1665 (first published in 1668), thoroughly answered the opponents of the organization.[22] However, in 1675, the clothiers presented a petition to Parliament decrying the Company, and other malcontents united in charging it with exhausting the treasure of the country and decreasing the consumption of its manufactures.[23] These accusations drew forth an able defense by

[16]Abbott, *op. cit.*, v. 2, pp. 56-58, 81-85; Bruce, *op. cit.*, v. 2, pp. 326-28, 671-72. See table toward end of this section.

[17]Craik, *op. cit.*, v. 2, pp. 76-77.

[18]For act of 1651 see Macpherson, *India*, p. 121, and Bruce, *op. cit.*, v. 1, p. 71. For other acts see 12 Car. II, cap. 18; 13 Car. II, cap. 14; 15 Car. II, cap. 7; also note William Smart, *Economic Annals of the 19th Century* (1821-31) (London, 1917), v. 2, pp. 101-03.

[19]Krishna, *op. cit.*, p. 330 and table toward end of this section.

[20]Lipson, *op. cit.*, pp. 95-97; Macgregor, *op. cit.*, v. 4, pp. 328-29.

[21]T. Ellison, *Cotton Trade of Great Britain* (London, 1886), p. 8.

[22]Craik, *op. cit.*, v. 2, pp. 81-83.

[23]*Commons Journal*, v. 9, p. 371; Macgregor, *op. cit.*, v. 4, pp. 329-30.

Thomas Papillion.[24] In 1681 the opposition again came to a focus. A petition was presented to Parliament by the silk weavers, and the Company was roundly denounced by its many opponents.[25] Josiah Child again appeared to defend the association. He pointed out the necessity of a joint-stock corporation to carry on trade; he indicated the great military, financial, and commercial value of the trade to the nation, the great national service which the Company was performing, and the selfishness and greed of its opponents.[26] The woollen and silk interests, however, would not be satisfied until a statute was passed in 1700 prohibiting the importation of Indian calicoes.[27]

After 1675 the interlopers' activity revived, but did not cause noticeable trouble until after 1688. They fomented opposition at home, stirred up trouble in India, and sent out a number of ships which competed with the Company.[28] Many interlopers were prosecuted, while others were repressed by the King. Defending themselves in the Sands case of 1681, the interlopers questioned the King's right to grant charters without Parliamentary consent. The Company won its case but the challenge of the King's constitutional right was soon to bear fruit.[29] Pirates in the East molested the Company to some extent, while a fire in London destroyed a large stock of its goods.[30] French competition also put in its appearance, while foreign wars were depressing to trade.[31]

On the whole the Company showed signs of prosperity. Its shares of stock, which were selling at 90-94 in 1661, rose to 245-300 in 1680, and were selling at 300 in 1690.[32] Its financial

[24]Thomas Papillion, *The East India Trade* (London, 1677).

[25]Macgregor, *op. cit.*, v. 4, p. 331; *Commons Debates* (1660-1680), v. 1, pp. 409-13.

[26]Josiah Child, *Treatise Concerning the East-India Trade* (London, 1681); Robinson, *op. cit.*, pp. 13-17.

[27]11-12 Will. III. cap. 3; also in 1690 they obtained a statute placing a heavy duty on calicoes. 2 W. and M. cap. 4; A. P. Usher, *Industrial History of England* (Boston, 1920), chap. 11 has an excellent discussion.

[28]Bruce, *op. cit.*, v. 2, pp. 351-54, 433-35, 463-65, 475, 480-81, 485, 522, 551, 628-30.

[29]Macpherson, *India*, p. 138; Kaye, *op. cit.*, pp. 118-21.

[30]Macgregor, *op. cit.*, v. 4, pp. 326-28.

[31]Cordier, *op. cit.*, v. 1, p. 16; Bruce, *op. cit.*, v. 2, pp. 166-68, 185-96, 310-25.

[32]Krishna, *op. cit.*, p. 316. See also appendix V.

condition improved greatly,[33] and the following figures of its trade prove beyond a doubt that it was established on a firm basis.

TABLE 2.—TRADE OF THE EAST INDIA COMPANY—TOTALS FOR FIVE-YEAR PERIODS*

Year	No. of Ships	Export £	Tonnage	Year	No. of Ships	Export £	Tonnage
1655–60....	36	390,583	11,585	1675–80....	59	1,949,051	28,920
1660–65....	47	677,124	14,730	1680–85....	90	2,798,413	39,125
1665–70....	44	733,287	14,400	1685–90....	31	1,267,679	17,834
1670–75....	75	1,512,370	28,505				

*Based on Krishna, *op. cit.*, pp. 286, 296-97. See also appendix VIII and IX.

This period saw the Eastern trade at last securely established. Holland and Portugal, the Company's old rivals, were on the decline. The association was on a firm foundation at home and its settlements in India were thriving. Under these circumstances conditions were ripe for expansion. One direction of this expansion was toward China.

2. *Factors Necessary for the Establishment of Trade with China*

There were at least four requisites to a successful trade with China.

1. It was necessary for the Asiatic trade to become stabilized so that the Indian and Spice Island factories might be used as bases for trade to China. Since factories had not been located there, and since the Chinese would allow no permanent fortified places on their shores, some outside base was essential.

2. The restoration of the Company's prestige and financial power was also necessary before any expansion movements could be undertaken. Both of these conditions were realized after 1660, as we have noted, while the remaining two were to be realized during the latter half of the 17th century.

3. The development of favorable circumstances in China was absolutely necessary to trade there. During the last years of the Ming dynasty, China was economically and politically on the decline. Civil strife rent the country, while agriculture, indus-

[33]See financial statements of the Company for years 1646, 1664, and 1690 given in Macgregor, *op. cit.*, v. 4, pp. 322, 327-28, 334.

try, and trade were disrupted.[34] The attitude toward foreigners seems, on the whole, to have been one of indifference, and the idea of Chinese hostility has been greatly over-emphasized.[35] In 1644 the Manchus proclaimed Shunche Emperor, and the greater part of his eighteen years of rule was devoted to the conquest of China and the suppression of uprisings.[36] There is no positive evidence that during the early years of his reign Shunche was particularly opposed to foreigners; rather, the civil war and various measures arising from it account for the unfavorable trade conditions which existed.[37] The English, however, took advantage of the civil war. They were allowed to open trade at Amoy and Formosa in return for supporting the opponents of the Manchus, who held this region for a time.[38] Between 1662 and 1667 there was a severe attack on foreigners at Peking. This ended when Kanghi assumed personal rule, but again a series of civil wars occurred which did not end until 1684.[39] After the conclusion of these civil conflicts, in 1685, Kanghi, who had always showed favor to the foreigners, threw open all Chinese ports to foreign trade.[40] It was during the subsequent period of peace, prosperity,[41] and imperial favor that foreign trade with China became established.

4. The final prerequisite to the development of a sound trade was the discovery of some staple products. These were supplied in the beginning by silks, and then in an ever increasing measure by tea, which at the beginning of the 18th century came into demand in England.[42] A fifth factor which aided the develop-

[34]Cocks, *Diary*, v. 1, pp. 219, 284; v. 2, pp. 172, 285, 324, 327; D. C. Boulger, *History of China* (London, 1898), v. 1, pp. 496-532; Gowen and Hall, *op. cit.*, pp. 169-73; Mabel Lee, *Economic History of China* (New York, 1921), pp. 104-08.

[35]See *postea*, chap. 6, sec. 3, and compare with Auber, *op. cit.*, pp. 130-34.

[36]Boulger, *op. cit.*, v. 1, pp. 534-81; John Macgowan, *Imperial History of China* (London, 1897), pp. 518-27; Williams, *History of China*, pp. 45-47.

[37]Lee, *op. cit.*, pp. 106-12; Martin, *op. cit.*, v. 2, p. 7; Eames, *op. cit.*, pp. 36-37, gives a quotation showing that the civil war was hurting trade, especially through the forced withdrawal of all the people eight leagues inland.

[38]Eames, *op. cit.*, pp. 26-32.

[39]Macgowan, *op. cit.*, pp. 528-33; Gowen and Hall, *op. cit.*, pp. 190-91; Corner, *op. cit.*, p. 82; Boulger, *op. cit.*, v. 1, pp. 586-96; Eames, *op. cit.*, pp. 32-35.

[40]E. T. Williams, *China*, p. 243; Williams, *History of China*, pp. 46-47.

[41]Prosperity is shown by the fact that the area of cultivated land increased from 5,493,576 chuans in 1661 to 6,078,430 chuans in 1686. See Lee, *op. cit.*, pp. 109-12, 396-97.

[42]See *postea*, section 4 of this chapter.

ment of the China trade was a demand in England that the Company should export large quantities of woollen goods. It turned northward into China in search of a market.[43]

3. *Beginning of Regular Trade with China—Taiwan and Amoy, 1670-1689*

A great deal of interest was shown in the China trade between 1657 and 1670. After the charter grant of 1657, the Company began to look toward the "Middle Kingdom." Letters were written from England to factories in India suggesting the possibility of opening trade in China.[44] Several interloping and private ships went to Macao, and in 1657 the *William* and most probably the *King Ferdinand* were there (the latter may have been at Macao in 1658).[45] In 1658 the *Richard and Martha* and perhaps the *Reformation* were at Macao. The former was reported as having made a profitable voyage. Two of these ships went away without paying their duties which caused the mandarines to lay a heavy tax upon Macao.[46] The Court of Directors proceeded with its plan to open trade with China, and in 1664 the *Surat* was sent to Macao. It encountered the severe opposition of the Portuguese, and was charged a heavy fee by these officials.[47] It carried a cargo of 9573 reals of eight, and paid a port duty of 2926 reals of eight. After four months of haggling with officials and merchants, it took on part of a cargo and sailed away.[48] It should be noted that this voyage came during the anti-foreign outbreak at Peking, and this may have accounted in part for the cold reception which the ship received. A supercargo described the situation thus:

> Under ye Tartar's govte. little security of person; . . . nor is there any certainty of trade in any part of China under ye Tartar; who is an enemy to trade and hath depopulated all ye vast quantityes of islands on ye Coaste of all maratime parts of Chyna 8 Leagues from ye Sea . . .[49]

[43]Bruce, *op. cit.*, v. 2, p. 460; Stevens, *op. cit.*, p. 197.

[44]*Factories in India* (1655-60), pp. 160-61, 206, 312; *Court Minutes* (1655-59), p. XXVI.

[45]Morse, *Chronicle*, v. 1, p. 33; *Factories in India* (1655-60), pp. 49, 60-61, 76-77, 142 and 152, 160-61, 203.

[46]*Factories in India* (1655-60), pp. 119, 133, 160-61, 196, 312; *Court Minutes* (1655-59), pp. XXVI and 206 n.

[47]Morse, *Chronicle*, v. 1, pp. 32-35; *Factories in India* (1665-67), p. 7; Martin, *op. cit.*, v. 2, pp. 7-8.

[48]Morse, *Chronicle*, v. 1, p. 35; Williams, *Middle Kingdom*, v. 2, pp. 445-46; Auber, *op. cit.*, pp. 137-38.

[49]Eames, *op. cit.*, pp. 36-37.

This really shows the effects of civil war measures rather than innate hostility to trade. The failure of this voyage discouraged the English considerably, and this together with the refusal of the Portuguese to allow anyone at Macao without the King of Portugal's permission prevented any more trade there for a number of years.[50] Interest in China, however, was maintained, and in 1668 the Presidency of Surat wrote to the Court of Directors proposing a direct trade to China.[51]

Trade was attempted at a number of places in and around the "Middle Kingdom." In 1667 the Company's agents had been ordered to send home 100 lbs. of tea, and as this trade developed the English became determined to secure a factory nearer the source of supply.[52] They first attempted to open an indirect trade by establishing a factory at Tonquin. The *Zant* arrived there in 1672, and began negotiations for trade. It was treated somewhat roughly, and was constantly interfered with by the officials. Most of the goods had to be disposed of to the king, and many presents and bribes were necessary. At one time the trader wanted to leave but the king refused. The cargo was finally sold and a new one procured. The ship sailed away leaving the factors to collect debts and prepare for a future season.[53] This trading post thus founded "struggled along for twenty-five years under a system of gifts, perquisites, and exactions; unable to sell for cash; unable even to buy for cash," and with the whole trade subject to the will of the king.[54] English goods and woollens did not sell well, but this port was the only source of supply for Chinese silks, and so the indignities were submitted to until 1697, when the factory was withdrawn.[55]

Taiwan and Amoy were the next places with which the Company tried to trade. The former was situated on the island of Formosa and the latter on the mainland. The son of the pirate king Koxinga, who had maintained his independence from the

[50] *Ibid.*, pp. 37-38.
[51] *Factories in India* (1667-96), p. 28; Bruce, *op. cit.*, v. 2, pp. 258-60.
[52] Bowman and Roper, *op. cit.*, p. 13; Bruce, *op. cit.*, v. 2, pp. 210-11.
[53] Bruce, *op. cit.*, v. 2, pp. 297-98, 322-25; Morse, *Chronicle*, v. 1, pp. 35-37; Auber, *op. cit.*, pp. 138-45.
[54] Morse, *Chronicle*, v. 1, p. 36; Eames, *op. cit.*, p. 38.
[55] Morse, *Chronicle*, v. 1, pp. 37-40; Auber, *op. cit.*, p. 145; Bruce, *op. cit.*, v. 2, pp. 431-32.

Manchus, controlled these ports at this time.[56] He issued an invitation to European traders. Acting upon this, the *Crown* and *Bantam* went to open trade at Taiwan in 1671. On the return voyage they appear to have been lost. They negotiated an agreement with the king, however, whereby: (1) the English might sell or trade their goods with whom they pleased; (2) the old Dutch state house was leased as a factory; (3) each ship was to bring a specific amount of arms, ammunition, and other goods which were to be sold to the king.[57] In 1672 the *Return* and the *Experiment* arrived at Taiwan from England. The king tried to monopolize the trade, thus violating the earlier agreement, so the ships sailed away without cargoes.[58]

In 1674 the *Flying Eagle* went to Taiwan and obtained, after a great deal of trouble, fairly good terms. It also secured licenses for trade at Amoy, and after dispatching these to Bantam continued on its homeward journey. With these licenses a ship sailed to Amoy in 1676 and established a factory.[59] Trade continued under varying conditions for a number of years. In 1681 this commerce was temporarily suspended due to the conquest of Amoy by the Manchus, who, a few years later, conquered Formosa. In 1686 Taiwan, the least prosperous and most vexatious of the two settlements, was abandoned.[60] At Amoy the Manchu officials dominated the trade, but on the whole they treated the foreign merchants fairly well considering the fact that the latter had been helping rebels. Trade was allowed provided enough presents were given. The measuring fee varied from T. 400 to T. 750, while presents amounted to several hundred taels.[61] In 1687 the customs duty was replaced by a single measuring fee.[62] The traders who came and went practically every year experienced the usual bargaining and quarreling, and

[56]Boulger, *op. cit.*, v. 1, pp. 586-96; Macgowan, *op. cit.*, p. 533; Corner, *op. cit.*, p. 83; E. T. Williams, *China*, p. 216.

[57]Eames, *op. cit.*, pp. 30-32; Morse, *Chronicle*, v. 1, p. 41; See, *op. cit.*, p. 49; *China Materials*, v. 1, pp. 76-82.

[58]Morse, *Chronicle*, v. 1, p. 41; Eames, *op. cit.*, pp. 31-32; Bruce, *op. cit.*, v. 2, p. 321.

[59]Morse, *Chronicle*, v. 1, pp. 44-45; Eames, *op. cit.*, pp. 32-33; Milburn, *op. cit.*, v. 2, p. 546.

[60]Eames, *op. cit.*, pp. 33-36; Morse, *Chronicle*, v. 1, pp. 45-49; Milburn, *op. cit.*, v. 2, p. 468; Williams, *History of China*, pp. 93-94.

[61]Morse, *Chronicle*, v. 1, pp. 52-55, 308.

[62]*Ibid.*, pp. 63-64.

the Chinese merchants were none too good at keeping their contracts. Twelve ships were sent to Amoy between 1676 and 1698, while three or four went to Taiwan.[63] Tea, camphor, sugar, and silks constituted the chief articles of export, while woollens, gunpowder, and lead were the chief imports.[64] No complete figures for the trade can be obtained but such as are available are given in appendix XIII.

Trade was also attempted at Canton during this period. In 1673 the *Return*, after unsuccessfully visiting Taiwan and Japan, put in at Canton, but after one year of fruitless bargaining went away without a cargo.[65] In 1677 the Viceroy of Canton invited the English to establish trade there.[66] The Court of Directors also showed interest in commerce at Canton in order to break more directly into the silk trade. These plans were somewhat interrupted by the civil war in China,[67] but in 1683 the *Carolina* put into Macao. The war had so impoverished the country, and the Portuguese were so hostile that no trading was done. The *China Merchant* which arrived the same year fared no better, and the opening of the Canton trade was delayed until later.[68] In 1689 the *Defence*, a ship of 730 tons, anchored at Macao. The merchants went to Canton, and after considerable bargaining and bribing ordered a cargo, and agreed to pay T. 1500 for measuring the ship and T. 300 (which was later increased to T. 450) to the Hoppo for the privileges granted. In the meantime the sailors became embroiled with the Chinese. An Oriental and an Englishman were killed and several English captured. The ship offered to pay T. 2000, but T. 5000 were demanded. It thereupon departed, leaving its supercargo and the seven sailors who had been seized.[69] This ended the attempts at Canton until 1699, which will be treated subsequently.[70]

[63] *Ibid.*, pp. 52-65; Eames, *op. cit.*, pp. 39-41 and appendix XIII.

[64] Morse, *Chronicle*, v. 1, pp. 47, 62, 86.

[65] *Ibid.*, pp. 41-42; Martin, *op. cit.*, v. 2, p. 8.

[66] Martin, *op. cit.*, v. 2, p. 8; See, *op. cit.*, p. 51.

[67] Bruce, *op. cit.*, v. 2, pp. 410-12, 459.

[68] Morse, *Chronicle*, v. 1, pp. 49-52; Eames, *op. cit.*, p. 39.

[69] Morse, *Chronicle*, v. 1, pp. 78-84; Martin, *op. cit.*, v. 2, p. 9; Auber, *op. cit.*, pp. 148-49; Eames, *op. cit.*, pp. 42-44.

[70] Eames, *op. cit.*, pp. 42-44, reports that the *Rebecca* went to Canton in 1688 and the *Loyal Merchant* in 1690; Morse does not agree and Morse's account is based directly upon the record of the Canton factory.

4. *Tea and the Establishment of a Successful Trade at Canton*

The development of tea as a commercial product was of utmost importance in the history of the English trade with China and will be briefly discussed.[71] Tea was an old product in the Orient, but it was practically unknown in Europe before the Dutch introduced it about 1610. It was little used upon the Continent and its merits were disputed by medical men.[72] The extensive consumption of tea was first developed by the English and was closely associated with the coffee-house. The first record of the use of tea in England is an advertisement in the *Mercurius Politicus*, No. 435, of September, 1658.

That excellent and by all Physitians approved China Drink called by the Chineans Tcha, by other nations Tay, alias tee, is sold at Sultaness Head, a cophee-house in Sweetings Rents, by the Royal Exchange, London.[73]

The use of tea was encouraged by advertising, and it became a fashionable drink. At first it sold for about 60*s*. per pound, and by 1700 it was selling at 30*s*. per pound.[74] In 1660 a duty of 8*d*. was levied on every gallon sold, which tax was replaced by a regular import duty of 5*s*. per pound customs in 1689.[75] In 1664 and 1666 the Company made presents of tea to the King, and in 1667 it placed its first order for 100 lbs. with its agents at Bantam. Practically every year after this saw the importation of some tea.[76] In 1684 it was put on the list of staples ordered by the Company from the East, and after this its importation steadily increased.[77] The high tariff on tea required a high selling price and hindered its extensive use, but in 1692 the duty dropped to 1*s*. per pound and five per cent *ad valorem*, on tea directly imported from the East.[78] The duty was raised to 1*s*. per pound and ten per cent *ad valorem* in 1698 and continued to be increased after that.[79] By this time, however, tea had become a well established article of import, and its hold on the English

[71]The best account of the development of the use of tea is to be found in Milburn, *op. cit.*, v. 2, pp. 527-42.

[72]*Ibid.*, pp. 528-29; Macgregor, *op. cit.*, v. 2, pp. 44-47.

[73]*Encyclopaedia Britannica* (Eleventh edition), v. 26, p. 476.

[74]Martin, *op. cit.*, v. 2, table opposite p. 152.

[75]12 Car. II, cap. 23 and 24, and 1 W. and M., cap. 6.

[76]Milburn, *op. cit.*, v. 2, p. 531.

[77]*Britannia*, v. 26, p. 476.

[78]4 W. and M., cap. 5.

[79]9 and 10 Will. III, cap. 23. It should be noted that after the duties on tea were raised, smuggling grew up to satisfy the English demand.

taste had become too great to be lost. Table 3 will show how its importation increased and why the Company was so eager to establish the China trade on a firm basis. Here more than anywhere else we find the cause for the development of the Anglo-Chinese trade. The day of the China trade was dawning.

TABLE 3.—TEA IMPORTED INTO ENGLAND*

Year	No. lbs.	Year	No. lbs.	Year	No. lbs.
1664.........	2 lbs. 2 oz.	1678.......	4,717	1695.......	132
1665.........	22¾	1685.......	12,070	1700.......	91,183
1670.........	79	1690.......	41,471	1706.......	137,748

*Based on Milburn, *op. cit.*, v. 2, pp. 527-30. For fuller statement see appendix XVIII.

Interlopers generally influenced the fortunes of the Company unfavorably, but this was not true in China. In fact the work of the rival English Company[80] virtually established the China trade on a firm basis. The *Wentworth* was sent by the Old Company to Canton in 1699 but went to Amoy. The voyage which actually opened and established trade at Canton was that of the *Macclesfield* sent out by the New Company in the same year.[81] Upon its arrival at Macao it found the officials very friendly and the merchants willing to trade. It refused to go into Canton harbor until the measuring fee had been definitely fixed. The officials were obliging and although the ordinary charge upon the ship would have been T. 1200 it was reduced to T. 480. The traders were also granted the following privileges: (1) freedom to trade with all merchants; (2) permission to go to and from Canton at pleasure; (3) exemption of their linguist from molestation, (4) and civil treatment.[82] After this arrangement the ship moved into the harbor; but trade was hampered by the "Mandarin Merchants," i.e., merchants representing officials, high prices, and the unreliability of the Chinese in the fulfillment of contracts. The ship finally had to sail with only one-fourth of the goods contracted for.[83] The charges on it totalled only T. 569, including but T. 89 as presents. Her entire cargo in

[80]A new organization called the English Company was created by Parliament in 1698. 9 and 10 Will. III, cap. 44.
[81]Eames, *op. cit.*, pp. 48-51.
[82]Morse, *Chronicle*, v. 1, pp. 86-93.
[83]*Ibid.*, v. 1, pp. 84-98, 100-102.

goods and silver amounted to £32,086, while her investments amounted to T. 44,928, and consisted of tea, silk, pepper, and other articles.[84] This voyage opened Canton to British trade. One ship was sent in 1700, two in 1701, and one in 1702, after which time vessels were directed regularly to Canton.[85]

It now remained for the English Company to open trade at Chusan. The *Trumball* anchored there in 1700 where it was joined by the *Macclesfield* after the latter left Canton. In this year Mr. Catchpoole also arrived at Chusan on the *Eaton*. He had been appointed president of the English Company's supercargoes, and was to be a permanent resident. He was also commissioned His Britannic Majesty's Consul for the Chinese Empire.[86] Mr. Catchpoole worked enthusiastically for several years to promote trade at Chusan and at times achieved some success. He met considerable trouble because of the insubordination of ship captains and supercargoes, the violation of contracts by the merchants, the demand for advances on contracts called "bargain money," and the duplicity and extortion of the officials. He failed to establish a permanent factory at Chusan, and in 1703 withdrew to the island of Pulo Condore (off the coast of Cochin China), where he hoped to establish a fort. The union of the two companies and the development of a profitable trade at Canton probably prevented the accomplishment of this project.[87] In spite of the above mentioned obstacles trade was carried on at Chusan by ships of both companies. The measuring fees were comparatively low, ranging from T. 300 to T. 400; however, considerable bargaining and bribery were necessary, contracts insecure, and supplies of goods poor. Between 1700 and 1703 seven ships visited Chusan.[88]

During this period trade was also pursued at Amoy by both companies, and eight ships were sent there between 1698 and 1703.[89] Competition between the two organizations was bitter until their union in 1702, at which time the united directors wrote to their respective supercargoes directing cooperation.[90]

[84] *Ibid.*, pp. 97, 308.
[85] *Ibid.*, p. 308. See also appendix XIV.
[86] *Ibid.*, pp. 109-10; Eames, *op. cit.*, pp. 51-56; See, *op. cit.*, p. 52.
[87] Morse, *Chronicle*, v. 1, pp. 109-21.
[88] *Ibid.*, p. 308. See also appendix XIII.
[89] *Ibid.*
[90] *Ibid.*, pp. 122-26.

With the union of the two companies the China trade may be said to have been established. Commerce was prospering at Canton, Amoy, and Chusan, in spite of minor vexations and difficulties. On the whole, the period was one of intense activity and great expansion, as Table 4 will show.[91]

TABLE 4.—ENGLISH TRADE TO CHINA*

Year	No. of Ships	Year	No. of Ships	Year	No. of Ships	Export of Goods and Coin £	Imports £
Prior to 1670...	7	1680–85....	7	1699.......	2	69,640....	15,309+
1670–75.......	1	1685–90....	5	1700.......	4	38,126....	41,758
1675–80.......	2	1690–95....	1	1701.......	6	108,020....	63,848
		1695–1700..	4	1702.......	7	210,285....	198,052

*Based on table in back of Morse, *Chronicle*, v. 1. See appendix XIII and XIV.

A study of this table and those given in the appendix, together with references already quoted, indicates a number of facts. First, after 1657 British interest in China was steadily increased and was enhanced by the English demand for silks and tea. Second, practically without exception, the Portuguese opposed the English at every turn. Third, between 1675 and 1698 Amoy was virtually the only port in China at which the British traded. Fourth, competition of the rival companies reacted favorably on the China trade and led to its development at Chusan and Canton. Fifth, the traders invariably encountered trouble with the officials and merchants, but these differences seem to have been due to greed and selfishness rather than to any deep-seated animosity. Sixth, no permanent factories were established; ships came and went, and each voyage was managed separately by the supercargoes in charge. Seventh, the duties and charges generally were not excessive, ranging between T. 300 and T. 2000, but their uncertainty and the bargaining and quarreling necessary were very troublesome. Eighth, the officials dealt directly with the European traders.

[91]Other authorities besides those already mentioned who give brief treatments of this subject are Milburn, *op. cit.*, v. 2, p. 468; Williams, *Middle Kingdom*, v. 2, p. 446; Macpherson, *India*, pp. 164-65; Davis, *op. cit.*, v. 1, pp. 38-40.

Some idea of what contemporaries thought of the Chinese is gathered from the following comments by Mr. Douglas of the *Macclesfield*:

Y^{e} many troubles & vexations we have mett wth from these subtile Chinese—whose principalls allow them to cheat, & y^{r} dayly practise therein have made y^{m} dextrus at it—I am not able to expresse at y^{s} time; and however easie others may have represented ye trade of China, neither I nor my Assistants have foūd it so, for every day produces new troubles, but I hope y^{t} a little time will put an end to them all.[92]

[92] Morse, *Chronicle*, v. 1, p. 98.

CHAPTER V

FIRM ESTABLISHMENT OF THE CHINA TRADE
(1703–1720)

1. *The Interlopers' Great Attack upon the Company, 1688-1702*

Before continuing the story of the China trade it will be well to take another glance at the status of the East India Company, which was responsible for that trade's development, and which was to manage it for nearly a century and a quarter more. The flourishing condition of the Company, when we last viewed it, had in large part accounted for the development of trade at Amoy and the attempts to trade at Canton during the 1680's. A glance at the statistics of Oriental trade after 1689 will show that only one ship was dispatched to China between that date and 1698,[1] the reason for this being the attack upon the Company which was taking place in England.

The change of governments in 1688 led to a great revival of the activity of the interlopers.[2] They petitioned Parliament to abolish the Company,[3] and it retaliated by petitioning both Parliament and the King for a confirmation of its charter and privileges.[4] The King addressed Parliament upon the subject, and after an investigation the following resolution was adopted in 1691: "that the East India Trade is necessary and beneficial to the kingdom; that it will be best managed by a joint-stock; and that a company to trade there in a joint-stock should be established."[5] Parliament, siding with the interlopers, aimed to create a new company with a capital of at least £1,500,000 to include the interlopers and the Old Company. The King's reply to this was a renewal of the Company's charter, which had been

[1]See appendix XIII and XIV.

[2]The best available account of this is to be found in Bruce, *op. cit.*, v. 3; see also v. 2, pp. 628-30.

[3]*Commons Journal*, v. 10, pp. 92, 120, 167, 324. A whole series of petitions was delivered every year against the Company and may be found in the *Commons Journal.*

[4]*Ibid.*, v. 10, pp. 363, 364, 397, 407, 408, 413, 541, 542, 554; Macgregor, *op. cit.*, v. 4, p. 334.

[5]*Commons Journal*, v. 10, p. 546; *Commons Debates* (1680-95), v. 2, pp. 390-91.

forfeited through a technicality.[6] This aroused Parliament, which declared in 1693 that "all subjects of England have equal right to trade in the East Indies, unless prohibited by Parliament." It also investigated the Company's affairs, and found that the latter had expended excessive amounts of money in getting its charter renewed, some of which had gone to the King.[7] The opponents of the Company next raised the question of the validity of its charter, which had not been granted by Parliament; however, this issue was decided in favor of the London Merchants.[8]

During the development of this quarrel between the Company and the interlopers, the British government encountered financial difficulties due to the war of the League of Augsburg. The upshot was that Parliament in effect held a public auction and offered a charter to the highest bidder. The Old Company offered a loan of £700,000 at 4 per cent to the government, while the interlopers offered £2,000,000 at 8 per cent.[9] The latter won. Parliament passed a bill in 1698 directing the King to grant a charter of incorporation to the subscribers of the loan; thus the rival English Company came into existence.[10] It was given exclusive privilege to trade with the East Indies, subject to a reservation of the concurrent rights of the London Company. This new company proved to be strong and powerful and there began a period of intense competition. This reacted favorably upon the China trade but unfavorably on the East Indian trade generally, causing a decline in the rate of increase.[11] It is doubtful if the favorable reaction would have continued in China. What was there needed was some special prod to start commerce, and good united effort to keep it going. The organization of the English Company in 1698 and the agreement for the union of the two companies in 1702 provided exactly this. This latter agreement was sanctioned by an act of Parliament in

[6] *Charters Granted to the East India Company*, pp. 141-152.

[7] *Parliamentary History* (1688-1702), v. 5, pp. 451-54, 828, 896-941; *Commons Debates* (1680-95), v. 2, pp. 457-74.

[8] Ilbert, *op. cit.*, p. 25.

[9] Macgregor, *op. cit.*, v. 4, p. 336; *Commons Debates* (1695-1706), v. 3, pp. 84-87.

[10] 9 and 10 Will. III, cap. 44; *Parliamentary History* (1688-1702), v. 5, pp. 1177-80; Cordier, *op. cit.*, v. 1, pp. 12-13.

[11] Krishna, *op. cit.*, pp. 323-34.

1708, and was formally completed by the Godolphin award later in the year.[12]

Thus a combination of circumstances, i.e., the sequence of competition and coöperation furnished by the two companies, and the favorable attitude of the Chinese Emperor,[13] united, just at the close of the 17th century, and enabled the English to establish trade upon a firm and lasting basis in China. Ten years' difference in time might possibly have changed the whole course of events.

2. *Impositions and the Gravitation of Trade to Canton, 1703-1716*

The union of the two companies ended the period of competition in China.[14] It was well that this happened, for the same year saw the beginning of systematic extortion on the part of the Chinese officials. Hitherto, exactions and troubles had been sufficient to discourage even the most energetic. "There is noe other way to bring them to better tearms, but either to divert the trade to Limpo [Ningpo] or Canton, or else to forbear some years; whereby the want of our Shipps may reduce them to a juster usuage and commerce," wrote a supercargo regarding conditions at Amoy.[15] Now in place of the old promiscuity, organized exaction appeared, which required the united efforts of the English if it were to be kept within bounds.

The "Emperor's Merchant," the first of the new innovations, was either the representative of some member of the Royal Family, or a person, who, by bribery at Peking, secured a monopoly of trade with the Europeans. He first appeared in 1702 at Chusan, where he soon drove out the other merchants and monopolized the trade for himself.[16] In 1703 he appeared at Amoy demanding six-tenths of the trade. In 1704 he organized the merchants into a closed corporation to trade with the Europeans, and so dominated trade that Amoy was practically aban-

[12] *Charters Granted to the East India Company*, pp. 243-316, 345-59; 6 Anne, cap. 17.

[13] See *postea*, chap. 6, sec. 3. Kanghi, the Chinese Emperor at this time, was very favorably disposed toward foreigners and foreign trade.

[14] Morse, *Chronicle*, v. 1, pp. 122-26; Cawston and Keane, *op. cit.*, pp. 120-24; Auber, *op. cit.*, p. 149; Cordier, *op. cit.*, v. 1, p. 13.

[15] Quoted by Morse, *Chronicle*, v. 1, p. 64.

[16] *Ibid.*, pp. 119-21, 138, 141-42; Morse, *International Relations*, v. 1, pp. 63-64; Martin, *op. cit.*, v. 2, p. 9; Lavisse and Rambaud, *op. cit.*, v. 8, p. 945.

doned.[17] In 1704 he appeared at Canton, claiming a monopoly of foreign commerce, and demanding several thousand taels per ship before he would allow other merchants to participate in the trade. However, he met with such opposition from the imperial customs officer and the merchants, both English and Chinese, that his monopoly was revoked and he disappeared.[18] The main objection to the "Emperor's Merchant" was that he never had a sufficient stock of goods to supply the traders and that his monopolistic character caused excessive exactions and prices.

In 1703 a new encumbrance appeared at Canton in the form of a 3 per cent *ad valorem* charge on the value of imports which was increased to 4 per cent the next year.[19] This charge was an addition to the ordinary customs duties, and 1 per cent of it was supposed to go to the linguist, while the other 3 per cent were charges which had formerly been squeezed from the Chinese merchants for their trading privileges.[20] In spite of loud protests by the supercargoes this duty was imposed and shortly after 1718 it was raised to 6 per cent.[21] There is no evidence that precisely similar charges were made at Chusan or Amoy, but it is certain that the irregular exactions there were so increased that Canton remained the most favored port.[22]

The recorded port charges of ships at Amoy seem to have averaged about T. 1500, while presents amounted to around T. 850, making the total measuring charges alone well over

[17] Morse, *Chronicle*, v. 1, pp. 124, 128-34; Eames, *op. cit.*, pp. 58-59.

[18] Morse, *Chronicle*, v. 1, pp. 134-45; Auber, *op. cit.*, p. 150; Eames, *op cit.*, pp. 56-58.

[19] Morse, *Chronicle*, v. 1, pp. 126, 139.

[20] *Ibid.*, pp. 139-40; Eames, *op. cit.*, p. 58; Auber, *op. cit.*, pp. 150-52; Martin, *op. cit.*, v. 2, p. 9.

[21] Morse, *Chronicle*, v. 1, pp. 106, 158, 175-77, 189. There is much obscurity regarding this duty. It at first appeared to be an import duty. Morse (p. 106) appears to say that in 1708 an export duty of 6 per cent was imposed. The date must be a misprint, for in 1718 (p. 158), the supercargoes petitioned for a removal of the 4 per cent without mentioning the 6 per cent, and in 1722 (p. 175) came the first record of this imposition in the supercargoes' notes. Information given on page 189 seems to indicate that the 6 per cent was both an import and export tax (See also Morse, *International Relations*, v. 1, p. 65). However at later dates the 6 per cent appeared to be only an import duty. (See Morse, *International Relations*, v. 1, p. 67). The safest conclusion is that the 3, 4 and 6 per cent during the early years certainly was an import duty and may have been an export duty also, but by 1760 it was an import duty only. It also seems certain that the 6 per cent came into existence between 1718 and 1722.

[22] Morse, *Chronicle*, v. 1, pp. 132-34.

T. 2000.[23] The measuring charges at Canton seem to have varied considerably. In 1702 the Hoppo, or imperial customs officer, demanded T. 1300 basic measuring fee and T. 1900 in presents, but the total was ultimately reduced to T. 1300. In 1704, the last year for which we have records until 1722, the charges on a 350 ton vessel seem to have run about T. 650 basic, and T. 210-220 as presents to officials, making a total of T. 860-870.[24] The tendency was undoubtedly toward an increase as the years went by. Milburn says that the present charge or "cumshaw," as it was known, became fixed at T. 1950 in 1704; this, however, seems to be an error.[25] In 1703 the Hoppo at Chusan demanded T. 10,000 measuring fee for three ships.[26]

In 1703, the last year of consul Catchpoole's service at Chusan, four ships were sent there, and three others visited it between that time and 1710, after which date no more recorded ships arrived until 1736. In 1703 Catchpoole left Chusan because of the obstructions. He established a base at Pulo Condore from which he attempted to direct trade for a time, but as commerce gravitated to Canton he disappeared from the picture as did his base at Pulo Condore.[27] In 1702, three ships visited Amoy, two came the following year, one anchored in 1707, and there were no more recorded arrivals until 1714. The *Anne*, which came in that year, made some contracts, and after waiting sixteen or eighteen months was expelled with the contracts unfulfilled. She seized a Chinese junk as compensation and sailed to India. This ended attempts to trade at Amoy until 1735.[28] Trade continued regularly at Canton. Ships went there each year except in 1710, paid their duties, sold and bought goods, and carried on trade with a certain amount of quarreling, but on the whole in a regular and orderly way. Four ships were sent in 1704, one in 1708, two in 1711, and three in 1716.[29]

[23] *Ibid.*, pp. 308-09.
[24] *Ibid.*, pp. 126, 135-36, 308-09.
[25] Milburn, *op. cit.*, v. 2, pp. 492-93; see *postea*, p. 111.
[26] Morse, *Chronicle*, v. 1, p. 120.
[27] *Ibid.*, pp. 120-30, 308-10; Eames, *op. cit.*, p. 64.
[28] Morse, *Chronicle*, v. 1, pp. 130-34, 150-53, 308-10; Eames, *op. cit.*, pp. 58-59, 70-73.
[29] For a complete statement of the ships and cargoes sent to Amoy, Chusan, and Canton, see appendices XIII and XIV.

The reasons for the gravitation of trade to Canton are not far to seek. At the other two ports the exactions were higher and more irregular; the "Emperor's Merchant" dominated at Chusan, while he together with eight other merchants and the officials controlled the Amoy trade in a crude and domineering way; contracts were insecure; the stock and quality of goods were low, and the harbors were poor. At Canton a more regular system was established due to the greater experience of this port with foreign trade, exactions were lower and not so bald and raw, the harbor was good, and reliable merchants were found in the persons of Hunshunquin and Linqua.[30] Supercargoes expressed their preference for Canton, and Lockyer, writing in 1711, said, "Merchants of Madras, have for these many years preferred it to Amoy; where they found the extravagant demands, charges, and abuses of the Mandarins, who pretended to have a Power over them, ready to swallow up the whole Profits of a Voyage."[31]

3. *Organization of Trade at Canton, 1715-1720*

By 1715 the trade at Canton had assumed a fairly regular form. Each year ships came and waited outside the Bogue until the Hoppo granted the ordinary privileges. In 1716 these customary privileges seem to have been reduced to a somewhat formal convention, and served, together with concessions granted two years later, as the basis of English rights in China for many years.[32] They were exceptionally reasonable, and if they had been lived up to by the Chinese, the foreigners would have found no cause for trouble. The privileges which were granted to the traders of the ship *Susanna* were as follows:

1. That we might speak with him [the Hoppo] at all times, without waiting.

2. That we have a Chop affixed at our Gate for a free Trade, and to forbid insults.

3. That we choose our Linguist, Compradore, and such other Servants we think proper, and discharge them at our pleasure.

[30]Morse, *Chronicle*, v. 1, pp. 99-100, 114, 116, 118, 126, 146-48; Eames, *op. cit.*, pp. 58-59, 64; Morse, *International Relations*, v. 1, pp. 63-64.

[31]Charles Lockyer, *Trade in India* (London, 1711), pp. 98-99; Morse, *Chronicle*, v. 1, pp. 133-34.

[32]Martin, *op. cit.*, v. 2, pp. 9-10; Sargent, *op. cit.*, p. 6; Morse, *International Relations*, v. 1, pp. 64-65. These authors give the date of this convention as 1712 and 1715 both of which are wrong according to documents cited in next note.

4. That the Supercargoes and Commander of [*Susanna*] shall not be obliged to stop, in coming from, or going to the Ship, at any of the Hoppo's boats; and that the Flag flying, shall be the Signal of their being in the boat.

5. That we have liberty to provide all naval stores, without duty, or any imposition whatever.

6. That we have at our request, the Grand Chop for leaving the Port without delay or embarassment.[33]

Two years later the *Carnarvon* requested three additional privileges which were granted.

7. If our English servants should commit any disorder or fault, deserving punishment, that the Chinese should not take upon themselves to punish, but should explain to us, and we would see them sufficiently punished according to the crime.

8. Liberty to fit up a tent ashore, and to refit casks, sails, and rigging.

9. That no customs should be paid on goods landed but not disposed of.[34]

To this list Auber adds a tenth, which was acquired at about this time.

10. That their escrutoires and chests might be brought on shore into their factory, and be carried on board again on their departure, without being searched.[35]

The supercargoes of the *Carnarvon* also demanded that the 4 per cent levy be lifted, but this was refused.[36] Trade was thus assuming a definite organization, and it seems advisable to examine more carefully its method, its character, and its quantity before proceeding.

The map (Fig. 1) will explain partially the geographical situation at Canton and will help to clarify the discussion which is based largely upon Lockyer's contemporary account.[37] A ship would arrive at Macao sometime in the late summer or early fall while the southwest monsoon had power to bring it into port.[38] At Macao a guide or pilot had to be obtained, and if the merchant were wise he would remain at Macao until he had been granted

[33] Morse, *Chronicle*, v. 1, pp. 155-56; Eames, *op. cit.*, pp. 59-60; See, *op. cit.*, p. 53. A "Chop" meant an administrative order, permit, or grant. The "Grand Chop" corresponded to a clearance paper.

[34] Eames, *op. cit.*, pp. 60-61.

[35] Auber, *op. cit.*, pp. 153-54.

[36] *Ibid.*, p. 154; Morse, *Chronicle*, v. 1, p. 158; Morse, *International Relations*, v. 1, p. 65.

[37] Lockyer, *op. cit.*, pp. 98-188; See also, Alexander Hamilton, *A New Account of the East Indies* (Edinburgh, 1727), v. 2, chaps. 50, 51, 52.

[38] Morse, *International Relations*, v. 1, p. 74.

the usual privileges, had made contracts for a cargo, and had his ship measured and the fee determined. During this bargaining the trader had to put on a bold front and threaten to leave unless the demands were reduced. Next the ship proceeded to the

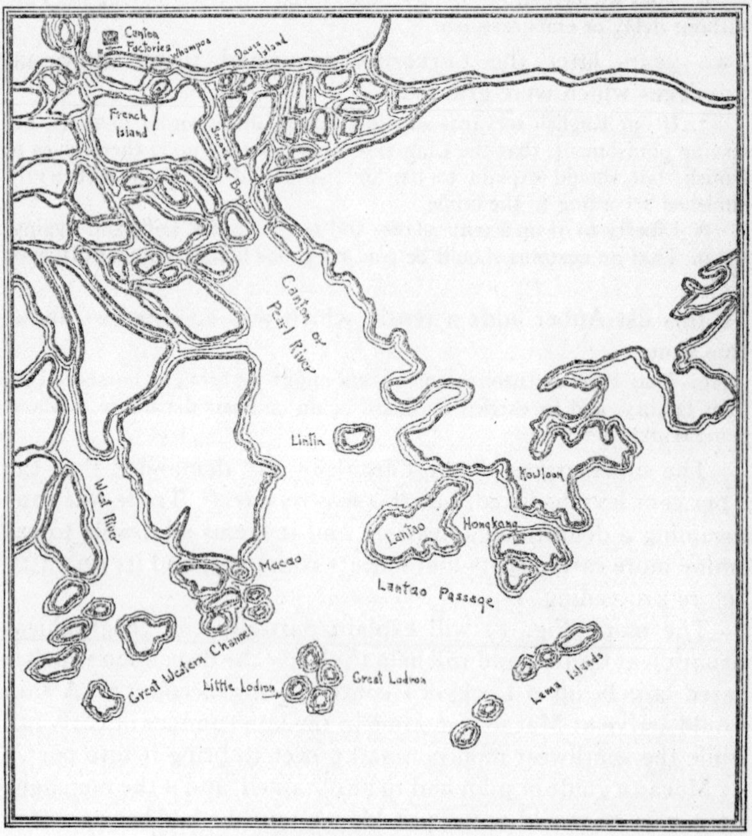

FIGURE I.—CANTON RIVER

Bogue, where the Hoppo's Chop, or order to enter the Canton river, would be granted. The Hoppo was the imperial customs officer, and at this time all measuring and customs duties were paid directly to him. He practically dominated trade, and many presents had to be given to him and to his officials.

The ship next proceeded to Whampoa, where a linguist or interpreter was engaged. He received I per cent on the value of the cargo from the trader and 1 per cent from the Chinese merchants. At this time he was generally regarded as a rogue and rascal who must be watched. A compradore or purveyor of supplies also had to be secured, but he did not yet have a monopoly of all purchases such as he later obtained. Supplies of food were abundant and of good quality.

The next problem was to rent a suitable factory from some merchant, and then to display the free trade Chop. The goods were then brought up from Whampoa in boats, which procedure entailed more expenses and presents.[39] Finally trade began. All types of merchants were ready to bargain, and a constant watch had to be kept for sharpers and crooks. All contracts had to be reduced to writing if the trader expected them to be fulfilled, and he must constantly watch for bad scales and defective goods. The Spanish dollar was the medium of trade and considerable trouble was experienced in determining money values. Much care had to be exercised in packing and caring for the return cargo.[40] During winter months when the trade was going on the officials often visited the factories. By late winter trade was finished, and all preparations were made to leave while the northeast monsoon had power enough to waft the ship down the South China Sea. In order to leave, a Chop had to be obtained from the Hoppo, and this entailed more presents.[41] The supercargoes generally came and went with the ships, but apparently there was no prohibition of their staying at Canton during the summer if necessary. Macao was not yet used as a summer residence.[42] Such was the method of trade at the beginning of the 18th century.

The supercargo managed the trade for the English, and each ship had its chief and several subordinates. His position was tremendously important, the success of the entire venture depending upon his honesty and trading ability. He had to be a person with business sense, capable of negotiating with all kinds of people, able to understand Portuguese, well informed as to the quality of goods, and acquainted with the problem of money values and exchange.[43] During the early years the supercargoes of different ships acted independently and often competed with

[39]Lockyer, *op. cit.*, pp. 99-108, 150, 167, 176.
[40]*Ibid.*, pp. 111-31; Eames, *op. cit.*, pp. 62-63.
[41]Lockyer, *op. cit.*, pp. 140-47, 185, 187.
[42]Morse, *Chronicle*, v. 1, pp. 99-108.
[43]*Ibid.*, pp. 66-71.

those of other vessels. The Court of Directors stopped this in 1715 by requiring the supercargoes of the various ships after arriving at Canton to unite and form a single council. The presidency of the board was to rotate, and the chief of each ship was to hold it for a week at a time. They were to live together, eat together, petition the Hoppo together, and buy and sell together as much as possible, thus presenting a united front to the Chinese.[44]

Considerable trouble was encountered in providing a system of pay which would encourage honest and efficient service. One voyage to China required perhaps three arduous years, and the temptation to misuse extensive power was very great. Much abuse arose through permission given to officers of the boat and to supercargoes to engage in private trade. Especially did they carry tea to the detriment of the Company. In 1714 the Court restricted private trade of the ship's officers to 3 per cent of the gross tonnage of the vessel, and placed a charge of 15 per cent on all teas brought.[45] Various methods of recompense to the supercargoes were tried without entire success, but by 1722 the following system was adopted, which, with slight modifications, lasted many years. The Court's instructions were addressed to Mr. James Naish and six others collectively, and constituted them a 'standing Council for managing our affairs in China, and to act in the same manner as any other Chief and Council at our Settlements abroad.' As had now become customary, they did not receive commission, but were incited to special efforts by having: (a) allowances of the result from trading with a portion of the Company's stock;[46] (b) permission to carry out a sum in foreign silver and invest it in gold; and (c) privilege of separate adventures in goods both ways, all in the following proportions:[47]

	Allowances £	Permission £	Separate Adventures £
Mr. Naish	3,000	1,500	200
Mr. Newnam	1,800	900	150
Mr. Savage	1,800	900	150
Mr. Pratt	1,200	600	100
Mr. Turner	1,200	600	100
Mr. du Bois	1,200	600	100
Mr. Talbot	800	300	100

[44] *Ibid.*, pp. 75, 154-55. Each ships' cargo accounts were kept separately however.

[45] *Ibid.*, pp. 73-77, 149; Eames, *op. cit.*, pp. 46-47.

[46] Morse, *Chronicle*, v. 1, pp. 74-75 for more complete explanation of this point.

[47] *Ibid.*, pp. 70-76, 171 for complete discussion of various methods used to pay the supercargoes.

The subordinate supercargoes were paid in the same way, but the amounts which they received were somewhat less.[48]

In spite of all the complaints raised against the impositions in China, they were not excessive: in fact, not as high as they were in England. The imperial import duty in 1700 on broadcloths was only T. 0.50 per 10 cubits (141 inches); T. 1.00 on an equal measure of camblets, and T. 0.30 on a picul (133⅓ lbs.) of lead.[49] About 1710 the imperial export duty on raw silk was T. 1.800 per picul, on rhubarb, T. 0.100 per picul, on sugar T. 0.100 and on tea T. 0.200.[50] This duty on tea was conspicuously low, amounting to only 16*d.* per 133⅓ lbs., while the import duty in England amounted to 5*s.* per pound.[51] The customs duties on the *London* amounted to T. 1147 in China, and when it arrived in England it paid T. 15,000 on tea alone.[52] The imperial duties, however, did not tell the whole tale, as Lockyer points out in the case of 1000 piculs of copper on which the imperial duty amounted to T. 400: 24 per cent on the customs charged by the Hoppo, percentages imposed on the transfer of money, and various other charges, such as the linguists' 1 per cent, and boat and coolie hire, raised this to T. 765. Add to this the 6 per cent *ad valorem* charge equalling T. 600 and we have a total of T. 1365 on the 1000 piculs, over three times the imperial duty.[53] But this was not nearly so high as charges in England.

On the whole the measuring fee and the "present" or cumshaw increased during the period as Table 5 shows. It must be noted also that the size of the ships increased, and that the charges on the *Macclesfield* in 1699 were exceptionally low. The basic charges did not increase much when we consider the growth in the size of ships, but the cumshaw did show a phenom-

[48] *Ibid.*, p. 154.

[49] *Ibid.*, p. 93. For a more complete statement see appendix XXII.

[50] Lockyer, *op. cit.*, pp. 148-50. For a complete statement of all custom duties see pp. 148-53. See also Morse, *Chronicle*, v. 1, pp. 106-07.

[51] Morse, *Chronicle*, v. 1, p. 106.

[52] *Ibid.*, p. 81.

[53] Lockyer, *op. cit.*, pp. 148-55. The 6 per cent is calculated from prices given in his table. See also Morse, *Chronicle*, v. 1, p. 107. For a complete statement of these duties see appendix XXII (c.)

enal rise. In addition to these there were numerous minor burdens which were a constant annoyance.[54]

The charges, therefore, which the Europeans had to meet were: (1) a low imperial export duty; (2) a low imperial import duty; (3) a series of impositions upon the value of these which increased their value by about 91 per cent; (4) a 6 per cent *ad*

TABLE 5.—CHARGES UPON SHIPS ENTERING CANTON*

Year	Ship	Tonnage	Basic Charges Tls.	Cumshaw Tls.	Total Tls.	Cumshaw percentage of the basic charges
1699	*Macclesfield*	250	480	89	569	18
1704	*Kent*	350	650	220	870	35
1728	*Macclesfield*	450	1059	1950†	3009	184

*This table is based on Morse, *Chronicle*, v. 1, pp. 106, 308-10.

†Between 1704 and 1722 there are no records of the measuring fees, and the ones in 1722, which are total measuring charges, including basic and cumshaw, run about T. 3000. The first separate record of the basic and cumshaw charges is in 1727, and the latter had then risen to T. 1950, where it remained for about a century.

valorem charge on all imports; (5) a basic measuring fee or tonnage duty of about T. 1000 on ships of 400-450 tons; (6) a cumshaw or accretion charge beyond the basic measuring fee which was fixed permanently at T. 1950 by 1727, and which was a present to the Emperor, Hoppo, and minor officials; (7) a series of miscellaneous burdens for boat hire, fees to minor officials, etc. There were also rent, provisions, and other sundry factory expenses. On the whole the charges were not exorbitant, and the dissatisfaction of the English seems to have been in reality a psychological one, growing out of the irregular manner in which the fees were imposed.

That these impositions did little damage to trade was shown by its increase during the period. Three or four Company's ships visited Canton every year, and their average size was from

[54]A few of these minor charges taken from Lockyer, *op. cit.*, p. 153, will show their nature.

Article	*Charge Tls.*
Boats of Hoppo and his men from Canton to Macao	3.00
Hoppo's custom at Macao	1.50
Ships passing Boco Tygris	5.60
Soldiers at Boco Tygris to drink	.70
Waiters at Whampoa	4.00
Custom boat at Fort	2.88
Hoppo's servant's accustomed present	10.00
Chunquan's Custom (opening the hatches)	50.00
Boat of Hoppo and his men to come to Whampoa	38.00

about 250 to 370 tons. An occasional Dutch or French ship put into Canton but most of the trade belonged to the Company. Table 6 of the English trade at Canton will speak for itself.

TABLE 6.—TRADE OF THE EAST INDIA COMPANY AT CANTON (1699–1721)*

Year	Imports Mdse. £	Imports Coin £	Total Imports £	Exports £	Tea Exported lbs.†	Silk Exported lbs.‡	No. of Ships	Tonnage
1699...	5,475	26,611	32,086	15,309	21,280	......	1	250
1704...	4,966	46,484	51,450	42,333	105,000+	......	4	1460
1707...	2,680	43,000	45,680	......	138,712	849¶	1	350
1711...	.....	......	33,635	......§	159,478	11	2	650
1716...	.....	......	89,167	18,000+	233,201	7,006	3	1060
1718...	5,278	56,000	61,278	......	672,669	23,700	2	640
1721...	6,476	109,000	113,476	108,921	783,967	512**	4	1670

*Most of the table is based on statistics in the back of Morse, *Chronicle*, v. 1. The figures are incomplete for the exports, and this accounts in part for their being lower than the import figures. It is also probable that some goods and silver were shipped in England which were never used at Canton. See appendix XIV.

†Of the figures in this column the year 1699 is based on Morse, *Chronicle*, v. 1, p. 97, as is year 1704, p. 136 (for one ship only). The rest are based on Milburn, *op. cit.*, v. 2, pp. 533-34. Based on sales in London by the Company. See appendix XVIII and XIX. The year following the date given in our table is the year used from Milburn to allow for the arrival of the tea from China, i.e., 1707 in our table is 1708 in Milburn.

‡Krishna, *op. cit.*, pp. 310-11.

§For one ship only.

¶For the year 1708.

**For the year 1720.

This table shows plainly that the total value of imports and exports was increasing, and that the imports consisted largely of coin. The silk export fluctuated considerably but on the whole increased, the year 1721 simply being a bad one. The most interesting features of the table are the figures on tea, which show plainly that its export was increasing rapidly, and that it was fast becoming the chief article of trade. Tea was purchased at prices ranging from T. 10 to T. 50 per picul (T. 50 = 29-30*d.* per lb.), and was sold in England at 16*s.* per pound.[55] The chief articles of import were broadcloths, long ells, other types of woollens, lead, and silver.[56] The most important exports, outside of tea and raw and woven silk, were: quicksilver, sugar, sugar candy, vermilion, camphor, china-root, alum, tutenague, china-ware, rhubarb, copper, fans, and gold.[57] The China trade was at last on a sound basis, and in tea it had an article that made its permanence a necessity.

[55]Lockyer, *op. cit.*, p. 150; Martin, *op. cit.*, v. 2, p. 152, table.

[56]Morse, *Chronicle*, v. 1, pp. 93, 123, 173, based on the cargoes of specific ships.

[57]*Ibid.*, pp. 97, 106, 110, 123, 124, 133, 144, 172, 176, 177, 178, based on the cargoes of specific ships.

It should be noted that this period in which the traders were granted such favorable privileges, and in which the trade became firmly established coincided with the last twenty years of Kanghi's rule; in other words with the closing period of imperial favor. In 1723, a new Emperor came to the throne and from that time on anti-foreignism grew rapidly. It was well that the traders won their concessions and established their customs during the first two decades of the 18th century or their subsequent plight might have been even worse.

4. *Troubles of the Company in Europe, 1708-1760*

Before considering the problem of anti-foreignism, which will be the subject of the next chapter, it seems advisable to look again at the fortunes of the Company in Europe. Besides the difficulties in China which have been mentioned, the London Merchants encountered some embarrassments in Europe which seem to have hampered their trade at times.

The attitude of the British government on the whole was friendly to the Company. There was already the growing tendency, which became very evident during the latter half of the 18th century,[58] for the government to identify its interests with those of the Company. Herein the government had found an easy way of collecting £800,000 or £900,000 revenue, and of advancing its colonial and commercial interests in the East, while at the same time insuring a supply of tea for its citizens.[59] It therefore favored the Company generally, by passing a series of acts to suppress interlopers and foreign competition, and by renewing the association's charter in spite of popular protest.[60]

The government, however, squeezed the Company unmercifully for revenue purposes. In 1708 it sanctioned the tripartite agreement for the union of the two companies, and extended the charter until 1726 upon the loan of £1,200,000 and the reduction of interest on all money owed by it to the Company to 5 per cent; providing that after that time, if the government should repay the money which it had borrowed from the Company and should give it three years' notice, the charter would auto-

[58]Cawston and Keane, *op. cit.*, pp. 120-130.

[59]Krishna, *op. cit.*, p. 330; 6 Anne, cap. 3; 10 Anne, cap. 29.

[60]Cawston and Keane, *op. cit.*, pp. 121-23; 7 Geo. I., cap. 21, sec. 12; and 5 Geo. I, cap. 21; 9 Geo. I, cap. 26; 5 Geo. II, cap. 29.

matically expire.[61] In 1712 Parliament extended the charter to 1733 subject to the same proviso, but without loans.[62] In 1730 it was extended to 1766, subject to the three-year notice proviso, and upon the donation of £200,000 and the reduction of interest to 4 per cent, provided that after 1736, upon one year's notice, Parliament might pay off all or any part of the debt.[63] In 1744, upon the payment of £1,000,000 at 3 per cent, the charter was extended to 1780, subject to the three-year notice proviso and repayment.[64] The government also oppressed the Company by levying excessive duties on tea, which policy resulted in smuggling. The duty on tea after 1747 was 44 per cent *ad valorem* and 1*s*. per pound excise.[65] The only notice which the government took of the popular outcries against the London Merchants resulted in a prohibition in 1720 upon the wearing of Indian calicoes.[66] The act against counterfeiting of tea, the East India Insurance Bill, and the statute of 1750 repealing duties on raw silk, were all favorable to the Company.[67]

Popular opposition to the Company was prevalent during this period. Shortly after 1710 the merchants of Bristol and Hull, aided by the woollen and silk weavers, attacked the Company and urged the government to lay open the Indian trade.[68] A detailed tracing of this opposition is unnecessary. Suffice it to say that many of the dissatisfied merchants soon disguised their interloping character in foreign companies and carried on a thriving smuggling trade, while the weavers were satisfied by the act of 1720. Even then the attacks continued, and the literature of the period is rich in pamphlets charging the Company with engrossing the Eastern trade contrary to common law, with being illegal according to Magna Carta, with raising prices

[61] 6 Anne, cap. 17.

[62] 10 Anne, cap. 28 and cap. 35.

[63] 3 Geo. II., cap. 14; Cawston and Keane, *op. cit.*, pp. 124-25; Macpherson, *India*, p. 173.

[64] 17 Geo. II, cap. 17; Macpherson, *India*, p. 414, has an account of monies paid by the Company to the government; Macgregor, *op. cit.*, v. 4, p. 350.

[65] For fuller statement see Martin, *op. cit.*, v. 2, table opposite p. 152, and Krishna, *op. cit.*, pp. 326-37. See also appendix XIX.

[66] 7 Geo. I., cap. 7.

[67] 4 Geo. II, cap. 14; 25 Geo. II, cap. 26; 23 Geo. II, cap. 9. The government's attitude is discussed by Robinson, *op. cit.*, pp. 31-44. Counterfeiting of tea refers to the sale of various types of non-tea leaves for tea.

[68] Cawston and Keane, *op. cit.*, p. 121; Robinson, *op. cit.*, pp. 31-32; *Commons Debates* (1706-13), v. 4, pp. 304-05.

and impoverishing the country, with exporting bullion, with causing smuggling, with encouraging foreign commerce at the expense of England, and with causing the decline of British trade.[69] The latter arguments came during the 1740's when foreign war was depressing trade.

Interloping activity and foreign competition became very acute at times. They grew primarily out of the smuggling business which was due directly to the high duties on tea in England.[70] The tea for smuggling was furnished by a group of European companies composed largely of erstwhile interlopers. For a time the latter imported tea directly under a law of the 3 and 4 of Anne, cap. 4; but when this provision (that tea might be imported into England by anyone in English ships with certificates and licenses) was repealed in 1720,[71] they had to rely entirely upon the smugglers. This trade assumed enormous proportions, some estimates contending that one-half of the tea consumed in England was smuggled. There was a great popular outcry against the smugglers, but also against the government's interference with personal liberty in trying to suppress them.[72] In spite of government bills against English interlopers and severe penalties for smuggling, the trade grew and damaged the Company considerably.[73]

In addition to the competition furnished by legitimate European organizations, such as the French and Dutch East India Companies, the London Merchants[74] met that of a number of foreign organizations especially created to suit the interests of English interlopers and smugglers. The first of these companies was the Danish East India Company, which was organized in

[69]Best collections of these arguments are to be found in McCulloch, *Scarce and Valuable Tracts on Commerce* (London, 1859), pp. 157-294 and 313-74; Cawston and Keane, *op. cit.*, pp. 120-30; Robinson, *op. cit.*, pp. 31-50; *Parliamentary History* (1747-53), v. 14, pp. 1207-1234; J. Walthoe, *Collection of Papers Relating to the East India Trade.*

[70]Macpherson, *India*, pp. 131, 208.

[71]7 Geo. I, cap. 21, sec. 12.

[72]*Commons Debates* (1734-37), v. 9, pp. 160-61, and (1733-34), v. 8, pp. 45-69; *Parliamentary History* (1733-37), v. 9, pp. 1-10, 236-62, 1045-1046; Daniel Defoe, *A Tour Through England* (London, 1927), v. 1, pp. 112-13.

[73]*Commons Debates* (1734-37), v. 9, pp. 230-37; *Parliamentary History* (1733-37), v. 9, pp. 1225-68; Macgregor, *op. cit.*, v. 5, pp. 50-54; 5 Geo. I, cap. 21; 9 Geo. II, cap. 35.

[74]Morse, *Chronicle*, v. 1, pp. 91-92; Lavisse and Rambaud, *op. cit.*, v. 8, pp. 947-50; Cordier, *op. cit.*, v. 1, p. 16.

1612, and which led a varied existence for a century.[75] The second, and most famous, was the Ostend Company chartered by the Holy Roman Emperor in 1717.[76] It aroused the ire of the English, so Parliament passed a law prohibiting any Englishmen but servants of the Company from going to the East Indies and providing special penalties for those who should do so under foreign patent, also allowing the Company to seize all such persons found in the East. Despite this and other laws,[77] the interlopers continued to work in the Ostend Company until the united action of the Dutch and English secured the repeal of its charter in 1727.[78] The interlopers now turned to Sweden, and the Swedish East India Company appeared as successor to the Ostend Company.[79] Despite Parliamentary laws prohibiting Englishmen from serving under foreign companies and severe laws against smuggling, the Swedish Company continued its existence until the end of the century.[80] The last of these organizations to be formed was the Prussian Company in 1750, but it showed little vitality. It called forth, however, another law from Parliament against persons other than the Company who might import tea.[81]

Besides the competition of these interlopers and smugglers the Company suffered greatly because of the War of the Austrian Succession.[82] A study of the trade figures of the Company and the imports and exports of Great Britain will show that both declined during the early years of the war.[83] This fact indicates that the Company's declining trade during the 1740's was due to the war and not to restrictions in China.

[75]Macpherson, *India*, pp. 285-93; Lavisse and Rambaud, *op. cit.*, v. 8, p. 954.

[76]Macpherson, *India*, pp. 295-303.

[77]5 Geo. I., cap. 21; 7 Geo. 1., cap. 21; 9 Geo. I., cap. 26.

[78]Lavisse and Rambaud, *op. cit.*, v. 8, p. 954; Macgregor, *op. cit.*, v. 4, pp. 343-48; *Commons Debates* (1716-27), v. 6, p. 384.

[79]Macpherson, *India*, pp. 305-10.

[80]5 Geo. II, cap. 29; 9 Geo. II, cap. 35.

[81]Macpherson, *India*, pp. 311-12; Lavisse and Rambaud, *op. cit.*, v. 8, p. 955; 28 Geo. II, cap. 21.

[82]Eames, *op. cit.*, pp. 71, 78; *Parliamentary History* (1737-41), v. 11, pp. 579-82.

[83]See appendix XIV; and table in Anderson, *Origin of Commerce*, v. 4, pp. 692-94.

CHAPTER VI

THE ORIGIN OF ANTI-FOREIGNISM IN CHINA

1. *Classical Explanations of Anti-Foreignism in China*

Having discussed the establishment of the East India Company's factory at Canton during the later years of the well disposed Emperor Kanghi, and having considered the fortunes and misfortunes of the Company in Europe, it seems advisable to examine the rise of the anti-foreign movement in China, which was to have a very decided effect upon the history of the English at Canton. In the matter of intercourse between the West and China, there is no problem of greater importance than that of the Chinese attitude toward the foreigner. It is certain that the government, and the people as a whole, were decidedly anti-foreign during the late 18th and the 19th centuries. Foreign penetration was systematically opposed, and only by force could the West win concessions. The question at once arises: has China always been anti-foreign?

Classical explanations of this point are inadequate and unsatisfactory. Without mentioning any specific examples, one may summarize the generally accepted view somewhat as follows:

> On the whole the Chinese have been opposed to foreigners. During the rule of the foreign Mongols, foreign intercourse was tolerated, but the Chinese themselves never became reconciled to outsiders. After the Mings, a strictly Chinese dynasty, defeated the Mongols, they closed the doors of China to foreign intercourse and only grudgingly let down the bars to the Portuguese in the 16th century. The early intercourse with the Western traders, i.e., Portuguese, Dutch, Spanish, and English, was so marked by violence, bloodshed, and disorder that in 1757 the Emperor confined all trade to Canton, 'at which place it was conducted under very onerous conditions.'

There is some truth in this explanation, but it is subject to three grave errors. First, it is entirely too sweeping and general. Second, it is hard to connect the decree of 1757 with the robbing and rapine of the 16th century. If the foreigners had continued to plunder and murder it appears that the Emperor would have closed the ports much sooner. Third, it ignores to a large extent the actual facts.

2. *Factors Which Should Be Considered in Discussing the Problem of Anti-Foreignism*

To treat this matter properly, one should avoid loose terminology such as the "Chinese" and "China" and look rather at the position taken by specific groups. First to be considered is the attitude of the mass of the Chinese people. There is little evidence to indicate their reaction to foreigners prior to the late 18th and early 19th centuries. We must, therefore, rely on analogy and experience. Europe during the Middle Ages affords a fair parallelism. Most of the people were engaged in agriculture or in the handicrafts where monopolistic guilds dominated industry. The members of these isolated, self-sufficient communities were conservative, backward, and very suspicious and hostile toward outsiders.[1] Witness, for example, the treatment of the Hansa Merchants in London and other European cities; it was little better than that of the European traders at Canton.[2] On the whole, then, we would expect the feeling of the common people to be one of settled distrust but not active opposition to the strange-looking aliens.

In our analogous Western society the great merchant was the forward-looking person. He desired trade, and tried to break down local barriers of conservatism and distrust. The same applies to the Chinese merchants, who wanted trade at all costs. Their activity and interest pushed them into the East Indies, to India, and even to Africa.[3] No better example of their desire for commerce is shown than the way they swarmed back to Manila in spite of massacres and harsh treatment by the Spaniards.[4] On the whole, then, we would expect the attitude of the merchant class to be consistently favorable to trade.

The officials offer a more complicated problem. They were naturally conservative and filled with an over amount of self-

[1]E. P. Cheyney, *Industrial and Social History of England* (New York 1927), chaps. 2, 3, 4, 5, 6; Lynn Thorndike, *Medieval Europe* (New York' 1927), chaps. 17 and 19; C. J. H. Hayes, *Political and Social History of Modern Europe* (New York, 1922), v. 1, chap. 2.

[2]W. Cunningham, *English Commerce and Industry During the Middle Ages*, pp. 241, 378, 392, 419; Henderson, *Short History of Germany* (New York, 1927), v. 1, p. 193.

[3]See, *op. cit.*, pp. 35-37; Martin, *op. cit.*, v. 1, pp. 378-79; G. N. Steiger, H. O. Beyer, C. Benitez, *A History of the Orient* (Boston, 1926), chap. 15, pp. 202-13.

[4]E. T. Williams, *China*, pp. 204-05; See, *op. cit.*, pp. 43-45; Parker, *China History*, pp. 90-92.

esteem and importance, as has been noted, and they were the zealous guardians of Chinese tradition and culture. Furthermore the trade of the foreigners offered opportunity for them to fill their pockets by threatening and extortion. Such an attitude would be injurious to trade, but could not prudently be carried so far as to kill the goose which laid the golden egg. It must also be distinguished from a settled position of hostility and dislike. On the whole, the mandarins looked with disdain on the foreigners but allowed them entrance into the country for financial reasons, so long as they confined their interests to trading and made no attempt to interfere with Chinese culture as did the missionaries, who thereby aroused the ire of the mandarins.

The attitude of the Emperor was particularly significant. Because of his great power, his personal likes and dislikes were of material importance. His position helped to determine the attitude and especially the policy of the mandarins, although their bias likewise influenced him. His feeling was also reflected in the stand taken by the masses.[5] The most important factor, then, in determining anti-foreignism at a particular time was the Emperor's position. This varied considerably because the ruler was but a single individual, and the opinions of different Emperors were not identical. Furthermore each ruler's attitude might be changed by the advice of his council and other pertinent circumstances.

A final factor to be considered was the situation at Canton. Several aspects there were quite different from the problem of anti-foreignism generally, yet they were closely connected with it. It seems that conditions at Canton were determined from the first more by financial considerations and personal prejudice than by a settled policy of dislike. These, although quite distinct from anti-foreign attitudes, were important in accounting for the decree of 1757.[6] On the whole it would seem that general anti-foreign sentiment was generated outside of Canton, and was transferred thither by the example of the mandarins and by public action elsewhere.[7]

With this rather lengthy analysis of the method of approach, we shall briefly analyze the problem on the basis of fact, keeping

[5]Huc, *op. cit.*, v. 1, pp. 144-51.
[6]See chap. 7, sec. 5.
[7]See sec. 5 of this chapter.

always in mind that the public attitude was one of settled distrust which would become active dislike if consciously fostered, that the merchants' feeling was constantly favorable, that the Emperor's position was important but subject to change, that the mandarins were indifferent until their sacred institutions were challenged (then, because of their influence over government, people, and Emperor, they became dangerous engines for generating anti-foreignism), and that conditions at Canton produced a goodly number of things detrimental to trade but which were quite separate from any settled anti-foreign prejudices. It is obvious, then, that the attitudes of the mandarins and of the Emperor were most important.

3. *Historical View of the Attitude of the Chinese toward Foreigners*

The Chinese were not particularly anti-foreign before the 16th century. Facts show that prior to the Mongol dynasty China carried on considerable communication with other nations. Overland trade was maintained with the West, India, and Asia Minor, while the Greeks and Romans also had dealings with the Chinese. Commerce was carried on by sea with the East Indies, India, and Arabia; and on the whole China seemed favorable to intercourse, but officials, even at this time, appeared bent on making it pay. This was also the period when Nestorian Christianity flourished.[8]

The age of the Mongols was generally favorable to foreign trade. It saw the trips of the Polos, a number of ambassadors from the West, the extensive development of the Arabian trade by land and sea, and the first period of the Catholic missionaries. Many contemporary writers of this period agree that China was open to intercourse and that the Mongol rulers were friendly to foreigners.[9]

At the close of the Mongol rule it is ordinarily assumed that the Mings shut themselves up and kept out the foreigners. It is

[8]Martin, *op. cit.*, v. 1, pp. 245-53 and 257-58; See, *op. cit.*, pp. 1-30; Williams, *Middle Kingdom*, v. 2, pp. 275-86, 410-14; Parker, *China History*, pp. 59-86; Harris, *op. cit.*, p. 377; Treat, *op. cit.*, pp. 45-46; E. T. Williams, *China*, pp. 158-59.

[9]Williams, *Middle Kingdom*, v. 2, pp. 287-89, 415-25; Martin, *op. cit.*, v. 1, pp. 258-59; Gowen and Hall, *op. cit.*, pp. 148-58; Ireland, *op. cit.*, pp. 32-37; Jernigan, *op. cit.*, pp. 222-24; Treat, *op. cit.*, pp. 46-48; E. T. Williams, *China*, pp. 176-81; Marco Polo, *Travels* (New York, 1926). Published by J. M. Dent and Sons.

true that European contact with China ceased and that the Catholic Missions died, but this seems to have been due to the long period of civil wars and disorders rather than to a settled policy of exclusion.[10] As a matter of fact, the Western nations, hindered by the break-up of communications in central and western Asia, and by civil wars in China, did not attempt to sustain connections with the latter. At least there are no records to indicate this. It is certain that during this period the Chinese continued to trade by sea with the East Indies, India, Arabia, and even Africa.[11] The best evidence which repudiates the old theory of Ming exclusiveness is a series of letters from the Emperor of China to the King of Persia dated between 1412 and 1417. In these letters the Chinese Emperor actually asked that free communication and trade be maintained.[12] The following statement coincides, to a large degree, with the present writer's own conclusions, and although it leans somewhat backward it will be quoted in full.

> Up to the opening years of the sixteenth century the general attitude of the Chinese toward aliens was exceptionally liberal and even hospitable. Strangers were received with cordiality, their commerce was encouraged, and no prejudice was shown against the practice or propagandism of their religions, however peculiar they might be. As a matter of fact, foreigners were placed on practically the same footing as the Chinese themselves; official positions were open to them, and they enjoyed the ample protection of the Imperial Government. In other words, the Chinese originally evinced none of the exclusive propensities with which they were finally associated in a very conspicuous manner. Such generosity has certainly never been accorded to outsiders by any other country in the world.[13]

If, prior to the 16th century invasion by Western traders, China did not evidence anti-foreign tendencies, how did she react to the first foreigners? Authorities agree that the first Portuguese to arrive at Canton were well received. This good will was enhanced by the exceptionally good conduct of Ferdinand Andrade, in 1517,[14] but was somewhat cooled by the actions of Simon Andrade, who arrived in 1518. He seized some land, began the erection of a fort, and committed other outrages,

[10]See, *op. cit.*, p. 36; E. T. Williams, *China*, pp. 196-201.

[11]See, *op. cit.*, pp. 36-37; Macpherson, *India*, pp. 8, 24, 53.

[12]Documents are printed in Martin, *op. cit.*, v. 1, pp. 253-57.

[13]See, *op. cit.*, pp. 37-38.

[14]Williams, *Middle Kingdom*, v. 2, p. 427; Martin, *op. cit.*, v. 1, p. 370; Milburn, *op. cit.*, v. 2, p. 462; Foster, *op. cit.*, p. 4; Eames, *op. cit.*, pp. 2-3.

with the result that he was driven from the country.[15] This, however, did not cause the Chinese to exclude foreigners. Trade was continued with the Portuguese and settlements were established at Ningpo, Amoy, and Lampaco near Canton. There must have been substantial commerce, because in the first outbreak against the Westerners eight hundred Portuguese and some thirty-five ships are said to have been destroyed.[16] If the government, the officials, or the people had been strongly anti-foreign, no such extensive trade could have been conducted. Evidences of good will were also apparent in the titles applied to foreigners. They were called "Franks," and Portugal was termed "Kingdom of the Great Western Ocean." Such derogatory titles as "Foreign Devils," "Barbarians," and "Red Hairs" were not heard.

The first period of anti-foreignism began about 1545 with an imperial order to exterminate the Portuguese wherever found. This decree had been issued because of their outrageous conduct, which had so aroused the public that they were driven with great slaughter from Ningpo. In 1549 another massacre occurred at Chinchew.[17] On the whole a period of intense restrictions began. The Portuguese were driven out of China except for Macao, and Russian ambassadors were refused audience at Peking.[18] The relaxation of trade restrictions in 1567[19] was the first indication of the close of this period. As years passed the old hatred seemed to be forgotten, and the Emperor and officials again allowed intercourse.

An attitude of indifference was, perhaps, most characteristic of the next century of Chinese relations with the West. There were times when the government and officials became aroused against foreigners, and times when they were especially favorable. There seem to have been no violent public outbreaks, and on the whole, the period was favorable to foreign relations. Missionaries were allowed to penetrate the Empire, and, with a

[15] Eames, *op. cit.*, pp. 3-4; Macgregor, *op. cit.*, v. 4, p. 292; Martin, *op. cit.*, v. 1, p. 370; Morse, *International Relations*, v. 1, pp. 41-42.

[16] Williams, *Middle Kingdom*, v. 2, pp. 427-28.

[17] E. T. Williams, *China*, p. 204; Morse, *International Relations*, v. 1, p. 42; Williams, *Middle Kingdom*, v. 2, p. 428; Eames, *op. cit.*, pp. 4-5.

[18] Morse, *International Relations*, v. 1, p. 59; Eames, *op. cit.*, pp. 5-7.

[19] Parker, *China History*, pp. 88-90.

few exceptions, were well treated.[20] By 1650 it was estimated that 150,000 Chinese had been converted.[21] The Dutch also attempted intercourse with China but were foiled by the Portuguese. They then laid themselves open to censure by attacking native junks, and by seizing the Pescadores in 1622, from which they were expelled by force and diplomacy. They retired to Formosa where they established a fort and carried on intermittent trade with the Chinese. In 1655 they sent an embassy to Peking, which, after performing the humiliating ceremonies demanded, was granted the privilege of sending an embassy and four trading ships to China once every eight years.[22] This was really quite a liberal offer, for China had never before received anything but tribute-bearing embassies and did not understand the Western idea of equality of nations.[23] Evidence from Cocks at Firando and from the English voyages to Macao show that the imperial will was not opposed to trade and that officials were willing, if enough "pocket money" was forthcoming.[24] On the whole the devastations and policies of civil war, together with the propaganda and actions of the Portuguese, seem to be responsible for the prevalence of the idea that the Emperor and officials had adopted a consistently hostile attitude toward foreigners.[25]

Most writers on China think that our difficulties in gaining permission to trade were due to a determination on the part of the Manchus to secure their conquests by prohibiting all intercourse between the Chinese and other nations. For this opinion there appears to be no real foundation. The policy of the Manchus at this time seems to have been directed toward encouraging foreign commerce.[26]

[20]Kenneth Scott Latourette, *History of Christian Missions in China* (New York, 1929), pp. 78-111; Williams, *Middle Kingdom*, v. 2, pp. 289-95; Parker, *China History*, pp. 89-94.

[21]Latourette, *Missions*, p. 107.

[22]Williams, *Middle Kingdom*, v. 2, pp. 433-36; Macpherson, *India*, pp. 41-50; See, *op. cit.*, pp. 45-47; Parker, *China History*, pp. 92-94; Morse, *International Relations*, v. 1, pp. 47-50; *State Papers, Colonial; East Indies* (1617-21), p. 346; Davis, *op. cit.*, v. 1, pp. 26-28; Lavisse and Rambaud, *op. cit.*, v. 5, pp. 907-09; Bau, *op. cit.*, p. 4.

[23]Williams, *Middle Kingdom*, v. 2, pp. 372, 406-07.

[24]*State Papers, Colonial; East Indies* (1622-24), p. 88; and (1617-21), p. 412.

[25]E. T. Williams, *China*, pp. 208-09 for examples of Portuguese opposition to the Dutch and English. See Eames, *op. cit.*, pp. 2-7, and p. 37 for a quotation which shows the bad influence of the civil wars upon trade and foreign intercourse. See also Martin, *op. cit.*, v. 1, p. 371.

[26]Eames, *op. cit.*, pp. 41-42.

With the exception of the years 1662 to 1667 this statement is true. There was, however, a period between the death of Shunche and the beginning of the personal rule of Kanghi during which a decidedly anti-foreign regency ruled. Father Schaal, who had been a good friend of the Emperor, was imprisoned, as were the other missionaries at Peking, and a policy of persecuting Christian teachers was adopted.[27] This reaction was apparently due to the opposition of the officials, whose ire had been aroused by the teachings of the missionaries, and by the favoritism shown them by the Emperor. A Dutch and a Portuguese embassy, which were sent to Peking at this time, were also forced to undergo very harsh treatment, and were dismissed with no concessions.[28] The only decree which directly affected trade was one ordering all inhabitants to move twelve miles inland. This was a war measure caused very largely by Japanese raids along the coast and was not directed against other foreigners.[29]

The great age of favoritism to Westerners corresponded with the personal rule of Kanghi (1667-1722). He himself was favorable to foreigners and missionaries, as was clearly shown in his legislation and acts. He immediately released the imprisoned missionaries, made Verbiest head of the Astronomical Board, and ended all persecutions. In 1692 he issued an edict of toleration to Christians, and, though he was forced to change this policy toward the end of his life, his reign was very favorable to Christians.[30] He also issued an edict in 1685 opening the ports of China to all nations.[31] Extensive trade was carried on with Russia, and several Russian embassies were especially well received, while Chino-Russian troubles in the Amur region were peacefully settled by the treaty of Nerchinsk (1689).[32] During his reign the French and Dutch, as well as the English, established factories at Canton and initiated the European trade upon

[27] Williams, *Middle Kingdom*, v. 2, p. 297; Latourette, *Missions*, pp. 115-16.

[28] Morse, *International Relations*, v. 1, pp. 42-43, 48; Williams, *Middle Kingdom*, v. 2, pp. 428-29, 438; Eames, *op. cit.*, pp. 107-08.

[29] Martin, *op. cit.*, v. 1, p. 371.

[30] Latourette, *Missions*, pp. 116-30; Bashford, *op. cit.*, p. 638.

[31] Milburn, *op. cit.*, v. 2, p. 468; Martin, *op. cit.*, v. 2, p. 9; Morse, *Chronicle*, v. 1, pp. 57-58.

[32] Hertslet, *op. cit.*, v. 1, pp. 437-39; E. T. Williams, *China*, pp. 232-33; Williams, *Middle Kingdom*, v. 2, pp. 441-43; Eames, *op. cit.*, pp. 108-15.

a firm basis.[33] Kanghi's attitude toward the Westerners is well represented in this statement made by him. "Europeans have always served me with zeal and affection. There are many Chinese who distrust [them], but, as for myself, I am so fully convinced of [their] uprightness and good faith that I publicly declare that [they] are deserving of every trust and confidence."[34]

We have a contemporary report on the treatment of foreigners by the Canton populace. "The better sort of People are Civil, and Complaisant to Strangers; but the Commonalty often Rude and Troublesome."[35] Evidence already cited shows the officials at the seaport rather favorable to trade but determined to milk it as much as possible.

Generally speaking Kanghi's reign was one of favoritism, but the seeds of trouble were growing during the period, and by the end of his rule the sky was clouded. It was well that the foreign trade became established before his death or it might have had to wait a century longer. The traders had learned to conduct themselves in an orderly fashion, and their quiet nibbling along the coast did not annoy the officials or the Emperor. But within the heart of the Empire, missionaries were working away, propagating doctrines which the officials hated, and making converts who gave their allegiance to a foreign ruler. Here, it seems, one may find the basis of 18th century anti-foreignism.

4. *The Missionaries and the Creating of Anti-Foreign Attitudes*

As has been noted, the reign of Kanghi was one of favoritism to foreigners. However, during this time there seems to have been generated a decidedly hostile attitude toward Westerners within the ranks of the literati-mandarins. Toward the end of his reign Kanghi himself became distrustful, for he said in 1717: "There is cause for apprehension lest, in centuries or millenniums to come, China may be endangered by collision with the various nations of the West who come hither from beyond the seas."[36] It is significant that this statement was made at the time of an edict proscribing the missionaries, and he must have

[33]Treat, *op. cit.*, pp. 54-55; Morse, *International Relations*, v. 1, p. 48; Macpherson, *India*, pp. 262-65; Cordier, *op. cit.*, v. 1, p. 16; Lavisse and Rambaud, *op. cit.*, v. 8, pp. 947-48.

[34]Quoted in Krausse, *op. cit.*, p. 103.

[35]Lockyer, *op. cit.*, p. 170.

[36]*Chinese Repository*, v. 5, p. 394.

been referring to them rather than to the traders.[37] It also seems that hostility toward the traders, other than a desire to extort money from them, was not present at this time, because they were allowed favorable privileges at Canton, including the exercise of extraterritorial jurisdiction over their people.[38] That the Emperor was not opposed to foreign traders was evidenced by the fact that he ordered the degradation of the two mandarins who had been responsible for the outrage against the *Anne* at Amoy in 1715.[39] Further, if trade was carried on only at Canton this was because it had gravitated thither due to commercial considerations, and not because of expulsion from the other ports. It seems unreasonable to lay blame for the widespread hostility to foreigners which developed in the 18th century to the nine or ten hundred Europeans who visited Canton every year, most of whom remained close to the ships and had little contact with the Chinese.[40] Furthermore, contemporary evidence shows that these traders were generally well behaved and that no outbreaks occurred against them.[41] For these reasons the tentative explanation is offered that the missionaries were mainly responsible for the anti-foreignism of the first half of the 18th century, that it was then transferred to all foreigners, and that once started it grew steadily.

The missionaries incurred the hatred first of the mandarins. As was noted above, they entered China during the closing years of the 16th century. Under the leadership of the Jesuits Ricci and Schaal, they made notable progress during the 17th century. These men were judicious in every way: they adopted the dress of the literati, used Chinese terminology in referring to God, and

[37] Latourette, *Missions*, pp. 156-58.

[38] See chap. 5, sec. 3.

[39] Eames, *op. cit.*, pp. 58-59. It is a significant fact that this outrage upon the *Anne* occurred at a time and place where the missionaries were strong, and when the mandarins were particularly angered against them.

[40] These numbers are obtained by considering the number of foreign ships arriving at Canton each year about 1720, and multiplying that by the average size of the crew which was about ninety. See appendix XXVI. There seem to have been no great restrictions placed by the Chinese on the freedom of movement of the foreigners. However, each ship had its rules of discipline and undoubtedly prevented its men from running about Canton to any great extent.

[41] The *Anne*, at Amoy already mentioned, was an exception, but this trouble really started over financial disputes and occurred when anti-missionary agitation as well was going on in the province.

did not interfere with ancestor worship.[42] They won the favor of the Emperors because of their astronomical and mathematical ability. Schaal was a particular favorite of Shunche. He was employed to reform the calendar and was given high official positions and honors. This favorable treatment of the Jesuits, at the expense of the officials, was the first step in antagonizing the latter actively against the missionaries.[43] In the course of time the Franciscans and Dominicans began to quarrel with the Jesuits over the term used to denote God and over the exercise of ancestor worship.[44] The missionaries were also active in the provinces, and some estimates indicate that there were 150,000 converts in 1650.[45] This dissension among the missionaries, and the active propagation of their faith throughout the Empire, annoyed the mandarins. At the same time, the fact became evident to them (it was brought more clearly to view by the quarrel between the groups) that the teachings of the missionaries attacked ancestor worship and Confucianism, the things which these scholar-administrators held most dear. They began to fear for themselves, their culture, and the Empire; so when Shunchè died and they came to power, persecution was instigated.

The attack was started by a memorial to the board of regents stating that

> . . . in Japan, nothing but intrigue, schism, and civil war was heard of, calamities that might sooner or later befal China if the criminal eagerness of the missionaries in enlisting people of all classes was not checked. The members of the different orders wore distinctive badges . . ., and were always ready to obey the calls of their chiefs, who could have no scruple to lead them on to action the moment a probability of success in subverting the existing political order and the ancient worship of China should offer.[46]

The regents replied by a decree in 1665 saying that "Schaal and his associates merited the punishment of seducers, who announce

[42]Latourette, *Missions*, pp. 102-06; Williams, *Middle Kingdom*, v. 2, pp. 289-94; *Chinese Repository*, v. 1, pp. 430-43; Ireland, *op. cit.*, p. 38; Lavisse and Rambaud, *op. cit.*, v. 5, pp. 911-12.

[43]Latourette, *Missions*, pp. 106-07, 115-16; Williams, *Middle Kingdom*, v. 2, pp. 296-97.

[44]Latourette, *Missions*, pp. 108-11, 131-39; Williams, *Middle Kingdom*, v. 2, pp. 299-303; Marshall Broomhall, *The Chinese Empire* (New York, 1907), pp. 8-9.

[45]Latourette, *Missions*, p. 107. See appendix XII.

[46]Williams, *Middle Kingdom*, v. 2, p. 297. Quoted directly from the memorial.

to the people a false and pernicious doctrine."[47] Schaal and his friends were thrown into prison, and persecution was instigated. When Kanghi took personal control into his hands, he restored the Jesuits and made Verbiest head of the Astronomical Board because of his superior ability. As the years advanced he became more indulgent to the missionaries, and finally in 1692, issued an edict of toleration to all.[48] There is no evidence that this imperial favor changed the attitude of the officials or of the literati; in fact, the missionaries' activity in making converts, the arrival of new groups of French Jesuits, the favors heaped upon the Christians by Kanghi, and the missionaries' "thinly-veiled assumption of superiority" only increased their dislike.[49] Because of Kanghi's attitude, however, the officials were forced to hold their peace and work to convert him.

The missionaries next incurred the opposition of the Emperor. The immediate factor which led Kanghi to adopt a somewhat less favorable attitude toward them was the decision of the Pope, contrary to his own, in the rites controversy. This discussion between the Jesuits and the Friars, over the term used to describe God and the practice of ancestor worship, had been going on since the middle of the 17th century, but was brought to a head about 1700 when the Jesuits appealed to the Emperor.[50] He decided in favor of the Jesuits and declared "*tien* [meant] the true God, and that the customs of China were political."[51] The Pope, on the other hand, handed down his final decision in 1704 to the effect that *Tien* (Heaven) must not be used to refer to God but only *Tien Chu* (Lord of Heaven) should be used, and that ancestor worship should be abandoned.[52] A papal legate was sent to reconcile the Emperor, but he only widened the breach, and in 1706 Kanghi, angered by the repudiation of his decision and by the adherence of missionaries

[47] *Ibid.*, p. 297.

[48] *Ibid.*, v. 2, pp. 297-99; *Catholic Encyclopaedia*, v. 15, pp. 346-47; Latourette, *Missions*, pp. 116-26; Gowan and Hall, *op. cit.*, p. 201; Boulger, *op. cit.*, v. 1, pp. 585-86.

[49] H. H. Gowen, *History of Asia* (Boston, 1926), pp. 154-55; Latourette, *Missions*, pp. 120-22, 126-30; Boulger, *op. cit.*, v. 1, pp. 629-32; Williams, *Middle Kingdom*, v. 2, p. 305.

[50] Latourette, *Missions*, pp. 131-40; Broomhall, *op. cit.*, pp. 9-10; Vinacke, *op. cit.*, pp. 29-30; E. H. Parker, *China Past and Present*, p. 117; Williams, *Middle Kingdom*, v. 2, pp. 299-303; *Catholic Encyclopaedia*, v. 3, p. 671.

[51] Williams, *Middle Kingdom*, v. 2, p. 301.

[52] *Ibid.*, pp. 301-02; Latourette, *Missions*, pp. 138-41.

to a foreign potentate, issued a decree proscribing all persons who refused to accept the Jesuit position and who adhered to the papal decree. This edict was not rigorously enforced, and the missionaries continued to work.[53]

If the rites controversy first caused the Emperors to oppose the missionaries, there were a number of more subtle considerations which finally caused the imperial attitude to become one of settled anti-missionarism. These centered about four facts. The first was the danger of the foreign teachings to Chinese culture and religion, which the officials and literati had long pointed out. Since ancestor worship and Confucianism were the very heart of Chinese culture, there was no doubt but that the missionary teaching struck at it.[54] The second factor was the danger to the imperial sovereignty which these missionaries and their teachings constituted. Not only by their attack on the religious-social system did the missionaries threaten to subvert the imperial power: but by their allegiance to a foreign ruler, by their conversion of several hundred thousand people who looked toward Rome, and by their building of a separate church organization in China which recognized the papal control, they tended to undermine imperial authority. The activity of the papal legate, followed by a bull, calling upon the Christians to obey the papal demand in spite of the Emperor, only strengthened this conviction.[55] A third factor which undoubtedly influenced the Emperor, the officials, and the public as well, was the rapid increase of missionary activity and converts between 1700 and 1715.[56] The fourth factor which converted the ruler was the propaganda of the literati and officials. This culminated about 1716 with a memorial from Kwangtung province which de-

[53]Williams, *Middle Kingdom*, v. 2, pp. 302-03; Latourette, *Missions*, pp. 141-50; Lavisse and Rambaud, *op. cit.*, v. 8, pp. 957-58.

[54]Williams, *Middle Kingdom*, v. 2, p. 303; Treat, *op. cit.*, p. 30; Martin, *op. cit.*, v. 2, pp. 60-63; Parker, *China History*, p. 95. We do not intend to show that the missionaries were any more dangerous to China than any other group of Westerners would have been. But it happened to be they and not the traders who were propagating Western cultural ideas. That the Western ideals actually were dangerous to Chinese civilization is proven by a glance at the cultural chaos in China today.

[55]Latourette, *Missions*, pp. 122-26, 141-47; Gowen and Hall, *op. cit.*, p. 201; Vinacke, *op. cit.*, pp. 29-30; Martin, *op. cit.*, v. 2, pp. 471-78; *Catholic Encyclopaedia*, v. 3, p. 672; Broomhall, *op. cit.*, p. 10.

[56]Williams, *Middle Kingdom*, v. 2, p. 303, says there were 100 churches and 100,000 converts in Kiangnan and Kiangsi provinces. By 1724, according to Martin, *op. cit.*, v. 2, p. 480, there were 300 churches and 300,000 converts

nounced the Christian teachers as dangerous to China. The final result was an imperial decree banishing all missionaries except those who obtained from the Emperor permission to remain.[57] Kanghi, however, had tolerated missionaries too long to change suddenly, and until his death the decree was not enforced with much vigor.

The whole problem of the imperial attitude was well summed up by a statement of Emperor Yung Cheng. "You wish [speaking to the missionaries] that all the Chinese should become Christians, and indeed your creed commands it. I am well aware of this, but in that event what would become of us? Should we not soon be merely the subjects of your kings?"[58] Yung Cheng, due to personal and dynastic reasons as well as general considerations, was anti-missionary, and with him the period of anti-foreign agitation began.[59]

Having noted how the mandarins and then the Emperor became anti-missionary, the next problem is to show how this feeling was transferred to the people and then directed against all foreigners. Anti-missionarism was transferred to the people by the persecutions during the reigns of Yung Cheng and Kienlung. With the imperial hostility definitely directed against the missionaries, the literati and provincial governors proceeded to arouse the people. Prior to this time we presume the public attitude had been one of tolerance mixed with distrust. Now, however, urged on by the propaganda and systematic opposition of the mandarins, the populace joined in the attack on the priests who were preaching against their sacred ancestors. The outbreak began in Fukien and Chekiang provinces where proclamations were issued against the missionaries as violators of the teachings of the Chinese sages. Attacks were organized, missionaries were driven out, and their churches were destroyed. A memorial was sent to the Emperor, who replied by issuing an

in China. Latourette, *Missions*, p. 128, says that around 1700 there were 500 conversions every year in Peking, and between 70 and 117 missionaries in China; see also pp. 129 and 158 for other figures; one estimate is 300,000 in 1705 and another the same amount in 1724. See also Boulger, *op. cit.*, v. 1, pp. 631-32 and appendix XII.

[57]Latourette, *Missions*, pp. 156-58; Boulger, *op. cit.*, v. 1, pp. 633-34; E. T. Williams, *China*, pp. 235-36; Gowen and Hall, *op. cit.*, p. 201; Macgowan, *op. cit.*, p. 538.

[58]Gowen and Hall, *op. cit.*, pp. 213-14.

[59]Latourette, *Missions*, p. 159; E. T. Williams, *China*, p. 235; Gowen and Hall, *op. cit.*, p. 213.

edict in 1724 condemning Christianity and banishing all missionaries to Macao. This edict was carried out by force but apparently without bloodshed.[60] Between 1730-32 a second series of persecutions occurred because many of the banished priests had returned in violation of the government's order.[61]

Kien-lung proved to be even more opposed to the missionaries than his father; he seemed, in fact, to be decidedly anti-European.[62] In 1736 he issued a decree proscribing the missionaries, ordering that the Christian faith be given up, and prohibiting officials from accepting it.[63] Fukien and Kiangnan provinces were centers of the Christians. The missionaries insisted on returning, and so between 1744 and 1747 another series of persecutions took place which did not entirely abate until the 1750's. Several missionaries lost their lives.[64]

These persecutions, in which the masses participated, served to arouse the people against foreigners, but this was undoubtedly accentuated by the hostile attitude of the Emperor and the mandarins which was constantly growing stronger. Another factor which encouraged public opposition was the over-zealous activity of converts, which resulted in the destruction of images and the flouting of old customs. Bigotry and ostentation on the part of the missionaries also helped to discredit them and make people dislike them.[65]

5. *Anti-Missionary Feeling Becomes Anti-Foreignism*

Anti-missionarism is not necessarily anti-foreignism, but in this case it became so. Missionaries were practically the only aliens whom most of the people ever met, and so the odium attached to them was placed on all foreigners by the indiscrim-

[60]Latourette, *Missions*, pp. 158-60; E. T. Williams, *China*, p. 236; Broomhall, *op. cit.*, pp. 10-11; Auber, *op. cit.*, p. 49; Williams, *Middle Kingdom*, v. 2, p. 304; for text of edict see Parker, *China Past and Present*, pp. 124-26. A few were allowed to stay at Peking for scientific purposes.

[61]Latourette, *Missions*, pp. 160-61; Gowen and Hall, *op. cit.*, p. 214.

[62]Williams, *op. cit.*, v. 2, p. 305. We have earlier noted (p. 37) that he immediately issued an order stating that whenever a foreigner killed a Chinese a foreign life must be exacted, and although he did relieve some restrictions on trade he imposed others.

[63]Latourette, *Missions*, pp. 161-62; Williams, *Middle Kingdom*, v. 2, p. 305.

[64]Latourette, *Missions*, pp. 162-65; Broomhall, *op. cit.*, pp. 10-11; Gowen and Hall, *op. cit.*, pp. 217-18.

[65]Williams, *Middle Kingdom*, v. 2, pp. 305, 312-13. Quotations from Bishop Caradre and Ripa, contemporary observers.

inating public mind. Nor were the mandarins loath to do the same. Years of domination on their part over the foreigners, and submission on the part of the latter, had bred a contempt for the Europeans which was easily transformed into open dislike.[66] Supported now by the imperial will, the mandarins increased their avaricious attitude toward the traders, used more insolent language, and heaped new restrictions and impositions upon them.[67] As the domination of the mandarins increased, so, too, did their insolence and contempt. All of China, taking its key from the Emperor, was slowly becoming anti-foreign.[68] Not only were the traders at Canton restricted more than formerly, but the conditions of the Russian trade were made more stringent. In spite of the fact that Russia was allowed a permanent embassy at Peking in 1727, the general intent of the treaty seems to have been the prohibition of Russian caravans from coming to Peking and their restriction to frontier posts.[69] It was also followed by an imperial order telling the merchants how to cheat the Russians.[70] Thus by the middle of the century Russian caravans had ceased to come to Peking, and the Russian embassy had vanished.[71] Two Portuguese embassies to Peking, one in 1727, and another in 1753, were dismissed with scant courtesy and no concessions.[72] On the whole, opposition to traders seems to have followed in the wake of the anti-missionary outbreaks, and by 1757 a policy of growing anti-foreignism seems to have fastened itself upon the country.

It was probably aggravated by the Dutch massacre of the Chinese at Batavia in 1740,[73] by the increasing number of Euro-

[66]Eames, *op. cit.*, pp. 73-74.

[67]See sec. 1 and 2 of chap. 7.

[68]Williams, *Middle Kingdom*, v. 2, p. 305. "The rulers were thoroughly dissatisfied with the foreigners, and ready to take almost any measures to relieve the country of them." For examples of mandarin and public dislike see Eames, *op. cit.*, p. 79, and *Chinese Repository*, v. 1, pp. 216-20.

[69]Hertslet, *op. cit.*, v. 1, pp. 439-46; E. T. Williams, *China*, pp. 236-38; Morse, *International Relations*, v. 1, pp. 61-62; Williams, *Middle Kingdom*, v. 2, pp. 442-43; Martin, *op. cit.*, v. 1, pp. 391-93.

[70]See in Martin, *op. cit.*, v. 1, pp. 137-39. Perhaps the most remarkable order ever openly issued by a government toward a supposedly friendly power.

[71]*Ibid.*, pp. 392-93; Williams, *Middle Kingdom*, v. 2, p. 442. The Chinese in reply to Macartney's demands declared that the Russians had not been permitted in Peking for many years. See Morse, *Chronicle*, v. 2, p. 249.

[72]Williams, *Middle Kingdom*, v. 2, p. 428-31; Morse, *International Relations*, v. 1, p. 43.

[73]Macpherson, *India*, p. 65.

peans who yearly came to Canton,[74] and by reports of European aggression in surrounding territories. The change in the public attitude is readily seen when this testimony, written in 1750-51, is compared with that of Lockyer quoted earlier.

> It is dangerous for a single person to venture too far [from factories at Canton] because he is in danger of being stripped to the very shirt. Though the curiosity of the Europeans may not be perhaps void of blame; yet the natives look as if they were glad to find a pretence to use violence against a stranger, especially when they are sure of overpowering him.[75]

The writer adds that children were reared to dislike foreigners.

In such a manner arose anti-foreignism in China.

[74]In the year 1751 there were between 2000 and 3000 foreigners in Canton alone, besides several hundred at Macao (Morse, *Chronicle*, v. 1, p. 292), while in 1720 there were only about 900 or 1000 at Canton (p. 101).

[75]*Chinese Repository*, v. 1, p. 216. From Pehr Osbeck, *A Voyage to China and the East Indies* (London, 1771). The voyage took place between 1750-51.

CHAPTER VII

THE EXPANSION OF TRADE AND THE GROWTH OF RESTRICTIONS AND CONFLICT (1720-1757)

1. *Restrictions and Conflict, 1720-1736*

Having in the previous chapter noted the development of anti-foreignism in China, it will be proper to resume the story of Canton trade, a story largely of new impositions on the part of the officials and of protests on the part of the English. The connection between these impositions and the development of anti-foreignism should not be too greatly emphasized, for most of the exactions originated in greed and avarice and were only enhanced by anti-alien attitudes.

The Co-hong (or merchant guild) was the first restriction which aroused the ire of the Europeans. It appeared in 1720 and consisted of sixteen prominent Hong Merchants. A Hong Merchant was a trader of "Substance or Credit," who, upon giving proper security, was granted permission and privilege to open a hong.[1] "The ostensible object of the guild was to check abuses, to foster foreign trade, and to protect foreigners from the malpractices of the unworthy among the merchants of Canton; and all of the thirteen articles of its charter [were] replete with these laudable aims."[2] From a study of the preamble to the guild patent and from the articles of its charter, one can hardly see why the Europeans objected. Its aim was undoubtedly economy for the merchants and protection to the foreigners. "To cheat foreigners is a crime our laws never pardon; if, for the future, anyone should impose false goods, he shall be liable to punishment."[3] It was not an official organ of exaction, but a purely private undertaking, which received the official charter. Its aim, however, was to monopolize trade.

[1]Morse, *Chronicle*, v. 1, pp. 161-70 and v. 5, p. 39. A hong was a large warehouse or factory. Cordier, *op. cit.*, v. 1, p. 15 defines the Hong Merchants and the Co-hong in the following terms: "Les *hannistes* ou *Hong Merchants*, étaient, à Canton, les marchands ayant le privilège exclusif du commerce avec les étrangers; leur réunion formait le *co-hong* ou *co-hang*."

[2]Morse, *Chronicle*, v. 1, p. 163.

[3]Eames, *op. cit.*, pp. 65-67, quoted from the charter of the guild.

The "grand cargo" was to be assigned to it, while the shopkeepers were to have the unimportant trade.[4] This was shown in 1721, when the Hoppo, supporting it, placed duties of 20 per cent on china-ware and 40 per cent on tea sold by outside merchants to the foreigners.[5] The supercargoes protested against the Co-hong at the outset, and in 1721 they refused to allow their ships to be measured until it was abolished.[6] As organized in 1720, it was a real corporation or Co-hong, acting and working as a unit, and as such had great power. Contrary to general belief, it was not re-established in such a capacity until 1760.[7] The individual Hong Merchants, however, continued to trade, and because of their greater repute were able to monopolize business. These men eventually became "security merchants" which gave them additional control over trade.

Competition of the Ostend Company next occupied the traders' attention. The supercargoes were ordered by the Court of Directors to purchase the entire supply of tea in 1720, if possible, and so prevent the Ostend Company's ships from trading.[8] This company was, as has been noted, a group of English interlopers which had received a charter from the Emperor of Austria, and the English government took immediate steps to have it suppressed. It was not popular at Canton, and in 1722 the Court directed its supercargoes to seize interloping ships whenever found. The Ostend Company continued until 1727, when its abolition caused the interlopers to find other means of keeping up their trade.[9]

The year 1722 marked the peak of privileges granted to foreigners, says Eames. The usual concessions were granted, but a change in attitude was in evidence in the fall of 1723.[10] In 1722 the supercargoes protested without success against the 6 per cent charge, but in 1723 the officials appeared with new demands. The military officers insisted upon the right to search ships for

[4] *Ibid.*, pp. 64-69.
[5] Morse, *Chronicle*, v. 1, p. 166; Martin, *op. cit.*, pp. 10-11.
[6] Morse, *Chronicle*, v. 1, pp. 166-67.
[7] See p. 136. For other discussions of this see Auber, *op. cit.*, p. 155. Latourette, *Early Chino-American Relations*, p. 20; Morse, *International Relations*, v. 1, pp. 65-66.
[8] Morse, *Chronicle*, v. 1, pp. 161-62.
[9] *Ibid.*, pp. 171-72; Macgregor, *op. cit.*, v. 4, pp. 343-48.
[10] Eames, *op. cit.*, pp. 69-70. Note that this was the first year of Yung Cheng's reign.

arms and apparently carried the demand into effect despite protests made to the Hoppo and to the Viceroy.[11] Martin states that the Chinese merchants were in a bad financial condition this year, due to high interest rates and the cornering of the tea supply by the Hoppo, who forced them to pay exorbitant prices; and that to help them, a 3 per cent duty (to form a Consoo fund) was established. The latter half of this statement seems to be untrue, but financial troubles of the merchants did depress trade.[12] In 1724 more vexations appeared in the rapacious character of the Hoppo, who was also governor of Kwangtung province. This double office placed great power in his hands, and he seems to have made such excessive demands that the supercargoes seriously considered going to Amoy, whither they had been invited the previous year.[13]

The year 1727 saw the first recorded imposition of the 1950 taels cumshaw, which amount became a fixed duty for the next century.[14] The following year the Viceroy demanded a 10 per cent *ad valorem* tax on all goods imported and exported, the reason being that the ships from Europe did not bring as bulky cargoes as did the "country ships," and so paid very little duty to the Emperor.[15] Despite the united protests of all foreign traders the tax was imposed, but the Chinese merchants were to pay it. When the foreigners went a second time to the Viceroy, he refused to see them, informing them that in the future all requests to him invariably should be addressed through Hong Merchants.[16] This year the Hoppo seriously restricted the freedom of trade by ordering that the foreigners should confine their commercial transactions to the respectable Hong Merchants.[17] The next year prices charged by the merchants had uniformly

[11] Morse, *Chronicle*, v. 1, pp. 174-78; Eames, *op. cit.*, pp. 69-71; Auber, *op. cit.*, p. 157.

[12] Morse, *Chronicle*, v. 1, pp. 175-76; Martin, *op. cit.*, v. 2, p. 11.

[13] Morse, *Chronicle*, v. 1, pp. 176-85.

[14] *Ibid.*, pp. 183-85; Eames, *op. cit.*, pp. 71-72; Davis, *op. cit.*, v. 1, pp. 40-41.

[15] Eames, *op. cit.*, pp. 71-72; Morse, *Chronicle*, v. 1, pp. 185-89. Eames says that the 10 per cent was an export tax while Morse says that it was both an import and export tax. At all events it was a separate and distinct duty from the 6 per cent which also had to be paid. "Country ships" were private Indian ships licensed by the Company. Most of the real Company ships came direct from England.

[16] Eames, *op. cit.*, pp. 71-72; Morse, *Chronicle*, v. 1, pp. 189-96; Auber, *op. cit.*, p. 160.

[17] Morse, *Chronicle*, v. 1, p. 188.

increased, showing that they had simply added the 10 per cent. Obstructions were becoming so great that the English talked of leaving Canton, and apparently decided to remove to Amoy, but they were dissuaded by favorable promises of the Hoppo.[18] The latter seems not to have carried out his promises, and restrictions became so embarrassing that the supercargoes sent the first recorded appeal to Peking in 1730.[19] The year 1729 was notable for the first imperial decree prohibiting the selling of opium in China and providing for the confiscation of ships that brought it. A penalty of death was to be imposed on anyone who would buy the drug or operate an opium smoking house.[20]

The difficulties which constantly had been growing came to a head in 1732. The supercargoes' linguist was put in chains because the English failed to observe the Hoppo's order not to fire guns.[21] The supercargoes of all nations sent a joint note of protest to the Hoppo, in which they demanded:

1. The issue of a Chop acquainting them with what the Emperor's duties were.

2. The abolition of the 6 per cent and the remittance of the 10 per cent.

3. That the compradore be charged less for his Chop so that he would not charge them so much for provisions. (He apparently now had a monopoly of the purchase of supplies).

4. The remittance of the T. 1950.[22]

To this the Hoppo returned a very general answer, and when the ships were ready to leave Canton, he refused the Grand Chop until all charges had been paid. He had discovered an effective weapon to enforce his demands. In 1733 the Company prohibited the carrying of opium in its ships.[23]

The foreign merchants continued their protests against impositions and restrictions. But when this proved futile, they changed their policy and threatened to go to Amoy. This again produced favorable promises but nothing more.[24] The Company did, however, send a ship to Amoy in 1734 and one in 1735, but they found the quantity and quality of goods there very defi-

[18] *Ibid.*, pp. 187-96; Martin, *op. cit.*, pp. 11-12. For details of the troubles of this year see also Auber, *op. cit.*, pp. 157-62.

[19] Eames, *op. cit.*, p. 72; Auber, *op. cit.*, p. 161.

[20] Morse, *Chronicle*, v. 1, p. 215.

[21] *Ibid.*, p. 210.

[22] *Ibid.*, pp. 210-14; Martin, *op. cit.*, v. 2, p. 12; Auber, *op. cit.*, pp. 161-62.

[23] Morse, *Chronicle*, v. 1, pp. 215-16.

[24] *Ibid.*, pp. 223-29; Martin, *op. cit.*, v. 2, p. 12; Eames, *op. cit.*, p. 72; Auber, *op. cit.*, p. 162.

cient, prices 10 to 30 per cent higher than at Canton, and the demands and extortions of the officials so exorbitant that the attempt to trade there was abandoned.[25] In 1736 a ship was sent to Ningpo, but it fared no better than the ones at Amoy, and so Canton remained the center of foreign trade.[26] The impositions seemed to be damaging business, for in the years 1733 to 1736 the number of ships sent to Canton decreased from an average of four a year to two.[27]

In 1736 Kien-lung came to the throne. Upon the payment of a considerable sum the Europeans had a petition presented to him. As an act of grace the Emperor abolished the 10 per cent because he considered it an illegal imposition, but demanded the revival of an old practice which required a ship to give up its arms before entering the harbor. Evasion of this last demand required the payment of a further sum.[28] Trouble also arose over the reception of the decree. The Hoppo insisted that the Europeans perform the *kotow* while it was read, but this they refused to do.[29] On the whole the Emperor's act of grace proved to be of little value. It did not take effect until the next year, and then, according to the supercargoes, prices did not decrease as had been expected.[30]

2. *Growth of the Security Merchant System and the Hongist Monopoly, 1728-1755*

The statement of the supercargoes that prices did not become lower is significant. It shows that the Chinese merchants had begun to pay the customs duties, which were then added to the price charged the Europeans. Just when this practice began is not known, but it probably originated with the development of the "security merchant." The first record of a security merchant, or person who became responsible to the officials for a

[25]Martin, *op. cit.*, v. 2, pp. 12-13; Morse, *Chronicle*, v. 1, pp. 220-23; Eames, *op. cit.*, pp. 72-73; See, *op. cit.*, p. 54; Davis, *op. cit.*, v. 1, p. 41.

[26]Morse, *Chronicle*, v. 1, pp. 239-46; Eames, *op. cit.*, p. 73; See, *op. cit.*, p. 55; Davis, *op. cit.*, v. 1, p. 43.

[27]Morse, *Chronicle*, v. 1, p. 310.

[28]*Ibid.*, pp. 247-51; Martin, *op. cit.*, v. 2, p. 13; Auber, *op. cit.*, pp. 162-63. The total cost of getting the decree past and avoiding its consequences was about T. 30,000.

[29]Morse, *Chronicle*, v. 1, pp. 251-53; Eames, *op. cit.*, p. 73; Davis, *op. cit.*, v. 1, pp. 43-44. It is interesting to note this example of personal humiliation demanded. It shows the growth of the anti-foreign attitude.

[30]Morse, *Chronicle*, v. 1, pp. 249-52, 257-61; Auber, *op. cit.*, p. 163.

ship, was in 1736.[31] In 1728, however, the supercargoes had been ordered to do business with certain Hong Merchants, and the Chinese traders were required to pay the 10 per cent as we have noted. The system of security merchants, therefore, probably arose during the early thirties. It seems not yet to have taken definite form, and there is no evidence that it was restricted to any particular merchants.[32] The system continued to grow and during the 1740's assumed definite form.

Its general characteristics and the main objections to it, both from the standpoint of the Hong Merchants, who in all cases were the securities, and the European traders, are well shown in the following extract from one of the supercargoes letters.

> The Merchant who takes upon him to be a Security for any Ship, is answerable for the Customs upon all Goods Imported on that Ship, wheather bought by himself or any other Person, in like manner he is accountable on the Export; so that unless he transacts every Article of our business, he advances considerable Sums of Money for all those who have any dealings with us, and 'tis often with great difficulty that he is reimbursed. A still further disadvantage is that the Security is looked upon by the Hoppo and other Mandarines, as the only Person to procure for them any Curiosities or Merchandize brought on that Ship, and this at the moderate Rules perhaps of One fourth of what the Security pays for them.
>
> Under such Circumstances it is no wonder that the Merchants are unwilling to engage themselves for our Ships, and we on our part are equally desirous they should be excused from it, for the consequences most certainly are, that either the Merchants must be impoverished, or the Company must make good the Expence in the Quality or Prices of the Goods bought from them[33]

as well as being troubled by long delays in obtaining a security or transacting business. It seems quite probable that the security merchant was also responsible for the port charges and harbor duties and for the good conduct of the foreigners, while it is quite certain that communications with the higher officials could be made only through the Hong Merchants.[34]

The records for the forties are scant, but it seems that trouble and vexation continued. In 1744, the *Hardwick* went to Amoy to avoid the Spanish ships of war outside Canton, but after long negotiations she was forced to sail away without a

[31]Morse, *Chronicle*, v. 1, p. 247.
[32]*Ibid.*, p. 260; Eames, *op. cit.*, p. 81.
[33]Morse, *Chronicle*, v. 5, p. 10.
[34]*Ibid.*, v. 1, pp. 278-79, 289, v. 5, pp. 5, 11, 29; Eames, *op. cit.*, p. 80.

cargo.[35] The Court continually sent out orders to protest against the T. 1950 and the percentage charges, but no permanent results were obtained.[36] The attitude of the populace was becoming so threatening that the lives of Europeans were often in danger, and it seems that the practice of confining the sailors to certain islands had begun.[37] Difficulties of trade increased, and the personal liberty of the supercargoes was becoming so restricted that they threatened, in 1747, to leave Canton if trade were not put on a firmer basis.[38] One ray of light during this time was the appearance of Mr. Flint in 1741. He began to learn the Chinese language and was to be of help to the Company later.[39] In 1751 the Hong Merchants apparently proposed an embassy to Nanking where the Emperor was celebrating his birthday. It was to carry presents and a petition, but the project was not carried out.[40] Trade seems to have been on the decline during the 1740's, but this was probably due more to the War of the Austrian Succession in Europe than to conditions in China.[41]

During the early fifties the difficulties became so oppressive that the supercargoes began a strenuous campaign for reform. During the season of 1753 they presented a petition to the Hoppo requesting the abolition of a number of minor abuses regarding commercial dealings and life about the factories, and demanding that they be not "troubled with Securities for [their] Ships, and that whoever [they] purchase[d] Goods of, or [sold] Goods to, . . . be answerable to the Government for the Duties to be paid on them." In 1754 they renewed their demands that the security merchants be abolished and held their ships outside the harbor until the matter might be settled. Long negotiations followed between the supercargoes and officials through the medium of the Hong Merchants. The English finally proceeded

[35]See, *op. cit.*, p. 57; Williams, *History of China*, pp. 96-97; Davis, *op. cit.*, v. 1, p. 45; Morse, *Chronicle*, v. 5, pp. 2-4.

[36]Morse, *Chronicle*, v. 1, pp. 281-93, v. 5, pp. 7-8; Auber, *op. cit.*, pp. 166-67.

[37]Eames, *op. cit.*, p. 77; Auber, *op. cit.*, p. 169. Dane's island according to Auber.

[38]Eames, *op. cit.*, p. 76; Morse, *Chronicle*, v. 1, pp. 289-93, v. 5, pp. 4-6; Martin, *op. cit.*, v. 2, pp. 13-14.

[39]Morse, *Chronicle*, v. 1, pp. 276, 286-87.

[40]Eames, *op. cit.*, p. 77.

[41]See table in the back of Morse, *Chronicle*, v. 1; Macgregor, *op. cit.*, v. 4, pp. 404-06, also appendix XIV.

in person to Canton, and after a long wait and many indignities were admitted to the Viceroy and presented their petition. He gave no direct answer to their demands, and the affair ended by the Hoppo ordering four Hong Merchants (despite their protests) to act as security and that the whole body of Hong Merchants be jointly responsible for all the charges which might be involved. The supercargoes, weary of the conflict and delay, accepted this arrangement and so the season ended.[42]

During the various disputes threats to leave Canton were apparently made, and in 1755, Mr. Flint, by order of the Court, went to Ningpo, where he was favorably received and where he procured a cargo. Two other ships traded at Ningpo in 1756, but in 1757 when the *Onslow* arrived she was refused entrance and permission to trade.[43] The answer of the Canton officials and of the Emperor to this attempt of the English at breaking the Canton monopoly was threefold: the creation of the Hongist Monopoly in 1755, the Imperial Edict restricting trade to Canton in 1757, and the establishment of the Co-hong in 1760.

In May, 1755, a series of edicts issued jointly by the Viceroy and Hoppo, as a result of petitions from the Hongists, identified the security and Hong Merchants, and gave to them a monopoly of foreign trade, thus insuring to the security merchant the necessary protection, were he to be responsible for a foreign ship. The purport of the edicts was as follows:

1. In the future security merchants were to be Hong Merchants, and a "Hongist Security" was to be "answerable for the Hoppo duties," while trade with the foreigners was to be conducted only by "Hongist Securities."
2. Shopkeepers were prohibited from engaging in any description of trade with the Europeans except in the name of a "Hongist Security," and they were to be organized into groups of five who were to be mutually responsible for each other.
3. The interpreters were to acquaint the "Hongist Security" before applying in his name for "Chops for dispatch."
4. In the future the "Hongist Security" and interpreter were to be responsible for any crimes committed by the supercargoes, captains, officers, and sailors, while the supercargoes and captains were to be responsible for the conduct of the sailors.
5. Order and quiet were to be maintained in the factories.

[42]Morse, *Chronicle*, v. 5, pp. 9 and 9-14 *passim;* Eames, *op. cit.*, pp. 78-80.

[43]Morse, *Chronicle*, v. 5, pp. 25-26, 49-53; Williams, *Middle Kingdom*, v. 2, p. 448; Eames, *op. cit.*, pp. 85-87; See, *op. cit.*, p. 57; Auber, *op. cit.*, p. 167; Davis, *op. cit.*, v. 1, pp. 48-49; Cordier, *op. cit.*, v. 1, p. 13. After long negotiations the *Onslow* was allowed to trade but was forbidden to return in the future.

The worst fears of the supercargoes had thus been realized, for the edicts threw the "whole business of the place into the hands of a few Merchants, that they [might] levy as a Recompense what prices they please on the Europeans." The supercargoes protested without success, but the shopkeepers raised such a remonstrance that supplementary decrees allowed them to deal "with private people, but not in any Goods imported for Accounts of the Companies." They were allowed to sell such products as china-ware, woven silks, and retail articles in general, but not tea or raw silk which were reserved for the "Hongist Securities." They were especially forbidden from buying "Curiosities of Value, such as Pearl, Coral, Chrystal, True Amber, & C^{a} all which being for the Emperors Use, no Shops [should] presume to Interfere."[44]

From all evidence the establishment of the Hongist Monopoly was largely a financial measure on the part of the government and officials. The security merchants had become a convenient tool for extortion from the foreigners. Officials held them responsible for all fees and dues, and levied demands upon them until the merchants themselves were opposed to the system. The only way in which the Chinese traders could meet these demands was to charge the foreigners more. The new combination simply increased the efficiency of this tool, and the decree of 1757 made its complete monopoly certain.[45]

3. *The Jurisdiction Questions, 1720-1757*

Jurisdiction over foreigners became an increasingly important question, and one which was significant in causing British interference in Chinese affairs. It is therefore necessary to understand its origin and development.

The common law of all nations holds that every completely sovereign state has unlimited right to control foreigners within its boundaries. In many cases, however, countries with different legal standards have granted, by formal treaty to foreign na-

[44]Morse, *Chronicle*, v. 5, pp. 28-44; Eames, *op. cit.*, p. 81; Auber, *op. cit.*, pp. 168-69; Martin, *op. cit.*, v. 2, p. 14; Morse, *International Relations*, v. 1, pp. 66-67; Milburn, *op. cit.*, v. 2, pp. 469-70; See, *op. cit.*, p. 57.

[45]Eames, *op. cit.*, p. 81 and Auber, *op. cit.*, pp. 168-69; Morse, *International Relations*, v. 1, pp. 66-67. See statements in the preamble of the edicts in Morse, *Chronicle*, v. 5, pp. 36-43. The decree will be dealt with later. See section 5 of this chapter.

tions, the right to exercise jurisdiction over their nationals within that country. This privilege was accorded England by China in 1843; however, since the British generally had refused to submit to the exercise of criminal jurisdiction by the Chinese for many years before this, it is necessary to examine the early history of the question. The first recorded case of this kind was in 1687 when a drunken sailor at Amoy broke into the customs house. The Chinese allowed the English to punish him, and one hundred blows were inflicted.[46] The next case occurred in 1690 when a Chinese and an Englishman were killed and several English captured in an affray at Canton. In this case the Chinese insisted upon a compensation of T. 5000 for the life of the man, and the British, because they refused to pay it, had to sail away without trade.[47] The matter was pursued no further, and, as we have seen (p. 81), the ships which came to Canton in 1718 were granted the right to punish their own men. This apparently was not a formal treaty binding for all time, and did not limit China's right of sovereignty in future cases if she chose to exercise it.

In 1721 some one from the *Bonitta*, a ship from Madras, shot a native by accident. The supercargo of the ship took refuge with the Company's supercargoes. Things remained quiet for eighteen days. Then a mate and four sailors of the *Cadogan* were seized by local officials. The supercargoes protested against this arbitrary action and threatened to leave Canton. The Viceroy and the Hoppo hastened to assure the English that the act had been done without their consent and proceeded to degrade the local officer. The men were released and there the matter rested.[48] The threat to leave Canton had accomplished its purpose.

The next year a gunner's mate on the country ship *King George* fired at a bird and by accident mortally wounded a boy. The matter was settled by the payment of T. 2000, only 350 of which went to the boy's parents.[49] In both cases, it would seem that the English recognized the Chinese right of sovereignty,

[46]Morse, *Chronicle*, v. 1, p. 64; Eames, *op. cit.*, p. 41.
[47]Morse, *Chronicle*, v. 1, pp. 82-84.
[48]*Ibid.*, v. 1, pp. 168-69; Auber, *op. cit.*, pp. 155-56; Eames, *op. cit.*, p. 69.
[49]Morse, *Chronicle*, v. 1, pp. 174-75; Auber, *op. cit.*, pp. 156-57; Eames, *op. cit.*, p. 69.

but in the first protested the illegal seizure of innocent persons. In the second a precedent of money compensation was established.

In 1729 the English attempted to get an extraterritorial concession. Supercargo Mr. Talbot, was able to have the following privilege added to the usual ones granted in the Chop for ships coming to Canton:

> That we desire there may be no Punch houses erected at Wampo, that so (sic) all quarrells between our Sailors and the Chineese may be prevented, and that we may not at Canton be accountable for any such accidents, it being impossible for us to be answerable for them at such a distance; and that if any of our people should be found to be the Aggressors in any Broils between them and the Chineese, that we ourselves only shall inflict such punishments upon them as they shall deserve and according to the Laws of our Country.[50]

This, however, lacked a good deal of being complete extraterritoriality because it was not a general formal grant by the central government, and in all likelihood applied only to the ships under Mr. Talbot's supervision which visited Canton that year.

In 1735 the ship *Richmond* fired at some boats which were hovering about. A woman was injured, but the physician dressed and cared for the wound and she recovered. Since the woman recuperated, the case was classed as accidental and was carried no further.[51] In 1736 a Frenchman, while out hunting, accidentally shot a Chinese. The French consul was seized and humiliated in many ways. The sailor was finally surrendered but it appears that he was not executed.[52] As has been noted, it was at this time that Kien-lung gave the decision that life for life should be exacted from the foreigners. The Chinese asserted their sovereignty in both of these cases and the Emperor's decision showed a determination to punish Europeans. It is also apparent that the carelessness of the foreigners was largely responsible for the accidents.

During the war of the Austrian Succession, French and English sailors were constantly coming into conflict. After the war such trouble continued, and in 1754 an Englishman was killed in one of these affrays. The English demanded justice and the Chinese stopped the French trade until the guilty man was

[50]Morse, *Chronicle*, v. 1, p. 193.
[51]*Ibid.*, p. 236.
[52]*Ibid.*, pp. 253-54.

given up. He was imprisoned for a time, but was freed by a royal act of grace. During the course of the dispute the Chinese urged the English to settle the matter with the French by a friendly arbitration, thus showing a willingness to surrender their extraterritorial jurisdiction where two foreigners were involved. It should also be noted that the English established a dangerous precedent in requesting the Chinese to punish a European for a wrong done to another foreigner. As a result of these affrays the French sailors were allotted French Island upon which to exercise, and the English were allowed Dane's Island. The problem of keeping the sailors under control while at Whampoa was real, for the temptations of the grog shop were many.[53]

Another problem was the treatment of English ships of war. Late in 1741, Commodore Anson of H. M. S. *Centurion*, put into the Canton river for supplies and repairs. Chinese law forbade foreign warships inside the Bogue, and it was only after many threats that he was allowed to go personally to Canton to get supplies. After repairs had been made Anson put to sea, captured a Spanish prize of war and returned to Canton. The officials now wanted to measure both ships and require harbor duties. He refused to pay them and found great difficulty in getting supplies. He threatened to use force and planned to interview the Viceroy in spite of the supercargoes' protests. At this point a fire broke out, and his men so aided in extinguishing it that he was granted a free audience. He protested the treatment of the King's ships and the impositions on the traders. The interview ended with the Viceroy's wishing him a speedy return to Europe.[54] Further conflict on this point also had occurred earlier in 1741, when the *Dorset*, an English ship, put into Macao with a Dutch prize of war. This incident delayed a merchant ship's Grand Chop for four days.[55]

[53]Morse, *International Relations*, v. 1, p. 101; Williams, *Middle Kingdom*, v. 2, p. 451; Eames, *op. cit.*, p. 80; Milburn, *op. cit.*, v. 2, p. 465; Davis, *op. cit.*, v. 1, pp. 47-48; Morse, *Chronicle*, v. 5, pp. 14-19.

[54]Morse, *Chronicle*, v. 1, pp. 284-85; Auber, *op. cit.*, pp. 163-66; Martin, *op. cit.*, v. 2, p. 13; Eames, *op. cit.*, pp. 74-76; Williams, *Middle Kingdom*, v. 2, p. 448; See, *op. cit.*, p. 56; Morse, *International Relations*, v. 1, p. 97; Davis, *op. cit.*, v. 1, pp. 44-45; Cordier, *op. cit.*, v. 1, p. 13; Lavisse and Rambaud, *op. cit.*, v. 8, p. 946.

[55]Morse, *Chronicle*, v. 1, pp. 277-81.

In 1747 Captain Congreve of the *Onslow* was attacked by some Chinese on French Island. The Europeans threatened armed reprisal, and under this threat, the local officials apprehended four guilty Chinese and sent them to Canton for punishment.[56]

On the whole it seems that the Chinese claim to sovereignty was sound, that they generally maintained it, and that the Europeans recognized it. Up to this time no European had been executed, but it appears that only the Emperor's act of grace in 1754 saved the Frenchmen. It further seems that the Europeans were very careless, and the prohibition upon firing guns and the confinment of sailors to different islands were justified. As to the treatment of H. M. Ships and prizes of war, the two countries' customs differed completely and no solution seemed possible.

4. *Progress of the China Trade*

Despite difficulties enumerated in the three previous sections, the Company's trade to China continued to grow, indicating that it must have been very profitable to the Company and of considerable value to England. Table 7 will show the general trend of imports and exports.

TABLE 7.—TRADE OF THE EAST INDIA COMPANY AT CANTON (1721–1760)*

Year	No. Ships	Tonnage	Import Mdse. £	Import Coin £	Total Imports £	Exports Tls.	Size of Average Ship Tons
1721	4	1670	6,476	109,000	113,476	326,763	390
1725	3	1230	.....	80,582	80,582	210,000	430
1730	5	2095	4,500	200,000	204,500	489,946	470
1735	2	1830	7,700	77,000	78,830	90,617	460
1741	6	2470	.....	......	136,500	....	495
1745	3	1494	.....	......	104,509	....	498
1749	4	2000	3,069	58,000	91,069	....	499
1756	..	....	42,193	244,868	287,071	....	...
1760	..	....	60,019	53,081	113,100	749,291†	...

*Based on tables in the back of Morse, *Chronicle*, v. 1, to the year 1749. Tables in Macgregor, *op. cit.*, v. 4, pp. 404-6 also agree in general with this table, and from 1749 to 1760 the figures are based on Macgregor. See appendices XIV and XVI for complete tables.
†For year 1762, from Morse, *Chronicle*, v. 1, p. 306. The figure is £243,097 or T. 749,291

This table shows a number of interesting items. Generally speaking trade increased until 1724, when it saw a decline, but it showed a rise in 1728 which reached a climax in 1731. It again

[56]Eames, *op. cit.*, p. 77.

declined due to impositions and troubles in China, reaching a low water mark in 1735. It then turned upward until 1741, when wars in Europe put a damper on it which continued to operate until the end of the conflict. Trade increased rapidly during the period of peace in Europe despite impositions in China, but with the outbreak of the Seven Years' War once more declined. This is conclusive evidence that European conditions affected trade more than did Chinese conditions. The table also shows that the volume of the import and especially that of the export trade increased during the period.

Another interesting fact is that bullion still constituted by far the most important of the imports into China, although the year 1760 was a decided exception. There was not yet a demand for English goods in China despite the Company's efforts to sell woollens. We also note that the tonnage figures had somewhat advanced, and that the average size of ships sent to Canton had increased by one hundred tons. The size of the crews varied from one hundred to one hundred and twenty men.[57]

Tea was the main article of export. Over the whole period it showed a phenomenal growth in both quantity and total sales receipts, despite the high tariffs previously mentioned. Here is reason for the Company's willingness to put up with the difficulties in China and its strenuous opposition to interlopers. Evidently tea drinking was becoming more popular in England despite the high prices of from 4*s.* to 12*s.* per pound.[58] If the amount of tea smuggled be added, a considerable consumption is indicated. Table 8 shows the trend.

TABLE 8.—TEA TRADE OF THE EAST INDIA COMPANY AT CANTON (1720–1760)*

Year	Pounds of Tea Sold at Co. Sales in London	Amount Realized on Sales £	Pounds of Silk Imported into England
1720	196,625	129,398	512
1729	1,416,028	446,836	4,550
1732	620,496	180,626	47,481
1737	2,895,529	592,504	......
1742	690,807	172,792	2,361
1746	2,524,165	573,028	2,116
1753	2,824,604	637,367	83,124
1760	2,626,552	831,894	75,693

*Tea figures are from Milburn, *op. cit.*, v. 2, p. 534, and silk figures are from Krishna, *op. cit.*, pp. 310-11. For full yearly statements, see appendix XVII and XIX.

[57]Morse, *Chronicle*, v. 1, p. 262.
[58]Appendix XIX; Defoe, *op. cit.*, v. 2, p. 550.

Both the silk and the tea trade show considerable fluctuations, but a steady rise. The curve of the tea sales would follow very much the same line as that of the general trade previously described. Other articles of export were tutenague (crude zinc), quicksilver, sugar, sugar candy, china-ware, nankeens, clothes, camphor, and china-root.[59]

Table 9 will show the prices paid at Canton on the principal articles of import and export in 1751.[60]

TABLE 9.—PRICES OF IMPORTS AND EXPORTS AT CANTON (1751)

Goods	Cost £ *s.* *d.*	Sold for Tls.	Profit percentage of gross
Imports			
Cloth, per yard	. 9 7	1.800	25.47
Camblets, per yard	. 3 2	0.500	4.75
Long Ells, per piece	2 1 6	7.500	20.01
Callimancoes, per piece	3 9 1	14.782	32.59
Lead, per picul	. 14 4	4.500	75.05
Tin, per picul	. .. .	14.000	....
Exports			Canton Purchase Price Tls.
Tea, Bohea, per picul			15.50
Tea, Pekoe, per picul			24.00
Tea, Congho, per picul			21.57
Tea, Souchong, per picul			31.94
Tea, Singlo, per picul			20.66
Tea, Hyson, per picul			41.13
Tutenague, per picul			6.00
Quicksilver, per picul			60.00
Sugar, per picul			3.05
Sugar Candy, per picul			5.05

The principal article of import was, of course, silver. The Chinese did not want European goods and would buy them only grudgingly. Woollens of various kinds constituted the chief merchandise import. The above shows that they realized a considerable profit, but after the freight rate of some £57 per ton and other expenses were deducted, the woollens throughout an average of years made practically no profit.[61] The Company

[59]Statement based on cargoes of several ships. Morse, *Chronicle*, v. 1, pp. 172, 255-56. See appendix XXIV for cargoes of special ships.
[60]Morse, *Chronicle*, v. 1, p. 291.
[61]Macgregor, *op. cit.*, v. 4, pp. 362-63.

carried them in order to satisfy public demands at home. Practically the only other notable articles of import were tin and lead.[62] There are no available figures showing the total quantities of these products, but they were very low as the total merchandise import indicates. Opium was not yet an article of trade, and what little was imported to China was brought by the Portuguese. Its importation by the Company's ships had been prohibited in 1733.[63]

Private trade by officers of the ships and by supercargoes was allowed to a limited extent. The latter were allowed to carry out a specified sum in foreign silver to invest in Chinese gold and ship back to Europe. They and the ships' officers also carried on private trade in tea and minor merchandise both to and from China, but the amount was limited. Commanders and officers were allowed 224 pounds for every 100 tons of the ship's tonnage, while the private investment of the supercargoes was fixed at specific amounts, depending upon their rank.[64] This business often rose to considerable quantities. The amount of private trade by the officers of one ship amounted to about T. 22,000 in 1733, while in 1731 the merchandise trade of the supercargoes amounted to £760 and their investments in gold to £15,000.[65] On a whole the tendency was for the Company to restrict the trade of its supercargoes and sea captains.

The "country trade" was that carried on between India and China by Indian and private ships licensed by the Company. There are no figures for estimating its extent at this time, but we do know from records of the cargoes of Indian ships that it existed. There are records of Indian ships at Canton prior to 1748, and in that year four country ships visited Canton, several in 1749, three in 1751, five in 1752, and five in 1753.[66] The Company also carried articles to and from India. The principal imports to China from India seem to have been raw cotton, sandalwood, and olibanum (fragrant gum), while the chief ex-

[62] Morse, *Chronicle*, v. 1, pp. 109, 283.
[63] *Ibid.*, p. 215.
[64] *Ibid.*, pp. 71-75, 149.
[65] *Ibid.*, pp. 207, 218-19. For further figures and discussion, see pp. 71-75, 149, 171, 196, 207, 208, 220, 230, 239.
[66] *Ibid.*, p. 292 and table in the back, and pp. 247, 261, 275, 282.

ports were sugar, sugar candy, china-root, tutenague, alum, and tea.[67] During this period the Company experienced much trouble in finding silver to finance the trade. As yet the private Indian trade did not supply a counterbalancing product in opium and cotton as it later did. The difference between the imports and exports had to be met by silver balances.

English commerce was predominant over that of any other single European country at Canton. The English, in fact, tried to monopolize the tea trade; but in this they were foiled by their own tariff walls, which enabled the interlopers and other foreign merchants to carry on a good business in tea under the cloak of foreign companies.[68] The French had been at Canton when the English first arrived,[69] while the Dutch and Danish came later. During the 1720's the severe competition of the Ostend Company was encountered. It sent about ten ships to Canton. Finally the Swedish and Prussian ships made their appearance, while an occasional Spanish vessel put into Whampoa.[70] The principal articles of export by these foreign ships were tea, woven silk, and china-ware.[71] Tables 10 and 11 show to some extent how the trade of other Western countries compared with that of England.

TABLE 10.—ENGLISH AND FOREIGN TRADE AT CANTON (1734)*

Companies	China-ware (No. chests)	Tea, Piculs	Woven silk pieces
English	240	4,427	16,028
French	154	3,313	3,375
Danish	248	7,024	3,488
Dutch	163	4,681	5,070

*Morse, *Chronicle*, v. 1, p. 229.

[67]*Ibid.*, p. 283 (based on ships' cargoes) for imports, and p. 172, for exports.

[68]Eames, *op. cit.*, pp. 78-79; A. L. Bowley, *England's Foreign Trade in the Nineteenth Century* (New York, 1893), p. 9. See also Morse, *Chronicle*, v. 1, pp. 160, 171.

[69]Morse, *Chronicle*, v. 1, pp. 91-92; Cordier, *op. cit.*, v. 1, p. 16.

[70]Macpherson, *India*, pp. 285-93 for the Danish; pp. 294-304 for Ostend Co., and pp. 305-12 for the Swedish and Prussian trade. See also Eames, *op. cit.*, p. 71.

[71]Morse, *Chronicle*, v. 1, p. 229.

TABLE 11.—TONNAGE OF THE VARIOUS COUNTRIES AT CANTON*

Year	English Company	Indian	French	Dutch	Danish	Swedish	Portuguese and Spanish at Macao
1739	2,465	950	1,700	1,650	700	700	.....
1740	990	...	2,000	1,950	800	.....	4,400
1741	2,250	350	1,450	1,450	850	2,600	.....
1751	4,700	...	1,800	3,150	950	1,590	.....
No. of ships of each in 1751	7	3	2	4	1	2	

*Morse, *Chronicle*, v. 1, pp. 275, 282, 292.

These figures show that the English, while being the predominant nation at Canton, were not more important than all the others combined. They also indicate that the combined export of tea by other countries was far greater than that of the British, although it must be noted that their tea trade was more fluctuating and irregular than that of the English. In fact their entire business was less stable and regular, and for this reason the British were preferred by the Chinese. The presence of a large number of different nationalities at Canton was important in that it increased the possibility of conflict and disorder.

5. *The Imperial Decree of 1757*

In 1757 Kien-lung issued an Imperial Edict which, together with supplementary decrees by the Viceroys of Min-Che (Fukien-Chekiang) and Canton, effectively prohibited foreign trade at any Chinese port other than Canton. To insure the confinement of trade to Canton the Emperor ordered that any European ship entering Ningpo or Chusan should surrender its "arms, guns, ammunition and sails, and pay double duties."[72]

In a sense this act was the culmination of the anti-foreign movement. It would probably not have occurred but for the hostility to foreigners; it was the Emperor's way of insuring the least trouble from them in the future, and at the same time reaping financial rewards from their trade. But there were very specific and obvious immediate causes for its issuance. It was the Emperor's and mandarin's reply to the foreigner's attempt

[72]Eames, *op. cit.*, pp. 85-86; Auber, *op. cit.*, pp. 170-71; Milburn, *op. cit.*, v. 2, p. 461; Morse, *International Relations*, v. 1, p. 67; Morse, *Chronicle*, v. 5, pp. 53-63. The decree may have been issued late in 1756, but it was not effectively made known to the Europeans until 1757. See pp. 53-54 of Morse.

to open trade at Ningpo. As was noted, a ship had been sent to Ningpo in 1755, at a time when the Emperor was also in need of money because of foreign war.[73] The desire of the sovereign to increase his revenue and the greed of the Cantonese officials led to the establishment of the Hongist Monopoly in the same year. In answer to this the English sent two ships to Ningpo in 1756 and one in 1757. In the meantime the Cantonese officials and merchants, aroused by the fear of losing this valuable trade, obtained the support of the Viceroy of Fukien and Chekiang, and dispatched a memorial, together with a large sum of money, to Peking requesting that trade be confined to Canton. Kienlung, fearing the loss of his newly created engine of revenue, also supported the Canton group.[74] Consequently, when the *Onslow* arrived at Ningpo in 1757, she was informed that it was the Emperor's will that foreigners should trade at Canton, but if they persisted in going elsewhere they would be charged double duties. The Emperor seems not absolutely to have prohibited trade at Ningpo, but left the matter to the Viceroy, who, being recently transferred from Canton, absolutely prohibited ships coming there in the future. These decrees constituted the necessary steps to make the newly created Hongist Monopoly completely effective as an organ of official exaction and imperial revenue.[75]

Other factors which probably influenced the Emperor's mind were the troubles with the missionaries, the recent homicide at Canton, numerous brawls among the European sailors, and the memory of the unhappy experience with Commodore Anson. By restricting trade to Canton he could insure against the occurrence of such trouble at other places within the Empire, and he could also limit the point of entry for missionaries who insisted on violating his exclusion decree. The edicts were therefore the result of a combination of private greed, imperial financial need, and public policy looking toward the future tranquillity of the Empire.

[73]Gowen and Hall, *op. cit.*, pp. 218-30; Lavisse and Rambaud, *op. cit.*, v. 8, pp. 935-43.

[74]Martin, *op. cit.*, v. 2, p. 14; Morse, *Chronicle*, v. 4, p. 318, v. 5, pp. 49, 53-56; Davis, *op. cit.*, v. 1, pp. 48-49; See, *op. cit.*, pp. 57-58 insists that the decree was a revenue measure.

[75]Eames, *op. cit.*, pp. 85-86; Williams, *Middle Kingdom*, v. 2, p. 448; Auber, *op. cit.*, pp. 170-71; Morse, *International Relations*, v. 1, pp. 67, 107; Morse, *Chronicle*, v. 5, pp. 53, 54, 56, 60-62.

6. *A Picture of Trade in 1757*

It will be well to stop at this point and take a cross-section view of trade and compare it with conditions as they had been between 1715 and 1720. We at once note the increase in the volume of commerce. Imports had doubled while exports had more than doubled. The annual number of English ships sent to Canton was twice what it had been,[76] while there were eight or ten other foreign ships a year where there had been only four or five during the earlier period. Roughly speaking, this meant an increase in the number of foreigners at Canton of from 1000 to 2500 annually.[77] Thus the possibilities of conflict had greatly increased, while the added value of trade made its continuation under less restraint more desirable.

Exactions and impositions had also increased considerably. The basic measuring fee had not been raised appreciably, now being T. 1300 to T. 1400 on an ordinary 499 ton ship, but the cumshaw had become fixed at T. 1950, making a total of about T. 3400 measuring fee on each ship.[78] Morse describes the measuring process and charges on a ship in 1739 as follows:[79]

Ships were measured for length from the centre of the foremast to the centre of the mizenmast, and for breadth from side to side close abaft the mainmast; no attention was paid to the depth. This length was multiplied by this breadth, both in Chinese coveds, cubits, or *ch'ih* of 14.1 English inches, and the product divided by 10; the result gives the units of measurage.

Ships of or exceeding 74 coveds long, or 23 coveds broad, were rated as first-rates; those 71 to 74 long, and 22 to 23 broad, as second-rates; those 65 to 71 long, and 20 to 22 broad, as third-rates; but all smaller ships were rated as third-rates, as in the case of the sloop in 1730.

First-rates paid measurage dues per unit Tls.	7.777
Second-rates paid measurage dues per unit Tls.	7.142
Third-rates paid measurage dues per unit Tls.	5.000

The *Augusta* measured 76.3 coveds in length and 23.3 coveds in breadth, and was therefore a first-rate. The calculation for her dues was as follows:

$$\frac{76.3 \times 23.3}{10} = 177.779 \text{ units.}$$

[76]See tables in appendices XIV, XVI and XXV.
[77]See p. 101 and appendix XXV and XXVI.
[78]See tables in the back of Morse, *Chronicle*, v. 1.
[79]*Ibid.*, pp. 267-68.

	Tls.
177.779 x 7.777	1,382.726
Deduct the 'Emperor's Allowance' of 20%	276.545
	1,106.181
Add 10% for the Copaen (Kungpan) or Hoppo's Controller	110.618
	1,216.799
Add 7% to make it sycee	85.176
	1,301.975
Add 2% on 1,106.181 for the Shupan or Clerks of the Hoppo's Office	22.124
Total, Current silver	1,324.099

This was the amount of the official dues, supplementary to which was 'the 1,950 taels' which, . . . was the established total of the 'Presents.' These were uniform for all ships, whatever their size, except that French ships paid 2,050 taels, and country ships (those from India) paid 1,850 taels. The 1,950 taels were distributed as follows:

	Tls.
To the Emperor on the ship's arrival	1,089.640
To the Emperor on the ship's departure	516.561
To the Liangtao (Grain Commissioner) for the poor	132.000
To the Security Merchant's Dispatchador	12.000
To the Writers (Shupan) on measuring the ship	8.400
To the Soldiers attending the measuring	5.560
To the Hoppo's soldiers on the arrival of the ship	16.780
To the Fuyuan on arrival of the ship	2.800
To the Kwangchow Fu (Prefect of Canton)	2.800
To the Penyu Hien with jurisdiction over Whampoa	1.700
To the Namhoi Hien with jurisdiction over the factories	1.200
To the Kunming Fu (military officer at Macao)	1.200
To two tidewaiters (preventive officers) stationed by the Hoppo on the ship during her stay at Whampoa	150.000
To the difference of the Emperor's weights, etc	9.359
Total	1,950.000

In addition to the measuring fee there were, of course, the imperial import and export duties. There is no record of them for this period, but presumably they were little higher than at the earlier date, and also subject to the same enormous increase, due to the manipulation of officials. The 6 per cent charge was still in existence. The pilot received a handsome sum; the linguist still secured his percentages together with other presents, amounting to about T. 50 for himself and T. 25 for the under linguist.[80] The compradore received about $200 and had

[80]Gutzlaff, *China Opened*, v. 2, pp. 85-87; Auber, *op. cit.*, p. 124; Morse, *Chronicle*, v. 1, p. 289.

a monopoly of buying supplies for the ships, from which concession he was enabled to derive considerable profit.[81] Besides these expenses there were the other annoying tips, charges, and demands which had to be met, in addition to the rent of factories.

Restrictions upon the liberties of the traders had increased even more than the impositions. The growth of most of these has been traced and they will now be briefly enumerated.

1. All trade except that of a minor sort was confined to the twelve or thirteen Hong Merchants and even that could be done only under license from them. (In 1720 trade had been free and open to all.)

2. All petitions to the officials had to go through the Hong Merchants, and direct communication with officials was prohibited. (Contrary to conditions in 1720.)

3. Duties and charges were paid through the Hong Merchants, whose members acted as surety for the ship. (Not directly to the officials as in 1720.)

4. The freedom of movement of foreigners was considerably restricted; the sailors being confined to certain islands, while the traders were restricted to the regions around their factories. (Seems also to be contrary to conditions in 1720).

5. The firing of guns by foreigners was prohibited, but this was apparently not enforced.

6. The study of Chinese by foreigners was prohibited.[82]

7. Arms and ammunition were to be deposited before the ship entered the port, but this was not enforced. (Just as in 1720).

8. Foreign battle ships were prohibited from entering the Canton River. (Probably the same as in 1720.)

9. The factories where the foreigners lived were under the control of Hong Merchants. (Probably the same as in 1720.)

10. Foreigners who committed crimes were to be punished by the Chinese to the limit of Chinese law.[83] (Apparently contrary to conditions in 1720.)

It is possible that there were other restrictions in existence at this time, but we have no definite record of them and so they will not be mentioned until they appear.[84]

The procedure of trade was much the same as in 1720. Pilots, who were taken on at Macao as before, guided the ship to the Bogue and Whampoa. The measuring fees no longer seem to

[81]Gutzlaff, *China Opened*, v. 2, pp. 85-86; Morse, *Chronicle*, v. 1, p. 205.

[82]Martin, *op. cit.*, v. 2, p. 13; Morse, *Chronicle*, v. 5, pp. 27-28.

[83]Martin, *op. cit.*, v. 2, p. 13. See chap. 2, sec. 7.

[84]Much of the preceding outline may be taken from the imperial decree of 1760 which seemed to be an enactment of existing customs. See Morse, *Trade and Administration* (London, 1913), pp. 283-84, and Morse, *Chronicle*, v. 2, pp. 56-57, v. 5, pp. 94-98.

have been bargained for at Macao but were settled either at the Bogue or Whampoa. Here the supercargoes demanded of the "Hoppo a continuance . . . of all the Privileges that the English Nation [had] enjoyed at this Port, and had his assurances that they should be granted."[85] The traders then proceeded to the Canton factories, there to make their contracts with the Hong Merchants for the sale of goods and the purchase of cargoes. Contracts were made probably a year in advance and accounts were settled at the end of each season. In all business the linguist featured as the medium of communication. When the season closed, the Grand Chop was issued, and the Company's ships and supercargoes departed. About this time the English began the practice of leaving an agent in China over the year. He resided at Macao during the spring and early summer when the ships were not at Canton.[86]

English trade after 1758 was managed by a permanent general council of supercargoes. The four senior members were termed the President and Select Committee, and were most influential in directing the trade. This closer organization had been found necessary in order to combat the power of the Hongist Monopoly, and to overcome the considerable dissension within the ranks of the supercargoes themselves.[87]

The factories at this time were rather shabby buildings and largely devoid of comfort. Life at Canton was rather base and uninviting, and it appears that the European colony at Macao had not as yet developed very far. The following account by a contemporary gives us a vivid description of Canton life:

> I had a mind to see the situation of the environs of the suburbs in that part where I had not yet been, and was forced to go by myself for want of company. As soon as I had passed the usual trading streets, the boys gathered about me in thousands, throwing sand, stones, and dirt at me; and shouted altogether, *akia*, *aque*, *ya*, *quailo*; and with this music they followed me through the whole town. . . . As I stopped here, and only gathered now and then a plant, my disagreeable company stopped their noise, especially when I turned to them. Here [sic] was no road which carried directly into the country, nor did I venture any further, but returned whence I came. However, in the afternoon, I went out of town, in a palankin, by this means avoiding my disagreeable forenoon companions.

[85] Morse, *Chronicle*, v. 1, p. 274.
[86] *Ibid.*, v. 5, p. 45 and preface p. V.
[87] *Ibid.*, v. 1, pp. 197, 232-38, 276, v. 5, p. 65; Milburn, *op. cit.*, v. 2, p. 469.

Returning again, I went on foot about the wall of Canton on the side from the country.

When we came to the first city gate, towards the side of the European burying-place, a mandarin, with a whip in his hand, joined us to accompany us about the city. Near this gate was a Chinese inn, where brandy and tea were sold. The people stood by the side of the round-house on the wall and stared at us; however, we got by without hurt, though not without fear, for we remembered that a person was sometime before pelted with stones from this very place. When we approached nearer to the suburbs, we everywhere, and almost close up to the wall, found houses; they were all full of men, and especially children and youths, who sang their old song, of which they were put in mind by grown people, if they did not begin it themselves. Yet we likewise found an old reverend man, who had more sense than the others, and made his children or grandchildren greet us civilly.[88]

Conditions at Canton in 1757 were unsatisfactory but endurable. The public and official attitude in China was becoming decidedly hostile and boded ill for the future. On the other hand the English were becoming more belligerent. They objected to conditions as they were, especially to the personal restrictions, the limitations on free trade, and the seeming irregularity of the demands and impositions—a change the Chinese would not grant, and the Court of Directors, rather than lose the trade, directed its agents to submit. This bred more contempt and aggressiveness on the part of the natives.[89] On the whole, however, the conditions were not such that the Company thought seriously of asking for government interference. Within the next forty years changes took place which led the English government to attempt to aid the Company. The causes are to be sought in two directions—the growth of restrictions and conflict, and the expansion of trade.

[88] *Chinese Repository*, v. 1, pp. 216-20 from Osbeck, *A Voyage to China* (Forster's translation), v. 2, p. 199; also in Eames, *op. cit.*, pp. 78-79.

[89] Eames, *op. cit.*, pp. 73-74.

CHAPTER VIII

INCREASED CONFLICT BETWEEN THE ENGLISH AND THE CHINESE (1757–1793)

1. *The Significance of the Decree of 1757*

The decree restricting trade to Canton aroused considerable protest and apprehension at the time, but its tremendous significance was not fully realized until later. From our present vantage point its importance becomes apparent, and during the subsequent seventy years of Anglo-Chinese relations its significance was progressively realized. The decree itself accomplished two things. (1) It precluded all possibility of expanding the rapidly growing British trade to other parts of China. This became particularly important when the newly created cotton industry began to demand ports in northern China, where its goods would find a more ready market. (2) It enabled the growing avarice and arrogance of the Canton officials to develop without fear or restraint. Formerly the Company had used the threat of another port as a means of combating the aggression of the Cantonese officials; now the power of this threat was gone. The growing anti-foreign sentiment could vent itself without restraint upon the foreigners; and as trade expanded and the number of contacts increased, the possibilities of trouble grew, while the restrictions became more and more irksome to the freedom-loving traders. Because of the decree there was no remedy, no way of combating the restrictions and arrogance, except by force—or by giving up the trade. In a certain sense the decree epitomized the growing anti-foreignism, and, by its exclusive and restrictive nature, clearly suggested the course of future developments.

2. *The Conflict over Trade Restrictions*

The period between 1757 and 1793 was marked by a steadily increasing conflict between the English—all foreigners for that matter—and the Chinese. The first point of conflict was over the matter of trade restrictions. The difficulties did not take so much the form of new impositions as of restrictions upon the freedom of the traders and of trade, stoppage of trade, and the enforcement of existing regulations. Conflict arising out of these disputes created attitudes of mind which were in themselves even more important than the restrictions.

Late in the year 1758 the supercargoes began another attempt to break the Canton Monopoly, relieve restrictions, and reform abuses. On December 28, a memorial was presented to the Viceroy stating the grievances of the Company and asking that they be abolished. His reply, issued on January 4, 1759, was evasive, denying that abuses existed and asserting the permanence and necessity of existing regulations. In March the supercargoes retorted to this, and the Viceroy replied with a threat to punish them if they caused any more trouble, but that if they had any further grievances they might see the Hoppo. A long struggle now ensued over the privilege of seeing the Hoppo. To strengthen their hands the supercargoes kept their ships outside the Bogue, and on June 13, conformable with orders from the Court of Directors, dispatched Mr. Flint, on board the *Success*, to Ningpo with orders to go to Tientsin if he failed at Ningpo. The struggle at Canton came to an end on July 16, when the Viceroy ordered the Hoppo to receive the supercargoes. They

demand'd to have no Securities and to pay [their] own Duties, repeating the several Reasons [they had] already mention'd . . . . He said it was impossible he could break through the old Custom but by an order from the Court. [They] then requested Him to represent it, and That in the meantime as [they] were convinced there [was] no Occasion for Securities so [they] were determined to appoint none, and if they must be, He Himself must do it, or [their] ships would not come into the River. [They] further inform'd Him the Merch^{ts} had many times refused being [their] Securities, which as [they] had no Occasion for, [they] would no more lay [themselves] open to a Refusal, That the Curiosities they [the merchants] were obliged to buy for the Emperor, had so distress'd them, that [they] [supercargoes] were now afraid to trust Them with the smallest sum . . . . [They] inform'd Him of the abuses of the Hoppo Houses, the Moneys extorted, from the Linguist and Compradores on the Ships arrival, By the Hoppo Houses between this and Macao, The Hoppo Boats being suffer'd to sell Samshew [spirits] to the Seamen, Shops tolerated to sell Samshew to them at Canton, And the Imposition of his Officers forcing the Security to pay 100 dollars per Ship before they [would] ship off a Chest of Silks. These Grievances he assured [them] should be redress'd. [They] mention'd the 1950 Tales, which he said was paid to the Emperor, and could give [them] no answer to That. He promised [them] Audience when [they] had anything material to say to Him, upon [their] presenting a Chop. [They] acquainted Him of the Detention every one of [their] Ships met with the last year, by not being able to obtain the grand Chop . . . , which he assured [them] should not happen again. [They] also insisted upon having Liberty to Deal with any Merchant [they] pleased wheather Hongist or not, which he made some difficulties about, but after confuting Him in his arguments, he said [they] might trade with whom [they] pleased.[1]

Trade was apparently opened, but not one of the promises was ever carried out. The center of interest now shifted to the activity of Mr. Flint. After being refused trade at Ningpo he pushed on to Tientsin where, on July 21, he presented, to the local officials for transmission to the Emperor, a memorial in Chinese setting forth the grievances of the English. The Emperor ordered an investigation, and dispatched a Tigen (Tachen, High Commissioner) and a Chuncoon (Tartar General) to Canton to conduct it. Mr. Flint accompanied them overland to Canton where they arrived on September 10. The results of the investigation were fair promises, the degrading of the Hoppo, and the limitation of some restrictions, but the cumshaw of T. 1950 and the 6 per cent received the imperial sanction. Soon after the Commissioners left Canton Mr. Flint and the supercargoes were summoned before the Viceroy. They were ordered to do the *kotow*, and when they refused, the Viceroy's men tried to throw them upon their knees. The Viceroy finally ordered his men to desist, and presented the supercargoes with an imperial decree, ordering that Mr. Flint be imprisoned for three years at Macao and after that be banished from the Empire. This was because he had attempted to trade at Ningpo, contrary to the imperial order. The man who had aided in translating the petition to the Emperor had been beheaded. Mr. Flint's sentence was carried into execution.[2]

About the only permanent result of the disturbance in 1759 was a memorial from the Viceroy of Canton proposing certain regulations regarding foreigners. These obtained the imperial sanction, and were issued at Canton on April 12, 1760. To a large extent this edict seems simply to have codified and legal-

[1]Morse, *Chronicle*, v. 5, pp. 79, 75-80.

[2]Eames, *op. cit.*, 85-87; Morse, *International Relations*, v. 1, p. 107; Morse, *Chronicle*, v. 1, pp. 301-05, v. 5, pp. 80-84; Williams, *Middle Kingdom*, v. 2, pp. 448-50; Milburn, *op. cit.*, v. 2, p. 469; Auber, *op. cit.*, pp. 170-73; Davis, *op. cit.*, v. 1, pp. 48-50; Cordier, *op. cit.*, v. 1, p. 13; Lavisse and Rambaud, *op. cit.*, v. 8, p. 946.

ized existing practices, but its very issuance was an indication of the determination to exercise a stronger control over foreigners.[3] Its provisions were as follows:

1. Foreigners were to trade and lodge with Hong Merchants only.

2. When the trading was ended and the ships dispatched for Europe the foreigners must go to Macao.

3. Hong Merchants were to settle all their accounts justly by the time of the departure of the ships, and were under all circumstances to finish their accounts and affairs before the return of the ships.

4. Hong Merchants were to be held responsible for the wrong doings of foreigners to whom they had rented quarters in the hongs to serve as factories, while other Chinese were not to build houses for rent to the Europeanes.

5. In the future foreigners were not to have Chinese servants except the "established" linguists and compradores.

6. Chinese were forbidden to borrow money from foreigners on pain of severe punishment and confiscation of property.

7. Foreigners were not to employ couriers to carry letters into the interior or to ascertain prices of commodities except with the advice and consent of the officials.

8. Additional troops under a mandarin of war were to be charged with the special duty of looking after the European ships and maintaining order.[4]

Not only were the supercargoes dismayed by the above trade regulations, but they were also confronted with the organization of an association of the Hong Merchants or Co-hong. When trade opened in the spring of 1760 the Hong Merchants presented a united front and demanded uniform prices. The English refused to trade with the association and complained to the officials. After considerable discussion the Hoppo informed them that the new procedure had been approved by the Emperor, that acceptance and conformity were imperative, and that the association had been formed to make the merchants jointly responsible for every trouble which the Europeans might make. After some further protest the supercargoes submitted and began making contracts.[5]

[3]This edict has often been said to have established the Co-hong, but there is nothing in it which would lead to this conclusion. Morse, *Trade and Administration*, pp. 183-84 summarizes the edict, but this is obviously a generalized account of the restrictions at Canton prior to 1834, and contains much more than was in the edict. See especially Morse, *Chronicle*, v. 5, pp. 89-90, 94-98.

[4]Morse, *Chronicle*, v. 2, pp. 56-57, v. 5, pp. 89-90, 94-98; J. R. Morrison, *Chinese Commercial Guide* (First Edition), p. 47.

[5]Morse, *Chronicle*, v. 5, pp. 90-93.

Thus at last the spectre of half a century had been realized, and the foreign trade at Canton was the monopoly of a closed corporation with unlimited control over prices and the support of the officials. The trade regulations and the organization of the Co-hong stereotyped conditions at Canton into a settled policy of restriction. It must be noted, however, that numbers five and six above mentioned were not enforced, while all the rest except number one were carried out indifferently.[6]

Instead of purchasing Mr. Flint's freedom as they should have done, the Court decided to send out a special mission to investigate conditions, protest against his imprisonment, and have restrictions upon trade relieved. The mission was entrusted to Captain Skottowe. He carried a letter from the Court to the Viceroy, and to emphasize his prestige, it was given out by the Company that he was the brother of the King's under-secretary of state. The mission expressed its disappointment at the exclusion from Ningpo, and the following requests were presented to the Viceroy:

1. That the imposition of the T. 1950, the 6 per cent on imports, and the 2 per cent charged on silver paid to the Hoppo be abolished.

2. That the supercargoes be allowed to pay the duties direct to the Hoppo, and that security merchants be abolished.

3. That the Hoppo would consent to hear complaints, and that appeals direct to the Viceroy be allowed from all decisions of the Hoppo.

4. That Mr. Flint be released.[7]

Number three was admitted with certain reservations, but seems never to have been lived up to, while all the rest were refused.

During the years that followed, the Court urged the supercargoes to avail themselves of every opportunity to complain to the Hoppo against the restrictions. It also urged that precautions be taken to prevent brawls among the sailors, and, in every way, to avoid offending the Chinese. The Co-hong seems to have been effective in raising prices and dominating trade.[8] Perhaps as a result of this, and to increase the effectiveness of their resistance, the council of supercargoes was more thoroughly

[6]Eames, *op. cit.*, pp. 89-90. Eames also gives an account of the decree of 1760.

[7]Eames, *op. cit.*, pp. 88-89; Auber, *op. cit.*, p. 174; See, *op. cit.*, p. 58; Martin, *op. cit.*, v. 2, pp. 14-15; Morse, *International Relations*, v. 1, p. 67; Gutzlaff, *China Opened*, v. 2, p. 105; Morse, *Chronicle*, v. 5, pp. 104-106.

[8]Auber, *op. cit.*, pp. 174-75; Morse, *Chronicle*, v. 5, pp. 107-122.

organized, and began to maintain a permanent residence in China during the sixties.[9] Protests against the Co-hong were continued, and in 1771 with the aid of the merchant, Puankhequa, to whom T. 100,000 had been given, the abolition of the Co-hong was obtained. The foreigners were, however, still restricted to the twelve or thirteen Hong Merchants who acted as security, but each merchant traded independently and not collectively.[10]

Because of their new solidified organization, and due to the fact that they had become imbued with a considerable amount of spirit and resistance, the supercargoes, through their head, the Select Committee, began a spirited opposition to the encroachments of the officials.[11] In order that some of the actualities of the troubles at Canton may be realized, the following pages from Morse's *Chronicles of the East India Company Trading to China* have been inserted:

> Just as the Council were leaving Macao for Canton, on July 2, 1775, it was made known to them that
>
> 'an Association of ten Merchants, was on the point of being re-established at Canton under the protection of the Tzuntoc and the other Chief Mandarines for the welfare of the trade of [the] Country.'
>
> The report was confirmed at Canton, and they called a meeting of the merchants, to whom they protested that they were expressly forbidden to deal with the body or association, and were allowed to trade only with individual merchants, each for his own account; and they declared that they would appeal to the Viceroy. . . . The matter was so far advanced that a public proclamation had been issued, and posted up in several places in the city and suburbs, in which it was ordered
>
> 'That the Europeans on the arrival of their several ships [were] to be informed that all imports must be sold to one of the body of the Security Merchants, who thereupon [would] become security for the ship.
>
> 'That of these Security Merchants they must purchase their returning Cargoes; as last year the Country ships on their departure were nearly empty, having bought nothing of the Security, but of the Shopkeepers, by which the Merchant was not repaid the Charges he was put to, and the revenue was trifling.
>
> 'That . . . the Linguists and Merchants must demand of the Supracargoes, to whom they intend to sell, and of whom they propose

[9]Auber, *op. cit.*, p. 178; Morse, *Chronicle*, v. 2, p. 2, v. 5, p. VI of preface.

[10]Auber, *op. cit.*, p. 178; Martin, *op. cit.*, v. 2, p. 15; Corner, *op. cit.*, pp. 107-08; E. J. Eitel, *Europe in China* (Hongkong, 1895), p. 8; Morse, *International Relations*, v. 1, p. 67; Lavisse and Rambaud, *op. cit.*, v. 8, pp. 945-46; Morse, *Chronicle*, v. 5, p. 153.

[11]Eames, *op. cit.*, p. 92; Morse, *Chronicle*, v. 2, pp. 1-2.

to purchase, till which [was] done, no one [would] be Security; consequently nothing [would] be permitted to be brought on shore, nor [could] the Ship remain at Whampo, but must depart incontinently.

'That supposing any Ship should offer to depart at the end of the season without having purchased a full Cargo from the Security Merchant, the Mandarines [were] determined to punish the Merchants and Linguists.

'That if the Europeans den[ied] to submit to the above orders, the Merchants and Linguists [were] to report the fact.'

And now occurred what at first sight appears to have been a tempest in a teapot, but was in fact an important element in the whole affair. On July 7th, the Hoppo went, as was the custom, on board the first ship of the season, the *Morse*, to measure her.

'During the ceremony of the measurage Yngshaw (the Security Merchant) informed [the supercargoes] that the Hoppo was extremely desirous of viewing the several Clocks and other pieces of Jewellery which he was informed was on board the *Morse*, which he said the Commander had assured him could not be done without the licence of the Supracargoes, and therefore desired that [they] wou'd give orders that the Hoppo's request might be comply'd with: He was told that most certainly the Hoppo must have received wrong information, for on Mr. Phipps's putting that question to the Captain, he had on his arrival; frequently since; and even that morning; declared to him, that there was neither Clocks or other Toys on board his Ship except a P^r of a very trifling nature belonging to one of his Officers: This being explained to the Hoppo, he seem'd much exasperated and order'd the Merchants to tell [the supercargoes], that [they] seemed very inclinable to give him a great deal of trouble and willing to impose upon him, as his Secretary had been informed of, and had got lists of the particulars; by means of the Linguists from the Proprietors; and if he was not to be permitted to see them, he wou'd not measure the ship. Captain Kent then reported to [the supercargoes], that to his great surprise, he had that instant learn'd there was certainly a quantity of Jewellry which had been smuggled on board by Mr. Foxall, his Second Officer . . . that he had not the least suspicion of such things being in the ship . . . The Hoppo's rage of [sic] gratifying his Curiosity by no means subsiding; the several packages were brought up from the steerage and carried into the roundhouse; where he retired and amused himself hours in critically examining each parcel, several of which he purchased, and immediately order'd into his Sampan.'

After allowing the Hoppo some time to 'return into good temper,' the supercargoes presented to him the memorial addressed to the Viceroy and the Hoppo, protesting against the proposed Gild; which, after a little more anger and much hesitation, and more explanations, the Hoppo consented to receive . . .

The importance of this episode [was] shown by the comment made on it by the Council:

> 'We cannot refrain from expressing our alarms, that the shew of Jewellery on board this ship at this critical juncture, will furnish Yngshaw and Munqua who are confidently reported to be the two great abettors of this pernicious monopoly with fresh arguments for the hasty conclusion of it, and serve as a corroborating proof of their assertions, that the charges on the trade are become so burthensome, owing to the extensive quantity of Toys and Machinery imported here (consequently obliged to be presented to the Mandarines) that no one private trader can support the weight of it. Such arguments strongly enforced, we have great reasons to fear, will draw the attention of the Mandarines, the consequence of which must most certainly prove fatal to the success of our remonstrance.'

The Hoppo's answer to the remonstrance was not long delayed, but was received on July 10th:

> 'That the Linguists were ordered to inform all Europeans that [came] to Canton to trade; it always [had] been the custom to have a Security Merchant and a Linguist; thro whom all their business must be transacted, and who [were] particularly appointed to take care that no deficiency in the Dutys does arise.
>
> 'That they [were] by no means to deal with Shopkeepers, as they [were] in general known to be bad men, and thro them the Emperor [became] defrauded of his Dutys.
>
> 'That it [had] every year been usual to affix a Chop in several parts of the City & Suburbs, to inform the Europeans that they [were] to trade with Hongists and no others.
>
> 'Therefore how [could] it be said, that the Conhong [was] re-established?
>
> 'The Trade [would] be carried on as heretofore.'

It was some time later, on August 20th that the supercargoes were relieved from their apprehensions.

> 'We hear all thoughts of the re-establishment of a Conhong are laid aside, owing to the great influence Puankhequa has with the Mandarines, whose remonstrances have been very strong in opposition to it.'[12]

After 1775, constant trouble of the type just mentioned arose. There were continual rumors of a revival of the Co-hong and constant personal differences with the officials and their servants. More important, however, was the growing indebtedness of the Chinese merchants to the foreigners. Little by little they raised prices and levied new charges upon commerce to meet their debts.[13] The final upshot of the debts problem and

[12]Morse, *Chronicle*, v. 2, pp. 13-16. The rest of this chapter s equally good for showing the petty nature of the quarrels. The indented material is quotations from the supercargoes' reports, while the rest has been supplied by Morse.

[13]Morse, *Chronicle*, v. 2, pp. 16-29, and 33 in particular.

the controversy arising over it was the establishment about 1779 of the Consoo fund, which was provided by a 3 per cent *ad valorem* levy on all imports except woollens, calicoes, and iron, and seems to have been engineered by Puankhequa. The fund was to be used for settling the debts of merchants to foreigners. Shortly afterward its administration was transferred to a number of Hong Merchants under official supervision. The fund failed to relieve the debt problem, and was constantly seized upon by the officials for personal use. It added another imposition to which the foreigners objected.[14]

Between 1780 and 1782 the Co-hong was virtually re-established. The debt trouble reached a crisis in 1779-80. It led to the failure of several of the Hong Merchants who, it will be remembered, had a monopoly on foreign trade, and so aroused the Emperor that he ordered the debts to be paid, and took steps to prevent a like condition in the future.[15] He directed, in 1780, that the Hong Merchants should cease competing among themselves, that they should fix a common price, and that a mandarin should be appointed to supervise them. Further, a sum of money was to be raised annually to be used in paying the debts and providing presents for the mandarins.[16] This money was apparently secured by transferring the administration and use of the Consoo fund to the Hong Merchants and by a tax on tea.[17] In 1781 a tax of 6 per cent was also levied on raw silk.[18] Prices were much higher and were identical among all the Hong Merchants in 1781, showing the result of the new machine. The mandarins had established fixed prices, and returned an insolent reply to the protests of the Select Committee, telling them either to pay the prices or quit the port.[19] In 1782 there were only four Hong Merchants who were solvent, and the Hoppo proceeded to force five other merchants to become

[14]Eames, *op. cit.*, pp. 98-99; Morrison, *op. cit.*, p. 33; *Correspondence Relating to China* 1840, p. 292; Morse, *Chronicle*, v. 2, pp. 39-49; Morse, *International Relations*, p. 68; Martin, *op. cit.*, v. 2, p. 15; sec. 3 of this chapter. There is some question as to whether the Consoo fund was established in 1779 or two or three years later, but 1779 seems most probable.

[15]Morse, *Chronicle*, v. 2, pp. 43-60.

[16]*Ibid.*, pp. 57-59; Eames, *op. cit.*, p. 100.

[17]Morse, *Chronicle*, v. 2, pp. 59, 69; Morse, *International Relations*, v. 1, p. 68.

[18]Morse, *Chronicle*, v. 2, p. 69. Whether this was a guild levy or a customs duty is not known.

[19]*Ibid.*, pp. 70-71.

Hongists; these were to be jointly responsible for each other. Thus by the orders of 1780 and 1782 virtually a new Co-hong had been created "under the control of the Hoppo, and was made the instrument for exacting a great revenue from the foreign trade, for the benefit primarily of the Hoppo, and indirectly, through him, of the Canton officials and the Court of Peking."[20] This new organization was supposed to have thirteen members; it had a monopoly of trade with the foreigners to whom it was to present uniform prices; it administered the Consoo fund, and each member was responsible for the debts of the whole.[21] It was not, however, a chartered corporation and some freedom of private trade seems to have been allowed.[22] Its control by the Hoppo made it an effective official instrument of exaction.

The remaining years prior to the Macartney Embassy were devoid of large economic troubles, but were filled with minor impositions and constant quarrels. In 1782, the Hoppo attempted to prohibit the export of raw silk in quantities larger than one hundred piculs per ship. Bribes and protests prevented this limitation, but, in 1784, it was definitely imposed.[23] The most important points of conflict during the period were: (1) the Hoppo's objection to allowing ships at Canton which did not buy cargoes; (2) heavy duties charged on goods going to and from Macao; (3) inaccurate weighing and measuring by the Hoppo. The Hoppo, however, refused to remedy these difficulties and continued his arrogant and aggressive attitude.[24]

Another fact that greatly aroused the English was the stoppage of trade. Ships were held and trade suspended over every little difference, while the larger controversies led to the delay of trade for weeks or months.[25] Moreover, the practice of placing a general embargo on trade toward the end of the year had been adopted by the Hoppo, because, "were the Hoppo to send up the Whole Produce of the Year, the Trade [thereafter] to decline so as not to produce an equal amount, the Consequences to him

[20] *Ibid.*, p. 82.
[21] Morse, *International Relations*, v. 1, pp. 68-69 and previous notes.
[22] Morse, *Chronicle*, v. 2, pp. 149-50; Milburn, *op. cit.*, v. 2, pp. 469-70.
[23] Morse, *Chronicle*, v. 2, pp. 75, 96.
[24] *Ibid.*, pp. 87, 96-98; Martin, v. 2, *op. cit.*, p. 17.
[25] Morse, *Chronicle*. 1884, 9 days, p. 105; 1885, 16 days, p. 111; 1787, about 25 days, pp. 127-28; 1788, 30 days, p. 145, and others see v. 2, *passim*.

might be disgrace and Ruin."[26] This stoppage was particularly objectionable because trade was now becoming so valuable.

In summary, one may say that a great amount of antagonism was created during this period by the persistent conflict between the two parties. As English trade grew in volume, the irksomeness of the restrictions became greater, and made the British more belligerent toward the Hoppo's increasing demands. By 1785 the British representatives in China began to feel that the restrictions were unendurable.

3. *Private Debts of the Hong Merchants*

Private debts of Chinese to foreigners were very closely associated with the impositions and restrictions on trade, the Consoo fund and the new Co-hong being caused directly by them. By creating considerable negotiation and disagreement between the natives and the foreigners; and by causing the failure of a goodly number of Hong Merchants, thus restricting the number with whom the foreigners might trade, they served as a second source of conflict.

By the decree of 1760 Chinese were prohibited from borrowing money from foreigners; but they were always eager to borrow, and the high rates of interest offered, ranging from 1 per cent to 5 per cent per month, attracted large amounts of private capital from India.[27] Moreover, the Company made yearly advances to the Hong Merchants upon contracts with the idea of tiding them over serious difficulties.[28] Debts began to be accumulated shortly before 1760, and were undoubtedly contracted, in part at least, to meet the demands of the officials upon the Chinese merchants. In 1777 Puankhequa told the Select Committee that he had already paid beyond his ability to satisfy the officials, and that he would have to have the Committee's help to survive. The Committee also experienced serious difficulty in collecting debts owed it by several of the Hong Merchants, and the governor of Madras wrote to it, asking for aid in the collecting of money owed by the Chinese to Mr. George Stratton.[29]

[26] *Ibid.*, p. 153—from a supercargo's statement. See also pp. 111-12.

[27] Morse, *International Relations*, v. 1, p. 68; W. C. Hunter, *The Fankwoe at Canton* (London, 1882), p. 39.

[28] Morse, *Chronicle*, v. 2, pp. 25-29.

[29] *Ibid.*, pp. 23-29; Morse, *International Relations*, v. 1, pp. 85-86.

The bankruptcy of the Hong Merchants and the debt controversy which were foreshadowed in 1777 culminated in 1779-80. In 1779, private merchants from India put forth a claim for $4,347,300 debts owed them by various Chinese. They addressed the Court of Directors in a memorial, and this body ordered the Select Committee to do all in its power toward collecting the debts.[30] After an investigation it appeared that only $1,078,976 had been borrowed, the rest being the result of accumulated interest. The most important debtors were the eight Hong Merchants, but it appeared at this time that, due largely to official extortion, two of them were bankrupt, two hopelessly involved, and only one had unassailable credit.[31] The merchants made various informal offers which were unsatisfactory. While these negotiations were going on the *Sea Horse* arrived, commanded by Captain Panton, with orders from Rear Admiral Vernon to present a demand to the Hoppo and Viceroy that the debts be paid. In spite of the Select Committee's protests—it being afraid that such action would lead to the establishment of a Co-hong—the memorial was delivered, and a vague reply received.[32]

As a result of this, the Hoppo demanded the amount of the debt, and was enraged at the answer he received. He called attention to the edict of 1760, but agreed to try to settle the matter. Negotiations with the debtors resulted in some arrangements but most of the propositions were unacceptable. Captain Panton renewed his demands, and sometime later a decree was brought from the Emperor ordering payment of the debts, and absolutely prohibiting the borrowing of money from foreigners in the future.[33] Two Hong Merchants were banished for running into debt and failing to pay the Emperor's duties, while arrangements were made for paying most of their debts to the foreigners in ten annual instalments.[34] As has been noted,

[30] Morse, *Chronicle*, v. 2, pp. 43-45; Auber, *op. cit.*, pp. 179-80; Martin, *op. cit.*, v. 2, p. 15. The figure $3,808,076 for the debts is also given but the one used seems to be the more careful estimate.

[31] Morse, *Chronicle*, v. 2, pp. 44-46; Eames, *op. cit.*, p. 99; James Matheson, *Present Position and Prospects of the British Trade with China* (London, 1836), p. 96.

[32] Morse, *Chronicle*, v. 2, pp. 46-49.

[33] *Ibid.*, pp. 53-57; Eames, *op. cit.*, p. 100; Morse, *International Relations*, v. 1, p. 68; Auber, *op. cit.*, p. 182.

[34] Morse, *Chronicle*, v. 2, pp. 57-59; Milburn, *op. cit.*, p. 470.

orders were also given for closer coöperation between the Hong Merchants, who were transformed into a virtual Co-hong in 1782. Thus, as a result of the debts and the interference of Captain Panton, the worst fears of the Select Committee had been realized. The Co-hong had been re-established under official control, a number of Hong Merchants had been bankrupted, and more conflict had been created.[35]

4. *His Majesty's Ships' Controversies*

The treatment of the King's warships while at Canton was the third source of conflict. We have already noted the case of Captain Anson in 1741, and during this period several serious disputes arose.

In 1765 H. M. S. *Argo* arrived at Canton with a cargo of silver for the Company. The captain claimed freedom from measuring, which the Hoppo refused to allow. When Captain Affleck refused to permit measurement of the ship, the Hoppo told the Select Committee that he held them responsible for Englishmen at Canton. They disclaimed any control of the King's ships, but offered to pay a fee equal to that on their largest vessel if it was not measured. The Hoppo refused and threatened to bamboo the security merchants and to drive the supercargoes from Canton if the ship were not measured. After four months of such negotiations the Select Committee, in order to save the trade which was in suspense, persuaded the captain to allow the ship to be measured. The Hoppo thus won his point.[36]

The *Resolution* and the *Discovery* arrived at Canton in 1779, but they remained outside the harbor and were given facilities for careening, refitting, and provisioning. The Select Committee aided as much as possible by furnishing money and supplies.[37] This was the period of the American Revolution, and war always increased trouble over battleships, because they had to be in the East to escort the merchant-men home. An example occurred in 1781 when McClary, a private Indian trader, seized

[35]Morse, *Chronicle*, v. 2, pp. 58-59; Eames, *op. cit.*, p. 100; Auber, *op. cit.*, p. 183; Davis, *op. cit.*, v. 1, p. 56.

[36]Eames, *op. cit.*, pp. 90-91; Auber, *op. cit.*, pp. 76-77; Morse, *International Relations*, v. 1, pp. 97-98; See, *op. cit.*, p. 59; Martin, *op. cit.*, p. 15; Davis, *op. cit.*, v. 1, p. 51; Morse, *Chronicle*, v. 5, pp. 127-29.

[37]Morse, *Chronicle*, v. 2, p. 43.

a Dutch prize of war at Whampoa within Chinese jurisdiction. This involved the Select Committee in considerable trouble with the officials, who ordered them to keep all ships of war outside the Bogue under pain of severe punishment.[38]

In 1791 the *Leopard* and the *Thames* arrived at Canton, their men suffering from scurvy, and badly in need of food and supplies. After considerable negotiation they remained outside the Bogue and supplies were sent out to them. The Select Committee was particularly pleased with the moderation and good judgment of Captain Blankett.[39] In their treatment of foreign ships of war, the Chinese were hopelessly at odds with English ideas, and this remained a constant source of agitation.[40]

5. *The Jurisdiction Conflict*

During the period under discussion the Chinese asserted their right of criminal jurisdiction very emphatically, and this matter was of the utmost importance in interesting the British government toward interfering in China. The first example of this, the imprisonment of Mr. Flint, which we have already noted, was followed by even more glaring evidences of growing hostility.

In 1772, a Chinese was wounded in an affray between the sailors of the *Lord Camden* and some natives. The clearance papers of the ships were held up, but the recovery of the injured man prevented serious trouble.[41] In 1773, a Chinese boy was accidentally killed at Macao; an Englishman, Francis Scott, was charged with the crime. A Portuguese trial completely exculpated him, but the Chinese threatened dire vengeance upon Macao if he were not given up. The Portuguese finally surrendered him; he was tried, convicted, and put to death by the natives. Thus occurred the first judicial execution of an Englishman by the Chinese, and it was considered a bad precedent.[42]

[38]*Ibid.*, pp. 63-64, 79-81; Gutzlaff, *Chinese History*, v. 2, p. 335; Auber, *op. cit.*, p. 182; Davis, *op. cit.*, v. 1, pp. 54-56.

[39]Morse, *Chronicle*, v. 2, pp. 182-83; Auber, *op. cit.*, pp. 191-92; Morse, *International Relations*, v. 1, p. 98

[40]Morse, *International Relations*, v. 1, pp. 98-99.

[41]Eames, *op. cit.*, p. 94; Auber, *op. cit.*, p. 178; Davis, *op. cit.*, v. 1, pp. 51-52; Morse, *Chronicle*, v. 5, pp. 173-75.

[42]Eames, *op. cit.*, pp. 94-95; Morse, *International Relations*, v. 1, pp. 101-102; Martin, *op. cit.*, v. 2, p. 15; Treat, *op. cit.*, p. 71; Davis, *op. cit.*, v. 1, pp. 52-53; Cordier, *op. cit.*, v. 1, p. 13; Morse, *Chronicle*, v. 5, pp. 182-85.

It will be noted that the jurisdiction trouble grew, to a large extent, out of the disorderly conduct of sailors. The Court adopted several expedients to preserve order and to prevent them from coming into contact with the Chinese, but these were often defeated by the natives, who sold spirits to the sailors.[43] Following are some of the orders issued in 1779 to every ship, with the purpose of preventing trouble with the Chinese:

1. Officers or men were not allowed to go shooting.

2. The ship's company was to be kept within the bounds of sobriety and decency.

3. English sailors were never to be allowed to go to French Island but must remain on Dane's Island.

4. When sailors were on Dane's Island they must not break into graves or molest the Chinese.

5. Ships were not to run away with goods (run goods = smuggle) on the pretense of saving custom or port charges.

6. The carrying to Canton by private individuals of clocks, watches, toys, or curiosities was forbidden, for the mandarins always wanted them and this caused trouble.[44]

In spite of these precautions difficulties continued, and in 1780, a case arose which caused much excitement. In this year, due to the European war, several affrays between sailors of different nationalities occurred. In one of these, a Frenchman, belonging to a country ship, killed a Portuguese. He took refuge at the house of the French consul. After several days of negotiation, and serious threats on the part of the mandarins, he was given up and was publicly strangled.[45] The Select Committee commented upon the event in the following manner:

> This is the first instance of one European being executed for the murder of another, in this Country, and appears to be a very dangerous precedent; as it may involve Europeans in inextricable difficulties; if even by accident one man should kill another. The man executed today could have no trial by common Justice.[46]

In 1781 a number of sailors were thrown overboard from a small boat in which some girls were being taken to a ship. A quarrel had apparently arisen over the number to be taken. The

[43] Morse, *Chronicle*, v. 2, pp. 37, 112, 145-49, 175-77.

[44] *Ibid.*, v. 2, p. 37.

[45] Morse, *Chronicle*, v. 2, pp. 59-60; Martin, *op. cit.*, v. 2, pp. 15-16; Morse, *International Relations*, v. 1, p. 102; Auber, *op. cit.*, p. 181; Eames, *op. cit.*, pp. 95-96; Gutzlaff, *Chinese History*, v. 2, p. 334; Treat, *op. cit.*, pp. 70-71; Williams, *Middle Kingdom*, v. 2, pp. 450-51; Davis, *op. cit.*, v. 1, pp. 53-54.

[46] Morse, *Chronicle*, v. 2, p. 59.

English complained and the Chinese officials punished the offenders.[47] Rum and women appear to have been frequent causes of trouble. In the same year a small boy accidentally shot a native with a gun which he got to frighten the Chinese, who was throwing stones at him; the boy was freed because he was under the age of responsibility.[48] In 1783, a Portuguese at Macao stabbed a Chinese, and after much trouble he was publicly shot by the Portuguese under the supervision of Chinese officials.[49]

The affair which most thoroughly aroused the English was the *Lady Hughes* case in 1784. A gunner of a country ship, the *Lady Hughes*, killed two minor mandarins while firing a salute. The jurisdiction of the Select Committee over the ship was indefinite, but the officials held them responsible and demanded the surrender of the gunner or some one else. Mr. Smith, a supercargo, was seized and held as hostage at Canton. The exchange of notes became heated, and British trade was stopped. The English prepared to give resistance, but finally, upon a promise that the man would be fairly treated, surrendered him. However, after a farcical trial, he was strangled. The result of this execution of a man innocent according to their own standards, determined the English never again to surrender a person to the Chinese, and caused them to prohibit the firing of salutes in the future.[50]

This was not an arbitrary act on the part of the Chinese, but rather the strict enforcement of their existing legal and judicial standards, the truth of which was shown the following year when they strangled a Chinese who had killed an Englishman, after complaints had been made by the Select Committee.[51]

It will have been noted that much of the trouble arose through the activity of country ships or private traders over whom the Select Committee's jurisdiction was very indefinite.[52]

[47] *Ibid.*, pp. 71-72.
[48] *Ibid.*, pp. 72-73.
[49] *Ibid.*, p. 86
[50] *Ibid.*, pp. 99-107; Martin, *op. cit.*, v. 2, pp. 16-17; Auber, *op. cit.*, pp. 183-87; Morse, *International Relations*, v. 1, p. 102; Milburn, *op. cit.*, v. 2, p. 470; Eames, *op. cit.*, pp. 96-97; Davis, *op. cit.*, v. 1, pp. 57-59; Cordier, *op. cit.*, v. 1, p. 13.
[51] Morse, *Chronicle*, v. 2, pp. 108-09; Auber, *op. cit.*, pp. 187-88; Morse, *International Relations*, v. 1, p. 107.
[52] Morse, *Chronicle*, v. 2, pp. 63-67.

As a result of the *Lady Hughes* affair this body wrote to the Court in the following fashion:

As repeated experience shews the utter imposibility of avoiding the inconveniences to which we are constantly subject from the imprudence or wilful misconduct of private traders, and the accidents that may happen on board their ships, it were to be wished that the powers, if any, which we really possess over them, were clearly and explicitly defined, or if no law, or construction of law, now existing allow of such a power, how far the absolute commands of the government under whose jurisdiction we are, will justify our compliance, and how far, in such cases, the commanders and officers of the Honourable Company's ships are bound to obey our orders; at present equally destitute of power to resist the unjust commands of government and to carry them into effect, we know of no alternative but retiring to our ships for protection.[53]

To this the Court replied: (1) that they were to conduct trade and avoid trouble as much as possible; (2) that resistance to the haughty and conceited Chinese government was useless; (3) that in case of accidental death they were to apply to the Chinese merchants to settle the matter (which meant by financial means); (4) that in case of murder they were to aid the Chinese officials in apprehending the criminal; (5) that the supercargoes had absolute power to seize private traders under 26 Geo. III. cap. 57, sec. 35, and that they had jurisdiction over the country ships.[54] The English thus submitted to Chinese law reluctantly, because they felt it to be unjust and barbarous.

6. *Minor and Personal Points of Conflict*

In addition to these great outstanding difficulties, many minor ones arose between the supercargoes and the officials, some of which were personal in nature, while others centered around the measuring of ships, the restrictions placed on the movement of supercargoes, living conditions, the treatment of their servants, and the insolent language used in addressing them.[55] In 1778 and 1779 robberies were committed against the English,[56] in 1781 the Hoppo objected to ships leaving Canton

[53]Auber, *op. cit.*, p. 186.

[54]*Ibid.*, pp. 188-91; Eames, *op. cit.*, p. 97. It would seem according to the terms of the statute that the Company's supercargoes had powers only over interlopers and not over lawful traders.

[55]Morse, *Chronicle*, v. 2, pp. 16-22, 67-68, 175-77, *passim*.

[56]*Ibid.*, p. 42.

without cargoes,[57] and in 1791 trouble arose over the prohibition of the importation of sea-otter skins and the carrying of opium.[58] Many minor affrays with the Chinese and between the various nationalities occurred, tending to heighten the tension and to increase the psychological strain.[59]

7. *Increased Chinese Hostility as a Cause of the Conflict*

It will now be well to turn from the conflict to its causes. The first which deserves mention was the increased hostility of the Chinese, which was in direct keeping with the growth of anti-foreignism. It was plainly seen on the part of the public in their numerous affrays with the soldiers, in their insolence to foreigners, and in the acts of depredation committed against Europeans. The activities and especially the language of the officials make evident their growing hostility. "You English are a lying and troublesome People"[60] runs one comment, while many similar ones may be found. The determined way in which Chinese jurisdiction was applied to foreigners, leading to the first execution, in 1780, followed by others, the new impositions on trade, restrictions upon the freedom of the traders, and the creation of the government Co-hong leave no doubt but that hostility was increasing.

Not only was antagonism manifested against the English, but it was shown by added impositions upon the Portuguese at Macao.[61] The Russian legation at Peking was also ended, and the Russian caravans ceased. A Russian embassy to the Chinese capital was not received, but had to wait at the border where a convention was signed relating to some boundary disputes.[62]

The causes for this increased hostility were numerous. In the first place it seems to have been due to imperial influence. Kien-lung was personally opposed to foreigners because of factors previously mentioned. He was a literatus and naturally disliked the missionaries, and the whole tendency of his reign,

[57]*Ibid.*, p. 62.
[58]*Ibid.*, pp. 185-91.
[59]*Ibid.*, pp. 112, 145-49, 175-77, 187.
[60]*Ibid.*, p. 65. See others *passim*; Auber, *op. cit.*, p. 192.
[61]Martin, *op. cit.*, v. 1, pp. 373-77.
[62]Morse, *International Relations*, v. 1, pp. 60-62; Williams, *Middle Kingdom*, v. 2, pp. 442-43; Martin, *op. cit.*, v. 1, pp. 391-94.

as expressed in his numerous edicts, was to place restrictions upon the foreigners.[63] However, he was inspired by ideas of legality and Chinese justice, and did not want to act arbitrarily, as was evidenced by his decree of 1736 and his order that the debts of the Hong Merchants be paid. The nation took its cue from him in this matter. It seems that his reign was generally one of administrative consolidation and tightening of government, which naturally caused the bonds to be drawn more closely about the foreigners. During his time the Empire reached its greatest power and consequently a peak of arrogance.[64]

A second factor which led to the quarrels and caused the growing Chinese hostility was, beyond doubt, official greed and avarice. Evidence has been submitted to show that the officials squeezed trade all they could; they even squeezed the Hong Merchants until they were bankrupt, and then had the Consoo fund and the Co-hong created to keep them going as organs of exaction. In extorting money the officials grew more overbearing and aggressive. Corruption was supposed to have spread during Kien-lung's reign, and it undoubtedly fits in with the attitude of the officials.[65] Bad conduct of foreign seamen and their numerous affrays also had its influence in increasing hostility. It was a cause as well as a sign.[66]

Krausse suggests an interesting possibility. In 1763 two Chinese visited Paris. These men were so impressed by the power and magnificance of the "barbarians" that when they returned to China they may have convinced the mandarins that the only way to save face was to close the Celestial Empire to foreigners, and so prevent the people from finding out the true greatness of the Europeans.[67] Between 1774 and 1784 a number of outbreaks against the missionaries occurred, which served to inflame the public and official mind against the traders. Some

[63]Boulger, *op. cit.*, v. 1, pp. 661-69. Note for example the order to exact "life for life," the decree of 1760, and the orders of 1760 and 1780 creating the Co-hong.

[64]Boulger, *op. cit.*, v. 1, pp. 664-714, 716-20; Gowen and Hall, *op. cit.*, pp. 217-31; Macgowan, *op. cit.*, pp. 544-53.

[65]Boulger, *op. cit.*, v. 1, pp. 727-28.

[66]Auber, *op. cit.*, p. 191.

[67]Krausse, *op. cit.*, pp. 79-80.

Chinese even went so far as to identify the Christian teachers and traders with the revolutionary secret societies.[68]

The final factor which caused the growing hostility was the English advance in India. The Chinese were probably opposed to this advance, but the thing which aroused them most was the belief that the English were giving aid to the Goorkas, a Nepalese tribe which had invaded Tibet. This was a serious impediment at the time of the Macartney Embassy.[69]

8. *Other Factors Causing the Conflict between the English and Chinese*

Two other factors of equal importance with the one already mentioned led to the conflict with the Chinese, but they will be dealt with to a greater extent in the next chapter and so attention will be called to them only briefly here.

The increased number of contacts, although a purely mechanical matter, was beyond doubt of great importance. This, of course, grew out of the expansion of the Canton trade. As the number of men who came there yearly increased, their contacts with each other and with the Chinese increased. With both sides in an unfriendly mood, and with the sailors often intoxicated, conflicts were common, in spite of regulations. The fact that the contending parties were of different races provided a color difference to which already existing difficulties might be attached. It is said that the conflict of two opposing groups increases in direct proportion to the number of contacts, and this seems to be true here. Table 12 will show how the number of Europeans at Canton increased.[70]

Increased aggressiveness of the British was the third factor in causing trouble. Many Englishmen deny this. They say that it was submission and the subordination of national honor

[68]Latourette, *Missions*, pp. 165-174; Broomhall, *op. cit.*, pp. 10-11; Williams, *Middle Kingdom*, v. 2, pp. 306, 312-13; Gutzlaff, *Chinese History*, v. 2, pp. 139-57; Corner, *op. cit.*, pp. 101-03; Boulger, *op. cit.*, v. 1, pp. 714-15, 729.

[69]Martin, *op. cit.*, v. 1, pp. 346-55; R. S. Gundry, *China and her Neighbors* (London, 1893), pp. 324-32; Auber, *op. cit.*, p. 199; *Chinese Empire*, pp. 281-88.

[70]This table is based upon various figures from Morse's *Chronicle* and from other authorities. It is arrived at by multiplying the average number of men per ship on those frequenting Canton at the different periods, by the number of ships. See also appendix XXVI.

TABLE 12.—INCREASE OF EUROPEANS AT CANTON

Year	No. of English Ships	No. of Englishmen	No. Ships of Other Nations	No. of Other Foreigners	Total Ships	Total Foreigners
1750	7	700	12	1,200	19	1,900
1751	10	1,000	9	1,289	19	2,289
1775	13	1,300	13	1,300	26	2,600
1785	28	2,800	17	1,700	45	4,500
1790	46	4,600	13	1,300	59	5,900
1796	40	4,800	14	1,680	54	6,480

to trade, which led to the impositions.[71] There is little evidence to uphold such a view. A perusal of Morse's *Chronicles* will show that the English attitude was always one of resistance, and that it increased in spirit as the years progressed.[72] This was natural, because as the value of trade grew, and as the outward pressure at home increased, the restrictions became more burdensome, in fact almost unbearable; while as English national greatness increased, the humiliation of the Chinese situation grated more and more upon the sentiments of the supercargoes in China.

9. *Effects of the Previous Developments on the Company's and Government's Attitude*

The trade restrictions that were most resented were the 3 per cent Consoo fund, the 6 per cent tax, the irregular way of paying the imperial duties, the cumshaw of T. 1950, the confinement of trade to Canton, and the Co-hong monopoly. As these things increased and as the volume of trade grew the Select Committee and the Court at home began to feel that something had to be done or trade would be ruined. It was this fact which turned the attention of the Select Committee, and of the Court to a much lesser degree, toward an embassy.

Personal limitations on the movement of traders at Canton, and the indignities suffered by them, were significant in creating

[71] Eames, *op. cit.*, pp. 73-74; Martin, *op. cit.*, v. 2, p. 17. It is true that any easy submission would have probably increased the restrictions, but there were no examples of this. Those cases where obstreperous naval officers refused to give in, and which many writers praise so much, seem to have caused more trouble than the graceful resistance and retreat of the Select Committee.

[72] Witness for example the following cases found in Morse's *Chronicle*, v. 2, "Troubles with the Hoppo," pp. 13-29; "Trouble over Debts," pp. 38-60, and "*Lady Hughes* Affair," pp. 94-109.

a demand for change on the part of the supercargoes. These things reacted much less upon the Court of Directors and the British government, who did not personally have to endure with such treatment.

The execution of British citizens, however, and the crude treatment of the King's ships reacted more directly upon the English government. These were insults to the national honor of one of the greatest countries in the world, and they could hardly fail to arouse protest. The executions especially served to increase greatly the demands of the Select Committee for a change, while their reaction on the Court seems to have been much less important.

The final problem, that of the debts to foreigners, was least interesting to the Select Committee and the Court. The merchants were not greatly in debt to them. On the other hand crude attempts at collection did react very unfavorably on the Company's commercial interest. Here again the British government, or at least the Indian government, felt itself in honor bound to demand the payment of debts and to back its demands by force.

Such were some of the considerations which led to the Macartney Embassy. Others were to be found in the development of trade itself.

CHAPTER IX

COMMERCIAL DEVELOPMENTS (1757–1795)

Since commerce, especially the trade in tea, was the factor which originally brought English and Chinese cultures together and which continued to tie them even more closely, some time may well be devoted to a study of its progress.

1. *Growth of the Company's Trade—The Commutation Act*

The most obvious thing in the commercial development of this period was the tremendous increase in the volume and value of trade. This was true not only of the Company's business, but of the private Indian trade, and of the commerce of all other nations, as evidenced by the number of their ships arriving at Canton each year.[1] This shows conclusively that the restrictions and impositions at Canton were not insurmountable. Table 13 will show how the Company's trade expanded.

TABLE 13.—COMPANY'S TRADE AT CANTON*

Year	No. of Ships	Size of Ship	Tonnage	Total Imports in Mdse. Tls.	Total Imports in Coin Tls.	Total Imports Tls.	Total Exports Tls.
1751	7	499	3,500	70,479	412,800	483,279	....
1762	..	....	......	....	....	364,305	729,291
1770	..	....	......	....	....	1,018,896	1,343,349
1776	8	758	......	419,921	....	419,921	....
1778-79	7	758	9,239	384,756	....	384,756	1,022,694
1785	19	758	......	687,299	....	687,299	2,965,000
1789	21	816	18,144	1,295,799	1,321,920	2,617,719	4,433,431
1796	23	1200	23,000	2,100,349	120,960	2,221,309	6,248,940

*See appendix XIV. The figures are based on Morse, *Chronicle*, see especially v. 1, p. 292. These figures correspond generally with figures of the Company's exports from England to China given in Macgregor, *Commercial Statistics*, v. 4, pp. 404-406. The following graph is based upon Macgregor, with the exception of the figures for tea, because his statistics are more complete. See appendix XVI and XIX.

The table, although incomplete, shows the general trend of both imports and exports to be decidedly upward. An especial tendency was the increased importation of merchandise accompanied by a corresponding decrease in the introduction of

[1]See appendix XXV.

bullion. The import of coin ceased between 1772 and 1785 with the exception of one year; then there was considerable import until 1792, when it ended again until 1796. A steady rise in the annual tonnage sent to China and an increase in the size of the ships from an average of 500 tons in 1750 to 1200 in 1795 is apparent. To aid in accurately picturing trade developments, the graph shown in figure 2 has been constructed. It is based upon figures of exports from England to China and upon the Company's sale of tea in London.

Figure 2 shows that prior to 1772 the tendency of the export (from England to China) curve was to follow very closely the export of coin, but after that date it was influenced more by the merchandise curve. Interesting to note is the great fluctuation in the coin curve, whereas the merchandise and tea curves are more stable, with a constant tendency to rise and a tremendous increase after 1783. Generally the curves show a fairly high level of trade during the peace following the war of the Austrian Succession, followed by a decline during the Seven Years' War, then a rapid rise in 1765 which glutted the market and caused a decline. Again there is a rapid rise to the greatest level yet attained in 1769-1771. The Company then fell into a bad financial condition, and had to ask the government for aid. The result was the famous tea act, the consequences of which influenced the outbreak of the American Revolution.[2] The curves remain low during the Revolution and the European war, but in the years of peace after 1783 a tremendous rise to unprecedented heights began.

The main cause for this rise was the Commutation Act, passed in England in 1784, with the purpose of preventing smuggling and of drawing the tea trade into British hands.[3] This act lowered the duties on tea, which then ranged from 75 per cent to 127 per cent, to a uniform 12½ per cent on the gross amount of the Company's sales, with drawbacks on tea exported to Ireland and British colonies in America. In its place was substituted a window tax which would throw the burden upon the wealthy.[4]

[2]7 Geo. III, cap. 56; 12 Geo. III, cap. 7; 13 Geo. III, cap. 64; 14 Geo. III, cap. 34; *Parliamentary History* (1771-74), v. 17, pp. 799, 921-31; Cawston and Keane, *op. cit.*, p. 142.

[3]24 Geo. III, cap. 38.

[4]Morse, *Chronicle*, v. 2, pp. 110-17, especially 116-17; Staunton, *Embassy*, v. 2, pp. 617-23; *Parliamentary History* (1783-85), v. 24, pp. 1008-13.

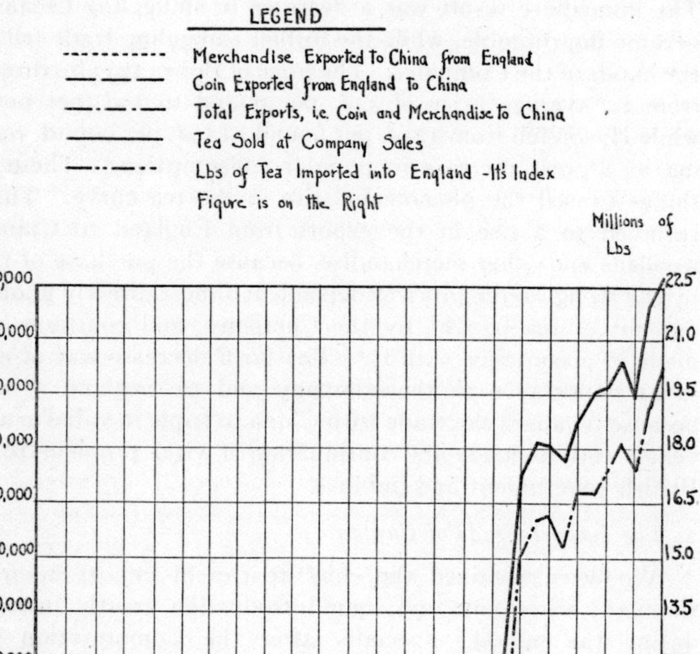

FIGURE 2.—ANGLO-CHINESE TRADE

Based on Macgregor, v. 4, pp. 404-06; Milburn, v. 2, p. 534. See also appendix XVI-XIX.

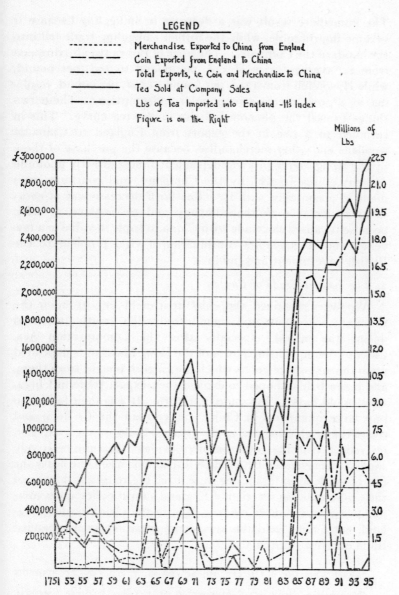

The immediate result was a decrease in smuggling because it became unprofitable, while the former smuggling trade fell into the hands of the Company. The price of Bohea tea also dropped from an average price of 44*d*. per pound to 19*d*. per pound, while Hyson fell from 121*d*. per pound to 59*d*. per pound, resulting in a great increase in popular consumption.[5] These two things caused the phenomenal rise in the tea curve. This in turn led to a rise in the export from England to China of woollens and other merchandise, because the purchase of these by the Hong Merchants was dependent almost directly upon the amount of tea bought by the Company, and contracts were made in accordance with it.[6] The tariff decrease was of enormous importance to the company and to England as well; because it caused the trade with China to triple in value in a few years, and so made its continuation a vital problem to the British government and public.

2. *The Import Trade of Canton*

Woollens remained the chief articles of import upon the Company's account, and their introduction greatly increased during the period, especially after the Commutation Act. Clearly, the purchasing power of the Hong Merchants depended upon the amount of goods which the English bought from them, and if the British hoped to expand their export trade in China, they would have to buy more in return. It was their failure to buy large quantities in China, rather than the Co-hong and restrictions, which served as the greatest brake on the expansion of trade.[7] Nothing could be more evident than the relatively small damage caused by Chinese restrictions when one notes the rise of trade after 1783, one year after the re-establishment of the Co-hong. The reaction of England's tariff policy upon commerce was never more evident than in the China trade. England, not China, held the key to the situation until expanded trade outgrew Canton.[8]

[5]Morse, *Chronicle*, v. 2, p. 116; Milburn, *op. cit.*, v. 2, p. 540. See appendix XIX.

[6]Macpherson, *India*, p. 210; Milburn, *op. cit.*, v. 2, p. 475; Morse, *Chronicle*, v. 2, p. 28.

[7]Sargent, *op. cit.*, pp. 54-57 gives some suggestions along this line.

[8]It is, however, obvious that the amount of trade which could profitably be carried on at Canton was limited. When increased English buying had expanded the Canton trade to its limit then the Chinese restrictions became a

The expansion of the woollen business was received with joy by the woollen weavers in England, and by the rising machine-spinning industry in yarns.[9] It encouraged them to support the China trade and to demand its expansion. Table 14 will show the growth of the woollen and merchandise trade of the Company.

TABLE 14.—COMPANY'S IMPORT TRADE AT CANTON*

Year	Woollens from England Tls.	Total Goods from England Tls.	Company Import from India—Mostly raw Cotton Tls.	Total Goods Tls.	Coin Tls.
1776..........	254,062	363,482	146,347	419,921	....
1780..........	403,462	433,657	45,522	474,179	....
1785..........	577,368	687,299	....	687,299	....
1790..........	1,192,263	1,621,201	211,672	1,832,873	2,106,041
1795..........	1,634,796	1,879,945	89,343	1,969,288	....

*See appendix XV for more complete figures which are based on Morse, *Chronicle*.

This table also shows that coin was no longer as important in trade as it had formerly been; however, a good deal of it continued to be imported for many years. Its relative scarcity during this period was due in part to the wars in Europe. In woollens, raw cotton from India, and opium, the English were beginning to find articles of exchange for tea so that they no longer had to depend on coin. All of the opium and most of the raw cotton was imported by the private Indian traders;[10] however, the money received for these articles was paid into the Company's treasury at Canton in return for bills on London, and so could be used by the organization in balancing its accounts.[11] The Company did import some raw cotton from India as the table indicates.

Opium, as an article of trade, had not developed to any great extent. Its day was in the future, but the first step which increased its importance had been taken. In 1773 the Company made the sale of Bengal opium a governmental monopoly.[12]

terrible burden. But such a condition was not reached until during the first half of the next century.

[9]P. Mantoux, *The Industrial Revolution* (New York), pp. 239-57, 409-42; Cunningham, *Growth of English Commerce and Industry: Modern Times* (Cambridge, 1907), part 2, pp. 639-68. Lectures delivered by Professor Dietz of the University of Illinois upon the Industrial Revolution.

[10]Sargent, *op. cit.*, pp. 53-54 and sec. 5 of this chapter.

[11]Morse, *Chronicle*, v. 2, p. 31.

[12]*Britannica*, v. 20, p. 130; Nathan Allen, *The Opium Trade* (Lowell, 1853), pp. 8-14; Kaye, *op. cit.*, pp. 146, 671-88; Robinson, *op. cit.*, pp. 132-33.

The object was to increase the revenues of India, and under such circumstances the Company (which governed India) would naturally favor expansion of the trade. By 1795 the amount realized from Company sales in Calcutta was £354,921, while the total revenue of Bengal was £5,937,931.[13] Opium had not yet become an apparently indispensable source of revenue.

The trade, even at this time, was carried on by smuggling. Between 1773 and 1794, the Company made some unsuccessful experiments in carrying opium on its ships.[14] Prior to 1773 opium delivered to China was brought by the Portuguese through Macao, but after that date the country ships began to bring it.[15] It was apparently sold without trouble over the wharf at Whampoa; it was also sold from supply ships anchored at Lark's Bay, south of Macao, and at Macao. On the whole no great difficulties were encountered in selling it during this period, but the demands were not great.[16]

The opium trade was undoubtedly of great lucrative value, but the figures are few and varied. Table 15, compiled from

TABLE 15.—OPIUM IMPORTED TO CHINA*

Year	Lowest Estimate Chests†	Highest Estimate Chests	Number of Chests sold at Bengal Sales	Selling Price per chest in Canton
Prior to 1767 per year	100	200	....	£200
1767	200	1000	....	£200
1773	1000	....	....	....
1780	....	....	....	$200–550
1781–1782	1400	1600	....	$200–300
1786	1300	2000	....	$388
1790	4054	5054	....	$370
1795–96	1070	1814	5183	....
1800–01	3224	4570	4788	....

*Morse, *Chronicle*, v. 2, pp. 140-41; Treat, *op. cit.*, pp. 63-65; Williams, *Middle Kingdom*, v. 2, pp. 377-78; *Britannica*, v. 20, p. 130; Martin, *op. cit.*, v. 2, pp. 175, 194; Morse, *International Relations*, v. 1, pp. 173-75; Allen, *op. cit.*, p. 19; Krausse, *op. cit.*, p. 104; Parker, *China History*, p. 96; Macgregor, *op. cit.*, v. 5, p. 74 and v. 4, p. 870.

†Chests from Bengal weighed 120 catties or 160 lbs.
Chests from Malwa or Bombay region weighed 100 catties or 133⅓ lbs.
See Morse, *International Relations*, v. 1, p. 173 note; Treat, *op. cit.*, p. 65. Most of the opium mentioned in the table was from Bengal.

[13]Milburn, *op. cit.*, v. 2, pp. 219-20; Romesh Dutt, *Economic History of India* (London, 1906), p. 288. George Campbell, *Modern India* (London, 1852), pp. 388-93.

[14]Allen, *op. cit.*, pp. 13-14; Morse, *Chronicle*, v. 2, pp. 77-79; Williams, *Middle Kingdom*, v. 2, pp. 377-78.

[15]Morse, *Chronicle*, v. 2, pp. 76-78.

[16]Williams, *Middle Kingdom*, v. 2, pp. 377-78; Allen, *op. cit.*, pp. 12-14; Milburn, *op. cit.*, p. 464; Morse, *Chronicle*, v. 2, p. 51; Morse, *International Relations*, v. 1, pp. 173-75; Martin, *op. cit.*, v. 2, p. 175.

several sources, shows the highest and lowest estimates, together with such price lists as are obtainable. In reality, the opium trade was dangerous to the merchandise trade from England, for it turned the buying capacity of the Chinese from British merchandise to Indian opium.[17]

Other important articles of import from England were: lead, being 2040 tons in 1785 and 785 tons in 1795, tin, with 55 tons in

TABLE 16.—INCREASE OF ENGLISH POPULATION

Year	Population in Thousands	Year	Population in Thousands	Year	Population in Thousands
1700	5,475	1750	6,467	1780	7,953
1720	5,565	1760	6,736	1790	8,675
1740	6,064	1770	7,428	1800	8,892

1788 and 1001 tons in 1795,[18] iron, copper, furs, linen, and various nicknacks.[19] In addition to the opium,—sandalwood, pepper, saltpetre, piece-goods, ivory, and like articles were the chief products of import from India.[20]

3. *The Canton Export Trade*

Tea was the chief export from Canton. Despite the high duties levied in England the amount exported rose slowly until 1784. The chief causes for this growth were: the gradual expansion of the tea-drinking habit to the lower classes of England, the increased consumption on the part of the upper classes,[21] and the increase of population generally, providing more mouths to be fed. Table 16 will show the increase of English population during the 18th century.[22]

The high tariff checked the Company's tea trade because it caused prices to be so exorbitant that smugglers were able to

[17]Sargent, *op. cit.*, p. 54.

[18]Milburn, *op. cit.*, v. 2, p. 476.

[19]Morse, *Chronicle*, v. 2, pp. 28, 192, 265, 315 from ship cargoes; Milburn, *op. cit.*, v. 2, pp. 147, 481.

[20]Morse, *Chronicle*, v. 2, pp. 6, 28, 173, 192, 265, and Milburn, *op. cit.*, v. 2, pp. 147, 481.

[21]The use of tea among the lower classes is shown by the following writers: Witt Bowden, *Industrial Society in England* (New York, 1925), pp. 224-26; W. R. H. Curtler, *The Enclosure and Redistribution of Our Land* (Oxford, 1920), p. 177; Gaskell, *Manufacturing Population of England* (London, 1833), pp. 24-25, 107, 217-18; Joseph Low, *The Present State of England in Regard to Agriculture, Trade, and Finance* (London, 1833), pp. 9-10 of appendix.

[22]Cunningham, *op. cit.*, part 2, p. 935.

flourish and most people could not afford to buy tea. The Commutation Act, as we have seen, struck with extraordinary success at both of these evils, and in the end rendered the tea trade a virtual English monopoly. The foreign companies, particularly those of Sweden and Denmark, aided by the French, Dutch, Prussian, Tuscan or Imperial, and Spanish, furnished tea for the smugglers. It is estimated by competent authorities, and the following table substantiates it, that before 1784 at least 7,000,000 pounds of tea were annually smuggled into England.[23] Table 17 will show how the legitimate import of tea into England increased after 1784 while the trade of the foreign companies decreased.

TABLE 17.—TEA EXPORTED FROM CANTON BY ENGLISH AND OTHER FOREIGN SHIPS*
(Figures in thousands of pounds)

Year	Exported by Company Lbs.	Exported by Europeans other than English Lbs.	Total Export Lbs.	Revenues to Br. Gov. in thousands £
1767–68	4,580	12,767	17,348	1,034
1775–76	3,402	12,841	16,243	1,221
1780–81	6,846	11,725	18,572	1,227
1783–84	9,916	19,072	28,989	1,289
1785–86	13,480	15,715	29,891	324†
1790–91	23,369	2,291	25,404	312
1794–95	23,733	4,138	29,311	352
1795–96	19,370	2,759	24,950	503

*Milburn, *op. cit.*, v. 2, pp. 486, 542, and Macpherson, *India*, p. 416. See appendix XIX and XX.

†Figures given in Martin, *op. cit.*, v. 2, p. 152 for the revenues are larger than Milburn's and Macpherson's.

The preceding figures definitely show that prior to 1784, foreign nations dominated the tea trade while after that date the English came to control it. Figure 3 will show more graphically precisely what happened. The decrease in price ruined the smugglers and enabled more people to use tea, at the same time actually increasing the Company's receipts.[24] The dependence of the English population upon the tea trade caused the public and the government to take an interest in China, the revenue being an added incentive to the government.[25]

[23]Anderson, *Origin of Commerce*, v. 4, pp. 550-54, especially 551. See appendix XX. It shows how the tea trade of these European companies flourished before 1784 and then began to languish after that date.

[24]Staunton, *Embassy*, v. 2, p. 625.

[25]For further details of this see Martin, *op. cit.*, v. 2, table opposite p. 152; also appendix XIX.

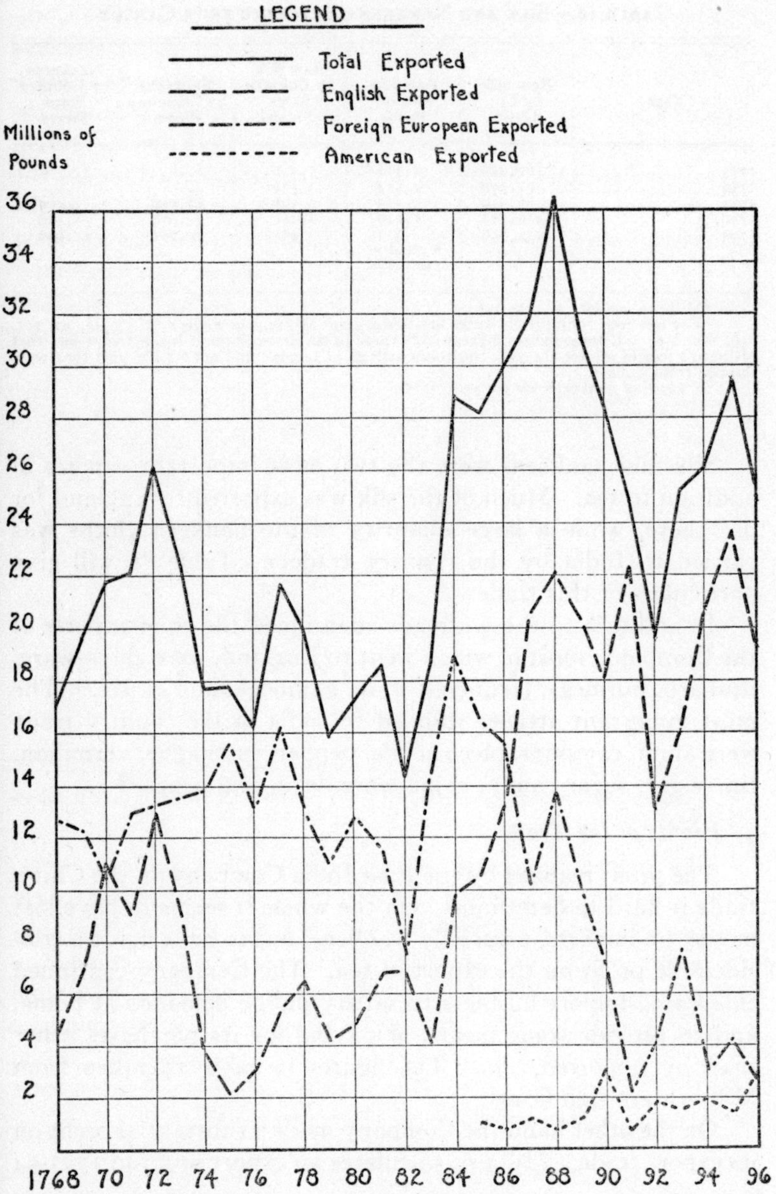

FIGURE 3.—TEA EXPORTED FROM CANTON

Based on table in Milburn, *Oriental Commerce*, v. 2, p. 486

TABLE 18.—SILK AND NANKEENS EXPORTED FROM CANTON

Year	Raw Silk by Co. Lbs.*	Raw Silk by Co.† Piculs	Raw Silk by Country Ships Piculs	Nankeens by Company Pieces	Nankeens by Country Ships Pieces
1775	167,229	2,112	1,196	......	......
1780	301,300	2,514	537	......	......
1785	98,920	525	298	40,000	2,000‡
1790	216,005	1,527	1,216	40,000	56,500
1795	154,590	711	460	80,000	45,000
		a picul = 133⅓ lbs.			

*Milburn, *op. cit.*, v. 2, p. 256.
†The last four columns of figures are based upon Morse, *Chronicle*, v. 2, pp. 11, 50, 111, 119, 180, 266. If these figures diverge from those in the first column it is due to the fact that Milburn's figures are for the year the goods arrived in London and not for the year they were shipped from Canton.
‡Figures of nankeens are for year 1786.

Silk and nankeens were the two most important exports in addition to tea. Much of the silk was exported to England for use there, while a large quantity of the nankeen cloths was carried to India by the country traders. Table 18 will give particulars of this trade.

In addition to those already mentioned the chief exports of the Company, most of which went to England, were china-ware, rhubarb, nutmegs, lacquered ware, gamboge, and cassia.[26] The most important articles shipped to India in the country trade were alum, camphor, piece goods, pepper, tutenague, vermilion, tin, sugar, sugar candy, china-ware, lead, and drugs.[27]

4. *Profits of the Trade*

The profit realized by the East India Company on the China trade is hard to determine. On the whole it seems to have lost money on imports, especially woollens, but to have made a considerable profit on the export of tea. The Company continued this losing import business to satisfy public demands at home, and to provide some means of paying for its purchases other than by imported coin. The figures in table 19 taken from Milburn are significant.

On the other hand the Company made a substantial profit on its export trade. Milburn calculates an export profit in 1793-94

[26]Milburn, *op. cit.*, v. 2, p. 481.
[27]*Ibid.*, p. 147.

TABLE 19.—PROFIT AND LOSS OF THE EAST INDIA COMPANY ON ITS CANTON IMPORT TRADE*

Year	Woollens £	Other Goods and Stores £	Bullion £	Total £	Profit £	Loss £
1781–82	129,179	12,555	....	141,734	......	3,830
1785–86	224,612	45,492	704,259	974,363	......	15,303
1790–91	431,385	109,788	....	541,173	......	13,509
Total for 11 yrs.	2,840,616	630,905	3,588,264	7,059,795	......	190,917
1792–93	587,421	160,485	....	747,906	14,045	......
1794–95	642,405	178,192	....	820,597	......	107,425

*Milburn, *op. cit.*, v. 2, p. 475. These figures are substantiated by others given in Morse, *Chronicle*, v. 2, pp. 6, 28, 192, 265.

of £529,814, in 1794-95 of £723,189, and in 1795-96, £917,652.[28] He also estimates that for a period of four years, 1776-79, the balance sheet of the Company presented the following average for each year.[29]

	£
Prime cost, including commercial charges	429,366
Customs paid from the Company's Treasury	241,937
Freight and demurrage charges	163,679
Charge of merchandise, estimated at 5% on sales	59,518
Total Cost	894,500
Amount of Sales	1,113,024
Balance to company profit	£218,524

Another indication of the Company's profits is shown by figures given in Morse, from which the annual increase or decrease in the value of the business (at Canton only) may be estimated. The figures are as follows.[30]

TABLE 20.—INCREASE AND DECREASE IN COMPANY'S BUSINESS (Canton only)

Year	Increase Tls.	Decrease Tls.	Page of Morse *Chronicle*, v. 2
1779	815,064	......	35 and 41
1783	......	477,337	83 and 94
1787	498,588	......	135 and 151
1792	882,523	......	192 and 205
1797	......	893,610	294 and 310
1799	2,925,868	......	322 and 347

28 *Ibid.*, p. 477.
29 *Ibid.*, p. 478.
30 Morse, *Chronicle*, v. 2. See pages cited in the table and calculate from figures given there as to the yearly increase or decrease in value of business.

These tables, while not conclusive, show that the Company must have been reaping a rich reward from the tea trade despite losses elsewhere and despite the troubles it encountered in China. The Commutation Act served only to increase its profit and hence its determination to free trade from the troubles that beset it in China.

The private Indian trade must also have been a lucrative business. Opium made a great profit, and apparently the raw cottons realized considerable gain. Table 21 showing balance sheets of a Company's ship will give an idea of the profit and loss on a specific cargo. It shows a large gain on the goods from India, and presumably the same thing was true of the cargoes in private Indian ships.

TABLE 21.—PROFIT AND LOSS ON AN IMPORT CARGO IN 1789*

	Prime Cost £	Realized Tls.	Profit + Loss − Per Cent
Cloth, 3,600 pieces	79,637	234,793	− 1.7
Long Ells, 93,640 pieces	237,060	701,092	− 1.4
Camlets, 640 pieces	5,169	23,447	+ 51.0
Tabinets, 140 pieces	1,355	4,066	+ 0.0
Lead, 1,401 tons	37,842	98,752	− 13.0
Copper, 180 tons	17,332	54,392	+ 4.6
Tin, 55 tons	4,488	14,332	+ 6.5
	382,883	1,130,874	− 1.6
Cotton, 6,468 piculs [Indian]	Rup. 128,330	Tls. 90,552	+116.0
Pepper, 4,958 piculs	$ 72,283	Tls. 74,373	+ 43.0
	Tls. 93,738	Tls. 164,925	+ 76.0

*Morse, *Chronicle*, v. 2, p. 173.

5. *The Private Indian Trade*

Private Indian trade was carried on under license from the East India Company, as has been noted. During this period it made an enormous growth and must have become equal to that of the Company in volume and value. Its chief exports from Canton were raw silk, nankeens, and to a minor degree tea and other articles, all of which have been previously noted. On the import list, besides opium already mentioned, were cotton and silver. Table 22 will give some idea of the volume of the country trade, and a few additional facts concerning it.

These imports were of value in aiding the Company to finance its trade at Canton without having to depend on im-

TABLE 22.—PRIVATE INDIAN TRADE WITH CANTON*

Year	No. of Company Ships	No. of Country Ships	Tea Exported by Country Ships Piculs	Cotton Imported by Country Ships Piculs	Silver Imported by Country Ships Chests
1776	8	16	731	......	17
1781	11	6	597	......	2
1786	29	24	175	65,130	..
1791	11 = 11,454 Tons	12 = 6,000 Tons	474	15,505	..
1796	23	17	1,202	118,668	..

*Morse, *Chronicle*, v. 2, pp. 12, 61, 119, 184, 278.

ported coin from England. We have already mentioned how the system worked. The following specific example from the year 1778 will bring this out more clearly, and at the same time show that the Company often carried goods from India for private traders in order to get money with which to finance its tea trade. The principal resources of the Council again came from payments against privileged Indian produce. Mr. Thomas Ferguson was to receive from the Governor and Council of Madras advances of 483,544 Sicca Rupees, in consideration of which he

> 'engaged to pay into the Treasury at Canton the sum of Spanish Dollars 205,555 [exchange 100 S. R. = 42.5 Sp. dollars] on condition he may be permitted to send 4,000 Bales of Cotton and 6,000 piculs of Tin freight free on the Hon'ble Company's Ships to China, to be consigned to one or more of the Supra Cargoes jointly with his agent and in case a sufficient quantity of the above goods should not be procurable to make up the Sum in Pepper, Silver or Gold.'

Mr. Charles Grant made a similar contract 'to pay 150,000 Current Rupees at the rate of 40½ Spanish Dollars for 100 C.R.,' and Mr. Thornhill for an amount not recorded. One of the conditions explains how it comes that the supercargoes pay such large sums into the treasury. Under these contracts large quantities of Indian products were in 1778 carried in the Company's ships, not directly for the Company, but for private merchants, besides other large quantities in country ships:

	Company's ships Piculs	*Country ships* Piculs
Cotton	7,020	19,344
Tin	5,473	10,304
Pepper	2,609	5,123
Putchuck	842	3,254
Sandalwood	980	1,468

Those who had paid silver into the treasury asked at an early date to receive their bills on London—payable at 12 months after sight, without interest—their intention being to send them by way of Suez or by a foreign ship.

'The Majority of the Council came to the Resolution not to deliver the Bills to those People who had paid Money into the Treasury, more than ten Days before the Departure of the first Ships . . . forwarding them by Suez or by some foreign conveyance [they conceived] to be not only highly improper, but contrary to the intentions of the Hon'ble Court, as they [might] by that means be presented for acceptance some Months before any Advices [could] possibly be received from [the] Council.'[31]

The private Indian traders objected to the Canton conditions. As their profits from the Canton trade increased, the restrictions and regulations became more distasteful. It would seem from the names of the members of Calcutta, Madras, and Bombay firms, that many were Englishmen doing business in India.[32] As they learned of the possibilities of the China trade they became interested in its expansion and its being completely thrown open to them. They were, therefore, together with the Indian government, supporters of any move to reduce restrictions which the Chinese imposed, but they were also ready to attack the Company's monopoly and demand free trade to China.

Besides these legitimate private traders there were a few others who remained at Canton—Mr. Smith and Mr. Beale being examples—in defiance of the Company or under commission from or protection of, a foreign government. Under earlier Parliamentary acts the Company was able to combat these men, and the supercargoes were ordered to seize them. In spite of this these private traders were a constant annoyance to the Company and always ready to attack it.[33] Moreover, commanders of ships and other officers still carried goods to and from China, which trade, in 1793-94, amounted to £258,981.[34]

6. *Economic and Political Developments in England*

Due to the territorial expansion of the Company in India the home government was confronted by a new type of problems. After a little hesitation it adopted a policy of regulating the

[31]*Ibid.*, pp. 31-33. The indented material is quoted directly from the Select Committee's report while the rest of the quotation is in the words of Morse.

[32]Milburn, *op. cit.*, v. 2, p. 170 and v. 1, p. 234.

[33]Morse, *Chronicle*, v. 2, pp. 4-5, 11-12, 31-33, 75, 85, 150; Auber, *op. cit.*, pp. 180-81; Eames, *op. cit.*, pp. 93-94; 10 Geo. III, cap. 47.

[34]Sargent, *op. cit.*, p. 53; Milburn, *op. cit.*, v. 2, pp. 479-80; Morse, *Chronicle*, v. 2, pp. 8-10.

Company rather than of eliminating it. In fact, a perusal of the Parliamentary debates and the statutes passed during the period reveals that English politicians identified the interests of the British Empire with those of the Company. They therefore sought to regulate the organization so that it might serve as a good colonial machine and at the same time furnish the government with considerable revenue. There was no thought of abolishing the Company or its monopoly, but only of regulating and helping it.[35]

Much of the discussion which went on during the period and many bad reports about the Company's administration in India did, however, help to build up an attitude of popular dislike. Furthermore, in the works of Adam Smith, an intellectual opponent of monopoly appeared.[36] In addition to this type of opposition, a real dynamic force with a great amount of potential danger to the monopoly was appearing in the newly created cotton kings. The Industrial Revolution was now in full swing in the cotton industry, and production was increasing rapidly.[37] The import figures for cotton wool indicate this expansion: in 1781, 3,198,000 lbs.; in 1785, 18,400,000; in 1790, 31,447,000; and in 1796, 32,126,000 lbs.[38] The first interest of the cotton kings was to insure a source of raw material and the second was to increase their market. They even talked with the Company of the possibility of its supplying them with raw cotton, but when this failed they became enemies of the organization.[39] In this the cotton kings were supported by certain Liverpool merchants, who as early as 1768 had petitioned for the opening of the East India trade.[40] Failure of the Company to find a market in China

[35]The materials for this subject are very full and are best found in the *Parliamentary History* and in the *Statutes*. A few characteristic bills and speeches which show a realization of this identity of interest, and which aimed to preserve the Company for the benefit of the nation, may be mentioned.

1. *Parliamentary History* (1766-68), v. 31, p. 25; 7 Geo. 3, cap. 47; 9 Geo. III, cap. 24, relative to allowing the Company to retain the territorial revenue of India.
2. 13 Geo. III, cap. 63, Regulation Bill of 1773.
3. 13 Geo. III, cap. 64, Indemnification Act of 1773.
4. 14 Geo. III, cap. 34, Tea Exportation Act of 1774.
5. *Parliamentary History* (1781-82), v. 22, pp. 108-38 (Lord North's speech), and 21 Geo. III, cap. 65 forcing the Company to renew its charter.
6. *Parliamentary History* (1782-83), v. 23, pp. 1187-1210, and 24 Geo. III, cap. 25, and 24 Geo. III, cap. 38, regulating the Company and passing the Commutation Act. See also Cawston and Keane, *op. cit.*, p. 142, and Robinson, *op. cit.*, pp. 85-112.
7. Macpherson, *India*, p. 414, for money contributed by Company to government.

[36]Macpherson, *India*, pp. 346-70.

[37]Mantoux, *op. cit.*, pp. 193-277.

[38]Cunningham, *op. cit.*, part 2, p. 930.

[39]Mantoux, *op. cit.*, p. 260; Ellison, *op. cit.*, p. 29.

[40]*Commons Journal*, v. 32, pp. 102, 108.

for cotton products still further alienated the cotton manufacturers. These various dissatisfied groups united, and raised enough opposition[41] to force a clause into the charter bill of 1793, requiring the Company to carry annually to and from India, 3000 tons of private goods.[42]

These interests were not so much opposed to the Company as such, as desirous of securing an expanded market. When the Company failed to provide such for them they opposed it. Some woollen weavers actually came forward with a petition to be allowed to furnish certain goods for the Company's export.[43] In these woollen and cotton interests we see a group which called for more extensive markets, and who would favor any change in the China trade which might secure this. They were willing, especially the cotton manufacturers, to do away with the Company and have free trade. Their desire, however, was largely hopeless, for the expansion of English goods in China depended upon the increase of English purchases in China, and at this moment England was not prepared for such expansion.[44]

From this discussion it appears why both the government, following out its idea of helping the Company, and the manufacturing interests of England came to favor an embassy to China with the aim of improving trade possibilities there.

7. *Foreign Competition in China*

Little regarding the competition of foreign companies with the English need be added. Enough has already been said to show that it centered around the tea trade. Smuggling nursed the Swedish, Danish, Prussian, Imperial, and Tuscan companies, and when that trade declined they declined also.[45] In

[41]Morse, *Chronicle*, v. 2, p. 152; Macpherson, *India*, pp. 214-15; *Critical Review*, v. 10, 1794, p. 459 and v. 8, pp. 459-60; *Annual Register*, 1793, v. 35, pp. 119-31; *Parliamentary Debates* (1792-94), v. 30, pp. 660-85. Dundas made a speech in which he took a great deal of time to point out the opposition to and to defend the Company. Ellison, *op. cit.*, p. 50; *Commons Journal* (1780-82), v. 38, p. 893.

[42]33 Geo. III, cap. 52.

[43]*Commons Journal*, v. 48, p. 779.

[44]Morse, *International Relations*, v. 1, p. 84, shows that the truth of this statement was realized in subsequent events.

[45]Macpherson, *India*, discusses the trade of these companies and gives figures of their tea trade.

(a) Danes, pp. 285-94; (b) Swedes, pp. 305-11; (c) Prussians, pp. 311-13; (d) Imperial Company of Trieste, pp. 313-19. Morse, *Chronicle*, v. 2, also gives a brief analysis of their annual trade in his statistical charts for each year.

TABLE 23.—TEA AND SHIPS SENT BY FOREIGN NATIONS OTHER THAN ENGLISH TO CANTON*
(Figures in thousands of pounds)

Nationality	1770		1775		1780		1785		1790		1795	
	Ships	Tea	Ships	Tea	Ships	Tea	Ships	Tea	Ships	Tea	Ships	Tea
Swedish...	1	1,494	2	4,088	2	2,626	.	.....	.	.....	2	2,759
Danish....	1	1,449	2	3,237	3	3,983	4	3,158	1	1,773	1	24
Dutch....	.	.....	5	4,911	4	4,687	4	5,334	5	5,106	4	4,096
French....	.	.....	4	2,482	4	2,102	4	4,960	1	294	.	.....
American..	.	.....	.	.....	.	.....	2	880	14	3,094	7	1,438

7 Imperial ships at Canton between 1779–1783†
5 Prussian ships at Canton between 1783–1791
22 Spanish ships at Canton between 1783–1795
4 Genoese ships at Canton between 1792–1794
2 Italian and Tuscan ships at Canton between 1787–1792

*Based upon Staunton's *Embassy*, v. 2, p. 624 and upon Macpherson, *India*, pp. 293, 310, 417. See also appendix XX and Morse, *Chronicle*, v. 2, p. 11. Figures for French in 1780 are really 1779, and in 1795 for the Swedish 1796.

†Based on Morse, *Chronicle*, v. 2. See appendix XXV and footnotes.

addition to these make-shift companies, the French, Dutch, and Spanish sent a large number of ships to China during the period.[46] In fact, at times some of these companies seemed about to forge ahead of the English, but the success of the Commutation Act, linked with the fact that England was the only country in Europe which used tea to any great extent, and that the wars of the French Revolution were beginning, saved the English and insured their supremacy.

In 1784, however, a new competitor appeared in the Americans, whose rivalry soon became very important. Expansion of the Chino-American trade to a position nearly equal to that of the English belongs to another chapter, and will be dealt with no further here.[47]

The presence of these various foreigners, of course, increased the possibility of affrays, and therefore the danger of trouble with the Chinese government. Table 23 gives an idea of the magnitude of foreign trade, other than British, at Canton.

8. *The Chinese Attitude*

It has often been stated that the Chinese did not care for the commerce of the West. This does not seem to be true, and we

[46]Macpherson, *India*—French, pp. 254-85; Dutch, pp. 41-72; Spaniards, pp. 319-35.

[47]Latourette, *Early American Relations with China*, pp. 10-18; Tyler Dennett, *Americans in Eastern Asia* (New York, 1922), pp. 44-64; Treat, *op. cit.*, pp. 58-59; Foster, *op. cit.*, pp. 27-37.

agree with Dr. Gutzlaff, when he says that the Chinese recognized the value of the trade.[48] The merchants thought a great deal of it, and the officials certainly realized its value. They wanted to exploit trade as much as possible, but they had no intention of closing up the gold mine.

9. *Significance of These Commercial Developments*

Having surveyed the commercial developments it is well to draw together their separate threads of meaning and see how they reacted upon the different parties affected.

As the value of commerce expanded, its importance to the Company and to the nation increased. Particularly significant in this connection was the growth of the tea trade. The English government, after securing this trade against the rest of Europe by the Commutation Act, was not willing to let it and its valuable revenue slip away because of difficulties in China. The dependence of the nation upon tea also made the British fearful of threatened dangers in China, while their best interests demanded its expansion and liberation. The Indian government through its opium revenue and its tariff on raw cotton found in the China trade a source of revenue, as well as a valuable commercial asset to enterprising English traders in India.

The woollen weaver, moreover, was finding an increasing market for his merchandise in China, while the cotton manufacturer hoped to find an outlet for his goods there. On the whole the great expansion of trade had seriously strained the existing order at Canton, and although the system did not in reality greatly hinder trade, its tightness and pettiness were daily becoming more irksome to the ambitious traders. The additional trade had furthermore increased the number of daily contacts and problems to be solved, and as these grew, the conflicts which they always involved multiplied. Thus, down at the base of things, the expansion of trade was working to create a situation which made all interested parties feel that something had to be done.

10. *Conditions at Canton in 1795*

In discussing conditions at Canton we shall depend almost entirely upon Milburn, who was a contemporary trader.

[48]Gutzlaff, *China Opened*, v. 2, pp. 60 61.

The supercargoes now remained in China all of the year. Their permanent residence was at Macao, where quite a foreign community had grown up. Their families stayed there the year around, while the traders went up to Canton during the trading season, although frequently returning to Macao. This passage was made expensive by various taxes, and it necessitated a great deal of red tape which was objectionable to the foreigners. They employed Chinese servants despite the imperial decree of 1760.[49]

When a ship arrived outside of Macao a pilot came aboard and conducted her to within six or seven miles of the town. Notice was sent to the mandarin, and as soon as he was satisfied that everything was all right he issued a Chop for the ship to proceed to Whampoa. Women had to get special permission to land. After about twenty-four hours' delay the river pilot arrived and the ship then sailed to the Bogue.[50] At the Bogue a mandarin examined the Chop and left one or two minor officials on board until the ship reached Whampoa. Near Whampoa were French and Dane's Islands, where the sailors were allowed to exercise. Provisions were plentiful and of a good quality. The commander of the ship and the supercargoes then proceeded to the Canton factories in small boats, and by special permission the Europeans were not molested by the various officials of the Hoppo between Whampoa and Canton. The factories were large and attractive, and were built at the water's edge with a flagstaff in front of them.[51] After the vessel was assigned a security merchant from among the members of the Co-hong, it was ready to begin business.

The next problem was the measuring of the ship and the payment of duties, the latter being handled through the security merchant. For this reason the exact amount of the duties was hard to ascertain.[52] (1) The actual measuring fee was larger than in 1757, but this was due to the increase in the size of the ships and not to an added charge. On an ordinary 1200 ton ship the basic measuring fee was about T. 2400 plus (2) the fixed T. 1950 cumshaw, making a total of approximately T. 4400. When the Hoppo and his officials came on board to measure the

[49] Milburn, *op. cit.*, v. 2, pp. 462, 474.
[50] *Ibid.*, p. 462.
[51] *Ibid.*, pp. 464-65.
[52] *Ibid.*, pp. 469, 472.

ship, trouble was likely to arise.[53] (3) The 6 per cent *ad valorem* tax and (4) the 3 per cent *ad valorem* Consoo fund levy had to be paid.[54] (5) The imperial import duty was collected but we have no figure relative to its amount. (6) There was the imperial export duty, amounting to T. 0.200 per picul on tea, which was about the same in 1710.[55] (7) These two duties were increased as in 1711 by additional percentages so that the actual duty was practically four times the original.[56] (8) Pilot fees amounted to $85 inward and $59 outward.[57] (9) An eighth charge was about 2 per cent on the value of the sales and purchases which went to the linguist, together with T. 70 as a present, while (10) the compradore received certain fees. (11) Presents and other unloading charges amounted to T. 11 per day, (12) while every ship upon leaving, had to give $40 as a present to the Hoppo.[58] (13) In addition there were numerous miscellaneous charges. These burdens were not excessive, but were so irregular in their assessment that they caused much trouble.

A few new restrictions upon the traders had developed since 1757,[59] but they were unimportant and not strictly enforced. They prohibited:

1. The lending of money by Europeans to Chinese.
2. The hiring of Chinese servants by Europeans.
3. And apparently prohibited foreign women from coming to Canton.[60]

All trade was, of course, confined to members of the Co-hong. Actual relations between the Select Committee and the merchants were generally very congenial, and they had the greatest confidence in each other.[61] The security merchant in charge of the ship usually had bought the cargo upon a previous year's contract, while he also supplied the ship with teas contracted for the year before. Practically all bargains had been made the season before and the amount of tea purchased bore a direct

[53]Morse, *Chronicle*, v. 2, statistical table in the back. See Milburn, *op. cit.*, v. 2, p. 492 for particulars of measuring.

[54]Both of these were fixed charges which apparently continued until the Opium War.

[55]Cf. Morse, *Chronicle*, v. 1, p. 106, with Milburn, *op. cit.*, v. 2, p. 494.

[56]Milburn, *op. cit.*, v. 2, p. 494.

[57]*Ibid.*, p. 495.

[58]*Ibid.*, pp. 493-95.

[59]See p. 136.

[60]Morse, *International Relations*, v. 1, pp. 69-70 and the last two chapters *passim*.

[61]Milburn, *op. cit.*, v. 2, p. 476; Morse, *Chronicle*, v. 2, p. 88.

relationship to the amount of woollens ordered. Money was generally advanced upon these contracts, showing a great amount of confidence.[62] Shopkeepers might trade with the foreigners if they received permits from the Hong Merchants, but these were so costly as to be a distinct disadvantage.[63]

11. *The Basis of Trouble*

Such, then, were the conditions of Canton trade, tremendously annoying but not out of reason. As we look over the picture we find that only one really substantial imposition had been added since 1757—the 3 per cent for the Consoo fund. A few more restrictions had been added but they were not enforced.

Wherein then lay the difficulty? No tremendous outcry had been raised in 1757. No embassy was mentioned then. It is to be found not in the increased restrictions, but in the expansion of trade, in the growing arrogance of the Chinese enforcement of restrictions, in the more belligerent attitude of the English, and most of all in the purely psychological condition growing out of the conflict.

The motive force back of it all was the expansion of trade and industry in England and of trade in China. Given the two cultures as they were, conflict was inevitable when they were drawn into intimate contact. Trade brought the two cultures together; economic expansion in England forced the British to demand and actively to agitate for a broader basis of trade in China. This the Chinese refused in an increasingly arrogant manner. As the number of persons yearly going to Canton grew, the old order was seriously strained, and when it failed to yield, became increasingly galling to the English. They considered themselves bound by an inflexible system, which vexed and annoyed them. Affrays, arguments, and disputes increased as the number of foreign persons at Canton increased, and as the tension grew. Finally a psychological situation was created which forced the supercargoes, and to a lesser degree the English at home, to demand a change.

[62]Milburn, *op. cit.*, v. 2, p. 473; Morse, *Chronicle*, v. 2, pp. 28, 268; 297-98, 315 has discussions relative to the contracts and gives a number of contracts actually entered into.

[63]Milburn, *op. cit.*, v. 2, pp. 494-95.

CHAPTER X

THE MACARTNEY EMBASSY

Little time need be spent upon this subject. Its fundamental causes have been discussed in the two previous chapters, and its positive results were practically negligible. All that need be done is to combine in a unified picture the immediate and underlying causes, and give an evaluation of this first English attempt to open official governmental relations with China.

1. *How the Idea of an Embassy to China Arose*

Mr. Auber explains the origin of the Embassy in the following words:

> In the month of January 1792 the Chairman and Deputy Chairman waited on Mr. Dundas, where they met Mr. Pitt, by whom they were informed that His Majesty's Ministers contemplated sending an embassy to China, for the purpose of placing our intercourse with that nation on a more firm and extended footing. The Chairs expressed great doubts as to the probability of a substantial and permanent advantage being derived by the Company or the country at large from the measure; but as contrary opinions had been adopted by some of the highest authorities, and as the nobleman proposed for the mission was considered to be particularly well qualified for the purpose, the Chairs thought, if the experiment must be tried, the opportunity ought not be neglected.[1]

In reality this is a very much simplified and distorted notion of what happened, although it does show two important things: that the Court of Directors was not enthusiastic about the Embassy, and that the British government was pushing the project. The series of specific events that led up to these final negotiations dates back to 1784 at the time of the *Lady Hughes* affair.

The dispute which arose over the accident and the stoppage of trade which ensued aroused considerable fear in England lest the trade of China be lost entirely—particularly the tea trade.[2] The execution of the gunner also excited the English public, and had a considerable effect upon the government.[3] The most important influence of the event, however, was upon the super-

[1] *Auber, op. cit.*, p. 193.
[2] Morse, *International Relations*, v. 1, p. 53; *Chinese Empire*, pp. 1-9.
[3] Williams, *Middle Kingdom*, v. 2, p. 454; Staunton, *Embassy*, v. 1, pp. 18-20.

cargoes at Canton. They were already greatly stirred by restrictions and insults, and the death of the gunner rendered the situation almost unbearable. They proceeded to demand some form of government aid, and seem to have suggested an embassy. There was a generally prevalent idea that the Emperor did not know what was going on at Canton, and that if an embassy would carry the information directly to him he would remedy the trouble.[4] The upshot of the whole matter was that the British government decided to send a mission to China to intercede with the Emperor in favor of the Company and to guard the welfare of English citizens and trade.[5]

It seems also that the personal interest of Mr. Dundas, president of the Board of Control in India, was influential in bringing about this decision.[6] The government felt that, in view of the importance of the China trade, because of the growing contact between England and China in India, and because of the international importance of Great Britain, it was high time the relations of its nationals with China be put on a more regular and legal basis.[7]

With this in view the government fitted out a mission under Lieutenant Colonel Cathcart and dispatched it at the Company's expense to China. It is an interesting fact that the Cathcarts were great patrons and friends of Josiah Wedgwood, pottery magnate, and one of the rising industrialists.[8] The Company paid the expenses of the Embassy amounting to about £10,000 for salaries, presents, and goods; the government provided the frigate *Vestal*. The ship sailed from Spithead on Dec. 21, 1787. On June 10, 1788, Cathcart died in the Straits of Banka and the expedition was forced to return home.[9]

Negotiations, which continued for some time between the government and the Company, seem to have been pushed by Mr. Dundas, and ended in the decision to send a much larger

[4]Staunton, *Embassy*, v. 1, p. 16; *Annual Register*, v. 34, 1792, pp. 178-179; Sargent, *op. cit.*, pp. 11-13.

[5]Krausse, *op. cit.*, pp. 104-106; Eames, *op. cit.*, p. 102.

[6]Martin, *op. cit.*, v. 2, p. 18; Morse, *Chronicle*, v. 2, pp. 212-15.

[7]Staunton, *Embassy*, v. 1, pp. 16-17, 24-27; Eames, *op. cit.*, p. 117.

[8]Mantoux, *op. cit.*, p. 405.

[9]Morse, *Chronicle*, v. 2, pp. 154-56; Ireland, *op. cit.*, p. 72; Williams, *History of China*, pp. 102-04; Eames, *op. cit.*, p. 117 f. £5000 were also taken on board the *Vestal* to provide for incidental expenses of the Embassy.

and more pretentious mission to China under Lord Macartney.[10] The Court of Directors was probably somewhat excited about the *Lady Hughes* affair in 1787, but by 1792 feeling had quieted down. The Court plainly saw that an embassy might do more than merely aid them; it might open China to other traders and so break their monopoly, or it might arouse so much opposition that their privileges would be entirely abrogated. For these reasons the Directors were not entirely favorable to the Macartney Embassy, and were very insistent that it coöperate with them.[11]

2. *Objects Revealed in the Instructions to the Ambassadors Show the Fundamental Cause of the Embassy*

The instructions given to Cathcart and Macartney were practically identical. They reveal the factors back of the Embassy, and for this reason may be summarized at some length. In anticipation, however, it may be said that the fundamental cause was one of trade expansion. The English people were very dependent upon the tea trade; the woollen interests were interested in an expansion of their market; the cotton interests were demanding new marts, and the Company hoped to improve its position. Secondary to this, but growing directly out of it, and out of the Chinese hostility and cultural differences were the growing problems of trade restrictions and impositions, and the matter of jurisdiction.[12]

The ambassador was to represent that, in view of the fact that more English were trading at Canton than nationals of any other country, and because of the great importance of the trade to both nations, His Majesty considered it his duty to extend his paternal regards to his citizens, "and to claim the Emperor of China's particular protection for them with that weight which is due to the requisition of one great Sovereign from another."[13] He was further to emphasize the interest which England held in

[10]Morse, *Chronicle*, v. 2, pp. 212-15.
[11]*Ibid*, p. 216.
[12]Other books that give a paragraph or so to the Embassy and its causes are: Macpherson, *India*, p. 215; Cornor, *op. cit.*, pp. 108-117; Milburn, *op. cit.*, v. 2, p. 470; Eldridge, *op. cit.*, pp. 19-20; Foster, *op. cit.*, pp. 22-24; Bau, *op. cit.*, p. 6; See, *op. cit.*, pp. 72-73; Krausse, *op. cit.*, pp. 80-84; Treat, *op. cit.*, p. 63; *Annual Register*, v. 34, 1792, pp. 179-89.
[13]Morse, *Chronicle*, v. 2, p. 232. Instructions to Macartney.

the great civilization of China and the mutual benefits that might arise from cultural exchanges.[14]

Further, the expansion of English control in India made it desirable to establish "sufficient means of representation and transaction of business with [their] principal neighbours there."[15] Here we see a first recognition of the future relations between China and India.

Interest in guarding the tea trade, and a desire to open China as a market for English manufactures and Indian products were expressed in the instructions, as the following quotation indicates:

> The measures lately taken by Government respecting the Tea Trade having more than trebled the former legal importation of this article into Great Britain, it is become particularly desirable to cultivate a friendship and increase the communication with China which may lead to such a vent throughout that extensive Empire, of the manufactures of the mother country and of our Indian Territories as beside contributing to their prosperity will out of the Sales of such produce furnish resources for the Investment to Europe now requiring no less an annual sum than one million four hundred thousand pounds.[16]

Next, the indignities suffered by supercargoes at Canton, the restrictions and arbitrary exactions on trade, and its confinement to Canton were mentioned as grievances which should be represented to the Emperor in the hope that he would relieve them.[17] In general the ambassador was to do his best to establish the commercial and diplomatic relations of the two nations upon a firm and equitable foundation.

The plenipotentiary was to request that a small detached piece of land be given to Great Britain as a depot for commerce. It was to be so far north that the English might find a ready sale for their woollens and be in more direct contact with the tea area. He was to request the right of English police regulation and jurisdiction over their own nationals at this depot. If this should be granted the British government promised to establish a person in charge with sufficient power to preserve order.[18] Here was a direct move to get away from the jurisdiction prob-

[14] *Ibid.*, pp. 233, 236-39. Instructions to Macartney.
[15] *Ibid.*, pp. 232-33. Instructions to Macartney.
[16] *Ibid.*, p. 233. Instructions to Macartney.
[17] *Ibid.*, p. 233. Instructions to Macartney.
[18] *Ibid.*, pp. 237-39. Instructions to Macartney.

lem and a definite indication of the interest in commercial expansion. It also suggests that the government was considering sending an official agent to oversee trade, because no officer of the Company could have had powers to enforce the extraterritorial rights desired. If these requests should not be granted, then the commissioner was to do all in his power to relieve the difficulties at Canton.

The ambassador was to observe how British trade might best be expanded in China, and to cultivate there a taste for English products. To this end he was to disperse a large assortment of goods among the natives of North China in the hope of stimulating their desires for British produce. He was given power to visit Japan and other Eastern islands and to negotiate for trade ports.[19] Here are plainly evidenced the wishes of the industrialists in England.

If Macartney found it necessary, he was to agree to the prohibition of opium, but he was to avoid the subject unless forced to deal with it.[20] He was also instructed not to press for the settlement of outstanding debts if he felt that more concessions could be obtained by avoiding the matter.[21]

An exchange of permanent ambassadors was to be proposed in case the other requests terminated successfully.[22] On the whole the Embassy was plainly directed to remedy existing difficulties, gain added privileges if possible, and above all else to look out for the expansion of English manufactures.[23] Its decided nationalistic aim, as contrasted with the narrow view of merely aiding the Company, was plainly shown, for, although the Embassy was ostensibly directed to help the Company, its demands entailed an opening of all China to trade, under British governmental supervision. When the Court requested that all privileges which an embassy might get be especially reserved for the Company in the agreement with China, Mr. Dundas rather

[19] *Ibid.*, pp. 240-41. Instructions to Macartney.
[20] *Ibid.*, p. 239. Instructions to Macartney.
[21] *Ibid.*, p. 243. Instructions to Macartney.
[22] *Ibid.*, p. 240. Instructions to Macartney.
[23] Other authors dealing with the subject of the causes of the Embassy and its aims are: Staunton, *Embassy*, v. 1, pp. 13-51; Morse, *Chronicle*, v. 2, pp. 212-23; *Critical Review*, v. 8, p. 461; Auber, *op. cit.*, pp. 194-96; Martin, *op. cit.*, v. 2, pp. 17-18.

curtly refused, but went on to say that it would enjoy these privileges as long as its present charter lasted.[24]

3. *The Embassy*

After having decided to send another mission to China the government looked about for a suitable person on whom the important trust might be placed. The choice fell upon Lord Macartney, a distinguished colonial administrator and diplomat. A former governor of Madras, he had been offered the position of Governor-General of Bengal, and had completed a successful mission to the Court of St. Petersburg.[25] In an exchange of notes with Mr. Dundas and the Company he expressed his ideas on the conduct of the Embassy.[26] It was finally decided that he should carry a letter from the King of England to the Emperor of China, and that the commercial nature of the undertaking should be disguised under the ostensible object of conveying the English King's congratulations and good wishes to the Emperor upon the attainment of his eighty-third birthday.[27] The entire cost of the Embassy was to be defrayed by the Company.[28] Macartney was given the privilege of choosing the persons to accompany him. He named Sir George Staunton secretary and minister plenipotentiary in absence of the ambassador, with power to complete negotiations in case of Macartney's death. H. M. S. *Lion* was commissioned to carry the ambassador. The Company's ship *Hindostan* carried a numerous assortment of presents for the Emperor, together with various types of English products which were to be distributed among the Chinese. The expedition included the tender *Jackal*, a military escort, and a large number of scientific men.[29] Some difficulty was encountered in securing interpreters, but finally two Chinese from a college in Naples were found.[30]

[24]Morse, *Chronicle*, v. 2, p. 155; *China Materials* (1787-90), v. 90, enclosure v/5. Letter, Dundas to Cathcart.

[25]*Ibid.*, p. 212.

[26]*Ibid.*, pp. 214-15.

[27]*Ibid.*, p. 219, and pp. 244-47 for King's letter to the Emperor; Auber, *op. cit.*, p. 197.

[28]Morse, *Chronicle*, v. 2, p. 216.

[29]*Ibid.*, pp. 215-20, 236, 240-41; Staunton, *Embassy*, v. 1, pp. 30-52; Eames, *op. cit.*, pp. 117-19.

[30]Staunton, *Embassy*, v. 1, pp. 38-41; Eames, *op. cit.*, p. 119.

In preparation, the Court sent a special Select and Superintending Committee to Canton to announce the coming of the Embassy. It was to do everything in its power to insure the success of the undertaking.[31] A large number of discretionary powers were left to Macartney, but he was strongly advised to sail directly to Tientsin and there to announce his arrival to the Emperor.[32]

The Embassy sailed from Portsmouth on September 26, 1792.[33] In March, 1793, it arrived at Batavia where letters were waiting from Canton, stating that the announcement of the Embassy had been favorably received by the Emperor, and that preparations were being made for its reception.[34] Later information indicated that the Canton merchants and mandarins were somewhat disturbed about the Embassy, but were nevertheless prescribing to the proper form in preparing for it.[35] The expedition did not touch at Canton but proceeded to Chusan and then to Taku, where it landed on August 5. It was well received by special imperial officials, and was conveyed with great pomp and ceremony to Peking and thence to Jehol where the Emperor was celebrating his birthday.[36] The Embassy was feasted and treated with the greatest courtesy, but the flags on the boats conveying it up the river carried the insignia "Ambassadors bearing tribute from the Country of England."[37] It is said that the entertainment cost the Chinese $850,000.[38] Some trouble was encountered over the matter of the *kotow*.[39] It was finally arranged that Macartney should pay the same homage to the Emperor that he would to his own sovereign.[40]

The ambassador was allowed two audiences with the Emperor at Jehol, but all discussion of the conditions of trade was

[31] Eames, *op. cit.*, pp. 118-19; Morse, *Chronicle*, v. 2, p. 216.

[32] Morse, *Chronicle*, v. 2, p. 235.

[33] *Ibid.*, p. 224; Cordier, *op. cit.*, v. 1, pp. 14-15.

[34] Staunton, *Embassy*, v. 1, pp. 235-41.

[35] *Ibid.*, pp. 390-98.

[36] *Ibid.*, chaps. 9, 10; v. 2, chaps. 1-4; Morse, *Chronicle*, v. 2, p. 224.

[37] Morse, *International Relations*, v. 1, p. 54; *Chinese Empire*, p. 319; Helen H. Robbins, *Our First Ambassador to China* (London, 1908), pp. 254-70.

[38] Williams, *Middle Kingdom*, v. 2, pp. 454-55.

[39] Staunton, *Embassy*, v. 2, pp. 48-67, 208-09.

[40] *Ibid.*, pp. 130-31, 135-37, 213-22, 232; Morse, *International Relations*, v. 1, pp. 54-55. The *kotow* "consisted of kneeling three times before the throne and, with each kneeling, striking the head three times upon the floor," E. T. Williams, *China*, p. 231.

avoided by the Chinese.[41] The mission then returned to Peking, where, on October 3, 1793, the ambassador presented the following requests to the Chinese government:

1. That the English be allowed to trade at Chusan, Ningpo, and Tientsin;

2. That they be allowed a warehouse at Peking;

3. That they be allowed some small unfortified depot near Chusan where their people might reside and their supplies be stored;

4. That a similar privilege be allowed near Canton;

5. That the transit duties between Macao and Canton be abolished or reduced to the standard of 1782;

6. That all charges at Canton above the imperial duties be abolished and that a copy of the imperial duties be given to the English.[42]

On October 7 the imperial reply was received, and on the same day the Embassy left Peking. The reply was a flat refusal of the first four requests and a vague assertion that justice would be done regarding the charges on trade. A clause was inserted saying that the propagation of the English religion could not be allowed.[43]

> To Conclude, as the Requests made by your Ambassador militate against the Laws and Usages of this Our Empire, and are at the same Time wholly useless to the End proposed, I cannot acquiesce in them. I again admonish you, O King, to act conformably to my Intentions, that we may preserve Peace and Amity on each Side, and thereby contribute to our reciprocal Happiness.[44]

Macartney accompanied the new Viceroy of Kwangtung overland to Canton. Their relations were very friendly, and the Viceroy so encouraged Macartney that the ambassador believed many of the troubles at Canton would be relieved.[45] Macartney presented him with a list of grievances which he hoped would be abolished.[46] The Viceroy was very favorably disposed at first, but after a series of conferences with the local officials his attitude changed, and the expedition was forced to sail without having received any definite answers.[47] The final result of the

[41] Staunton, *Embassy*, v. 2, pp. 224-39, 240-48, 248-55.

[42] Morse, *Chronicle*, v. 2, pp. 224-25; Staunton, *Embassy*, v. 2, pp. 320-336; Robbins, *op. cit.*, pp. 333-39.

[43] Morse, *Chronicle*, v. 2, pp. 226-27, 247-52.

[44] *Ibid.*, p. 251.

[45] *Ibid.*, pp. 227-30; Staunton, *Embassy*, v. 2, pp. 432, 470-71, 483-87.

[46] Morse, *Chronicle*, v. 2, pp. 252-54.

[47] *Ibid.*, pp. 230-31; Staunton, *Embassy*, v. 2, pp. 530-34.

whole affair was the recalling of the favorably inclined Viceroy and the continuation of conditions as before.[48]

4. *Results of the Embassy*

"The ambassador was received with the utmost politeness, treated with the utmost hospitality, watched with the utmost vigilance, and dismissed with the utmost civility," says Auber.[49] It is contended by some that the failure of the Embassy was due to suspicion of England created by the reports of her advance in India, and by the hostility of the Tibetan general who believed that the English were aiding the Goorkas against the Chinese.[50] This may have had some influence but was fundamentally of little importance. The basic reason for its failure was the aversion of the Chinese government to foreign intercourse. A settled policy of anti-foreignism, arrogant superiority, and absolute exclusiveness prevailed, and, although the Emperor was willing to receive an Embassy of tribute and congratulation, never in his wildest dreams did he think of opening his Empire to the troublesome "barbarians." There was a party in China which favored open trade, but it was too small to be influential.[51] The Emperor, perhaps, was favorable to some slight reform at Canton, but the greed and avarice of the Canton officials was too

[48]This brief account of the Embassy has dealt in the main only with those things of direct interest to our subject. The whole Mission was a brilliant and colorful affair, and the large group of Europeans who accompanied it availed themselves of every opportunity to study and learn about Chinese customs and manners. The increased knowledge about China which resulted from it was perhaps its most important accomplishment. There are three extensive accounts of it which are recommended to anyone who is interested in the descriptive details. Staunton, *Embassy*, in two volumes, is perhaps the best. *The Chinese Empire*, published anonymously, in London in 1798, and *A Narrative of the British Embassy to China* (London, 1795) by Aeneas Anderson, one of the members of the company, are good. Most of the documentary material relating to it is to be found in Morse, *Chronicle*, v. 2, chap. 43 and appendices, and chap. 49 and appendices. Brief accounts from which we have drawn are found in Auber, *op. cit.*, pp. 193-200; Eames, *op. cit.*, pp. 103-29; Macgowan, *op. cit.*, p. 533; Gutzlaff, *Chinese History*, v. 2, pp. 336-44; Morse, *International Relations*, v. 1, pp. 53-55; Williams, *Middle Kingdom*, v. 2, pp. 454-55; Cornor, *op. cit.*, pp. 108-17; Krausse, *op. cit.*, pp. 80-84; Lavisse and Rambaud, *op. cit.*, v. 8, pp. 949-52.

[49]Auber, *op. cit.*, p. 200.

[50]Eames, *op. cit.*, pp. 119-21; Staunton, *Embassy*, v. 2, pp. 48-67, 131-35, 208-09; Morse, *Chronicle*, v. 2, p. 223; Gutzlaff, *Chinese History*, v. 2, pp. 336-44.

[51]Morse, *Chronicle*, v. 2, pp. 225-26.

great to be overcome by a well-meaning Viceroy. After a temporary gleam of light, conditions settled back into the old routine.[52]

The failure of the Embassy was significant for several reasons: (1) "The only permanent effect left upon the Chinese was that England was promptly enrolled on the list of tribute-bearing nations," says Eames.[53] (2) China would not recognize European countries as its equals, but considered them as inferior nations with whom it would have no official settled intercourse. (3) The conditions of the China trade were to remain unchanged for a generation, because as yet the British government did not consider the problem sufficiently important to warrant the use of force in breaking the Chinese cultural barrier. (4) Perhaps the most important result was the knowledge which members of the Embassy obtained about China and the interest thus created in the ancient culture of Cathay.

[52] *Ibid.*, pp. 226-30.
[53] Eames, *op. cit.*, p. 127.

CHAPTER XI

CONCLUSION

England's interest in and early contact with China grew out of her own internal expansion, the adventurous spirit of the Renaissance, and the desire of merchants to break into the profitable spice trade. Yielding to the petitions of London merchants, and following out the "concentration of National Power" policy of the Tudors, Elizabeth created the East India Company, the tool for expanding English trade in the East and for opening English intercourse with China.

The early years of the Company were very successful and after establishing itself in India, the Spice Islands, and Japan it turned toward China, hoping to find a market for woollens and a source of supply for raw silk. Disorderly conditions in China, linked with the opposition of the Portuguese and the Dutch, prevented the success of these early experiments and created an impression that China was decidedly anti-foreign.

Before this error could be corrected the Company fell into decline due to the competition of the Dutch, the lack of royal support at home, popular opposition in England, financial trouble, and the rivalry of interlopers. The Company lost its base in Japan, and was virtually excluded from the Spice Islands, while its position in India was precarious; it was thus in no position to undertake the opening of new ports. Furthermore, China at this time offered no products which were invaluable to trade, and during the middle of the 17th century the country was so torn by wars of the Manchu conquest that foreign intercourse was practically impossible.

From 1660 on, however, the fortunes of the Company revived, due to royal patronage, the suppression of the interlopers, favorable commercial policies of the government, and the decline of its greatest rivals. It was enabled to re-establish its trade to the Spice Islands, and so to come once again into more direct contact with the Chinese traders. Tea was introduced into England, and it so rapidly captivated British taste that the establishment of a firm base where tea was produced became imperative. The Company, desiring to enlarge the field of its commerce, to find a greater supply of raw silk, and to increase the vent of English woollens, began, during the last quarter of the 17th century, to experiment in the China trade. It opened relations at Amoy and tried to trade at Canton, but without success.

At this point, due to the Glorious Revolution and a split between Josiah Child and Thomas Papillion, leaders of the Company, a new and powerful organization of interlopers was formed. This eventually obtained a charter from Parliament, and around 1700 the two Companies competed vigorously for mastery of the China trade. A result was the opening of business at Canton and Chusan. The rival groups finally were amalgamated and from that time presented a united front to all opponents of their monopoly.

The period between 1670 and 1700 had been one in which the Manchu Emperor, Kanghi, was particularly favorable to foreigners. Under his countenance missionary work expanded, and the English, French, and Dutch trade became established at Canton, while a profitable business developed between Russia and China in the north. The missionaries, however, aroused first the enmity of the mandarins, and then that of the Emperor, and after 1703 there was a growing tendency for the officials and the rulers to look with dislike upon all foreigners.

Officials, however, found foreign trade so profitable that they were willing for it to continue, provided it furnished sufficient compensation. To better enable the mandarins to milk the foreign trade, institutions of systematic exactions such as the "Emperor's Merchant," the "Mandarin Merchant," and the various percentage charges appeared, while the irregular demands were increased. The result of this policy of extortion was the gravitation of trade to Canton, where the exactions were less and certainly more cleverly veiled. In the closing years of Kanghi's rule of foreign favoritism trade at Canton became established upon a firm and lasting basis, while tea became a staple and invaluable product for English consumption. Favorable privileges were negotiated, giving the merchants almost complete freedom of commerce and personal movement, with only nominal charges upon trade.

After 1722 the auspicious conditions began to disappear. A new Emperor, opposed to Europeans, came to the throne. With his support the mandarins stirred up the public to attack the missionaries. This dislike of the missionaries was transferred to all aliens and led to a growing anti-foreign attitude, which, linked with the natural avarice of the officials, led to a number of restrictions. These were of two kinds: restrictions upon the personal freedom of the foreigners, and restrictions upon the freedom of trade, with the object of exacting greater profit from it. Actual direct impositions on trade were increased for a time, but the new charge of 10 per cent was lifted by Kien-lung in 1736. However, at the same time he inaugurated a policy of strict jurisdiction over foreigners who violated Chinese law.

During this period of growing restrictions and regulations a number of new institutions and practices were evolved, including the security merchants, the Co-hong, to which all trade was confined, the 1950 taels cumshaw, and the addressing of all appeals to officials through the Hong Merchants. To meet these conditions the English supercargoes organized into a single committee, with a president, and adopted the practice of making contracts a year in advance with the Chinese merchants.

The steady growth of restrictions led the British to look toward other ports. To prevent the loss of their valuable monopoly the Cantonese interceded with the Emperor. He, due to financial reasons, and a desire to free his Empire from the troublesome Europeans as far as possible, acceded to the demands of Canton, and in 1757, prohibited European trade at any other Chinese port. Thus culminated the anti-foreign movement which began with the opposition to missionaries and which grew in proportion to the number of foreigners coming to Canton.

Despite Chinese complications and the competition of interloping groups, the East India Company's trade grew steadily. High duties on tea at home, however, prevented its monopolizing this trade. Commerce also suffered during the periods of European conflict; the wars being more harmful than the restrictions in China. By 1757 conditions in the Orient were undesirable, but not so bad as to warrant government aid.

After 1757 the hostile attitude of the Chinese continued to grow while the total volume and value of trade greatly increased; especially did the tea and woollen trade expand after the passage of the Commutation Act. Growing Chinese dislike led to many new personal restrictions, while the controversy over debts led to the establishment of a new 3 per cent imposition in the form of a Consoo fund and in 1782 to the virtual re-establishment of the Co-hong, which had been abolished in 1771. The increased number of persons coming to Canton each year, plus growing hostility between the two groups, led to an increasing number of affrays and the killing of several Chinese. The latter insisted on a life for a life in most cases, a policy which was stoutly resisted by the English. These increased restrictions and the precariousness of life, property, and trade grew steadily more galling as the volume of business expanded. It seemed to the English merchants that their very existence was being endangered. The truth of the matter was that the Chinese system remained much the same as before: trade was out-growing it.

The whole period of conflict created a psychological condition which received relief only when the traders demanded government aid. The British government, impelled by considerations of maintaining the tea and woollen trade, of opening new markets for cottons, of affording better protection to the lives and property of its citizens, of guarding its revenues and the welfare of India, and of asserting its national greatness, decided to send an embassy to the Emperor.

The mission ended in failure, not because of the inefficiency of the ambassador or the unjustness of the cause, but because of the fundamental difference in the cultures of the two nations. China was haughty and aloof; England was equally haughty but not so aloof. Their cultural ideas and practices were far removed, which fact was the basis of all the difficulty. Trade merely served to bring the two cultures together. Ultimate conflict was inevitable but for the moment was averted, because England was not vitally enough interested, and because she was then engaged in the wars of the French Revolution.

In conclusion the following generalizations may be put down as basic.

1. England's first interest in China was promoted by the desire of private traders, as organized in the East India Company, to make profits, and to find a market for woollens and a purchasing place for silk.

2. The monopolistic East India Company continued to be the sole connecting link between England and China until 1833 despite governmental attempts to establish relations in 1793 and 1816.

3. The tea trade served as the great binding link between the two peoples.

4. A very extensive anti-foreign attitude did not exist in China before the first quarter of the 18th century. It was generated by hatred of the missionaries, and was then increased by quarrels with, and arrogant treatment of, the steadily increasing number of foreign traders who came to China.

5. Between 1723 and 1757 the most prominent feature in the relations between the English and the Chinese was the growth of restrictions. Between 1757 and 1795 the most important factor was the growth in the volume of trade, and the increasingly arrogant way in which the Chinese applied the restrictions.

6. The fundamental cause of the trouble between the English and the Chinese was a cultural one. Conflict was inevitable if the two civilizations were once brought together in an extensive way. It was the function of trade to bring them together, and as contacts, driven on by the basic factors of economic relationship, increased, the conflict of cultures grew. War in the end followed and China gave way. But still more basically than this, the two cultures continued their silent struggle, until finally the more dynamic West made a breach in the Chinese system—as the 17th century mandarins had feared. The result is the chaos of today, the final outcome of which no one knows.

As the 18th century drew to a close the period of great reciprocal cultural influences between China and Europe was just opening. If in the century and a quarter to come Sinic civilization was to embrace many things from the West (so many indeed that one sometimes wonders whether it may not ultimately be submerged), at this time it was the West which had borrowed most. The missionaries had made a few converts and had presented a few Occidental ideas, but had made scarcely an imprint upon the real Chinese culture. The only thing from the West which had interested China was mathematical and astronomical knowledge, and this had not passed beyond the Imperial Astronomical Bureau at Peking. The baneful habit of opium smoking was just beginning to be fastened upon the Middle Kingdom with the assistance of greedy Western traders. On the other hand China had converted England into a nation of tea drinkers, to say nothing of the United States and parts of Europe. Oriental silks and china-ware were in demand, and Europeans were struggling against prohibitory Chinese laws for opportunity to learn the language. The cultural relations of the Macartney Embassy and the earlier contact with the Orient were having important influences upon the customs, manners, and literatures of Europe.

The pernicious opium habit remained for years the only visible influence of the Occident upon the aloof and exclusive Orient. The West, however, showed an active interest and a readiness to adapt itself to things Chinese and to borrow freely when it seemed desirable. If in the long run Western culture proves to possess a higher degree of permanence than that of China, the explanation will perhaps be found in its greater adaptability.

APPENDIX I

WEIGHTS AND MEASURES

A. Currency[1]

The tael (T. or Tls.) is the ounce of China, weighing from 525 to 585 grains; as currency it is a tael of silver of a weight and fineness dependent on the banking convention of the city concerned. During the period covered by this work the tael of Canton had a conventional fixed value of 6*s.* 8*d.* (one pound sterling = Tls. 3).

The dollar ($) during the period covered by this volume was always the Spanish (Carolus) dollar, with an intrinsic value of 4*s.* 2*d.* and an exchange value in China ranging from 4*s.* 6*d.* upward. Between 1619 and 1814 it was invoiced at 5*s.*

B. Weight[1]

The picul is 133⅓ lb. av. or 60.453 kilogrammes.
The catty is 1⅓ lb. av. or 604.53 grammes.
The tael is 1⅓ oz. av. or 37.783 grammes.
One picul = 1⅕ cwt. English = 1⅓ cwt. American.
16.8 piculs = 1 long ton.
15.0 piculs = 1 short ton.
16.54 piculs = 1 metric ton.

C. Length[1]

The li is nominally ⅓ mile or ½ kilometre.
The "foot" or "covid" or "cubit" is 14.1 English inches.
The chang is 141 English inches.

D. General[2]

1. The Cash is the lowest unit of Chinese money.
   10 Cash = 1 Candareen.
   10 Candareen = 1 Mace.
   10 Mace = 1 Tael.
   1 Tael = ⅓£ or 6*s.* 8*d.* or 1£ = 3 Taels.
   1 Tael = $1.63 in U. S. money or $1.57 Spanish.
   1 Spanish dollar = 0.72 Tael or 5*s.* (£ = 4 Spanish dollars.)

[1]Morse, *International Relations*, v. 1. Note before page 1.
[2]Milburn, *Oriental Commerce*, v. 2, pp. 470-72; Morse, *op. cit.*, p. 26; Morse, *Chronicle*, v. 1, opposite p. 1.

2. 1 Tael = 1⅓ oz. av. or 37.783 grammes.
   16 Tael = 1 catty or 1 lb. 5 oz. av.
   100 catties = 1 picul.
   1 Picul = 133 lbs. 5 oz.
3. Malwa opium chests = 100 catties or 133⅓ lbs.[3]
   Bengal opium chests = 120 catties or 160 lbs.

E. Signs Used in This Book

1. Tael is used to refer to money value and is identified by T. or Tls.
2. R 8/8 = reals of eight. Later called the Spanish dollar.
3. £ = pound sterling.
4. *s.* = shillings; 20*s.* = 1 £.
5. *d.* = pence; 12*d.* = 1*s.*
6. 1*d.* = 2 cents in American money.

[3]Treat, *The Far East*, p. 65; Morse, *International Relations*, v. 1, p. 173n.

APPENDIX II

CHINESE EDICT—THE EMPEROR'S ACT OF GRACE, 1736[1]

By order of the Emperour.

All Ships belonging to the English and other Europeans that arrive at Wampo in Canton shall Deposite in the Mandarine's hands, all their Powder, Cannon and Arms, before they enter into any Trade or Contract, and when their Trade and Business is over and the Ships are upon their departure, their Powder, Cannon and Arms shall be deliver'd to them. As to the Dutys, the Measurage of each Ship shall be Two thousand Tales or thereabouts, and on all merchandize imported and exported they shall pay Dutys according to the Old Custom. For what reason have you suffered of late years the Europeans to keep their Powder, Cannon and Arms on board their Ships, and for what reason have you made them pay ten per Cent on their Goods, giving me to understand it was a voluntary present from them. This was not the Custom formerly. I think the Antient Custom was that all European Ships that arrived at Wampo were obliged to deliver up their Powder, Cannon and Arms. Now I Order that hereafter all European Ships that arrive at Wampo shall deliver up their Powder, Cannon and Arms, and as for the 10 per ct. it was not My Will to receive Presents from Foreigners, For which reason I Order that on the arrival of the Chuntuck at Canton, He, the Foyeen, and Hoppo, shall consult together and do herein what they shall see necessary.

[1] Morse, *Chronicle*, v. 1, p. 249.

APPENDIX III

EXAMPLES OF CHINESE TORTURE[1]

Let us describe a few of the simplest modes of torture. The upper portion of the body of the culprit having been uncovered, each of his arms—he being in a kneeling position—is held tightly by a turnkey, while a third beats him most unmercifully between the shoulders with a double cane. Should he continue to give evasive answers, his jaws are beaten with an instrument made of two thick pieces of leather, sown [sic] together at one end, and in shape not unlike the sole of a slipper. Between these pieces of leather is placed a small tongue of the same material, to give the weapon elasticity. The force with which this implement of torture is applied to the jaws of the accused is in some instances so great as to loosen his teeth, and cause his mouth to swell to such a degree as to deprive him for some time of the powers of mastication. Should he continue to maintain his innocence, a turnkey beats his ankles by means of a piece of hard wood, which resembles a schoolboy's ruler, and is more than a foot long. Torture of this nature not infrequently results in the ankle bones being broken. Should the prisoner still persist in declaring his innocence, a severer mode of torture is practiced. This may be regarded as a species of rack. A large heavy tressel is placed in a perpendicular position, and the prisoner, who is in a kneeling posture, is made to lean against the board of it. His arms are then pushed backward and stretched under the upper legs of the tressel, from the ends of which they are suspended by cords passing around the thumb of each hand. His legs are also pushed backward and are drawn, his knees still resting on the ground, towards the upper leg of the tressel by cords passing round the large toe of each foot. When the prisoner has been thus bound, the questions are again put to him, and should his answers be deemed unsatisfactory, the double cane is applied with great severity to his thighs, which have been previously uncovered. Prisoners have been known to remain in this position for a considerable time, and the quivering motion of the

[1]Gen. Ki Tong Tcheng and John Henry Gray, *The Empire of China*, pp. 94-96.

whole frame, the piteous moans, and the saliva oozing freely from the mouth, afforded the most uncontestable evidence of the extremity of the torture. Upon being released from the rack, they are utterly unable to stand. They are therefore placed in baskets and borne by coolies from the court of justice, falsely so-called, to the house of detention on remand. In the course of a few days they are once more dragged out to undergo another examination. Even this torture occasionally fails in extorting a confession of guilt. In all such cases another still crueler torture is enforced. The prisoner is made to kneel under a bar of wood, six English feet in length, and is supported by two upright pillars or posts of the same material. When the back of his neck has been placed immediately under it, his arms are extended along the bar, and made fast by cords. In the hollow at the back of his knee joints is laid a second bar of equal dimensions, and upon this two men place themselves, one at each end, pressing it down by their weight upon the joints of the prisoner's knees, between which and the ground chains are passed to render the agony less endurable. This bar is occasionally removed from the inner part of the prisoner's knee joints, in order that it may be made to rest on the tendon Achillis. When in this latter position, the same amount of pressure is applied to it, with the view of stretching the ankle joint.

APPENDIX IV

CAPITAL STOCK OF THE EAST INDIA COMPANY*

Year	Name of Stock	Amount £	Year	Name of Stock	Amount £
1599.....	London Adventures	30,133	1640.....	Failure to raise Fourth Stock	22,500
1600.....	First Charter Stock	57,543	1641.....	Single voyage	67,500
1601.....	First voyage	68,373	1641–49..	First General Voyage	105,000
1604.....	Second voyage	60,450	1649–57..	United Joint-Stock	157,000
1606–07..	Third voyage	53,500	1649–57..	Second General Voyage	30–35,000 ?
1607–08..	Fourth voyage	33,000	1657.....	New Stock	786,000
1608–09..	Fifth voyage	13,700	1676.....	Estimated at	739,782
1609–10..	Sixth voyage	82,000	1694.....	Permission to add	744,000
1610–11..	Seventh voyage	71,581	1698.....	English Company	2,000,000
1611–12..	Eighth voyage	76,375	1708.....	Permission to raise	1,200,000
1612.....	Ninth voyage	7,200	1708–09..	United Stock	3,200,000
1612–17..	First Joint-Stock	429,000	1787.....	....	4,000,000
1617, 1621, 1631....	Second Joint-Stock	1,629,040	1789.....	....	5,000,000
1631–41..	Third Joint-Stock	420,700	1793.....	....	6,000,000

*See notes for appendix X, also Bruce, *Annals of the East India Company*, v. 1, pp. 146-165, 306, 363-64, 372, 381, 390-91, 436, 441, 503, 529. *Charter Granted to the East India Company*, p. 157; 9-10 Will. III, cap. 44; 6 Anne, cap. 17; Macgregor, *Commerical Statistics*, v. 4, pp. 508-09.

APPENDIX V

SELLING VALUE OF THE COMPANY'S STOCKS*

Year	Selling value %	Year	Selling value %	Year	Selling value %
1617	203	1696	67–38	1739	121–169
1629	80	1697	65–47	1740	104–164
1661	90–94	1698	75–33	1741	155–164
1665	60–70	1699	59–41	1742	157–178
1668	130	1700	142–58	1743	186–195
1669	108–130	1701	119–75	1744	168–194
1670	111	1702	120–77	1745	163–187
1672	80	1703	134–106	1746	154–184
1677	245	1704	139–117	1747	151–177
1680	300–245	1705	128–93	1748	156–184
1681	365–460	1706	123–87	1749	174–191
1682	150–260	1707	115–103	1750	184–188
1683	170–122½	1708	108–98	1751	184–195
1684	210	1709	105–104	1752	187–195
1685	500–360	1731	174–198	1753	191–191
1690	300	1732	154–178	1754	182–192
1691	200–158	1733	136–163	1755	148–180
1692	158–131	1734	135–149	1756	133–145
1693	146–90	1735	145–169	1757	133–142
1694	97–66	1736	169–178	1758	132–148
1695	93–50	1737	174–181	1759	123–141
1695	67–38	1738	121–176	1760	134–142

*Krishna, *Commercial Relations between India and England*, pp. 316-319.

SELLING VALUE OF THE ENGLISH CO. STOCKS†

Year	Selling value %	Year	Selling value %	Year	Selling value %
1699	50¾–106½	1703	219–151¾	1707	272–254½
1700	154–126	1704	260–202½	1708	258½–240¼
1701	140½–100	1705	258¼–234	1709	114–112
1702	161–125¾	1706	260–238½	....	....

†Krishna, *Commercial Relations between India and England*, p. 316.

APPENDIX VI

CHARTERS OF THE EAST INDIA COMPANY*

Year	Persons Granting Charters	Characteristic Feature
1600	Elizabeth........................	Exclusive trade to the East for 15 years
1609	James I........................	Perpetual
1657	Cromwell........................	
1661	Charles II........................	Perpetual—with limitations
1677	Charles II........................	Perpetual and more liberal
1683	Charles II........................	Perpetual and more liberal
1686	James II........................	Perpetual and more liberal Forfeited by a technicality in 1693
1693	William III.....................	Confirmed former privileges subject to reservations
1698	Parliament.....................	Granted to English Company until 1714
1708	Parliament.....................	Provided for the extension of the United Co. to 1729
1712	Parliament.....................	Extended charter to 1736
1730	Parliament.....................	Extended charter to 1769
1744	Parliament.....................	Extended charter to 1783
1781	Parliament.....................	Extended charter to 1794
1793	Parliament.....................	Extended charter to 1814
1813	Parliament.....................	Extended charter to 1834 and abolished the Indian trade monopoly
1833	Parliament.....................	Abolished the China trade monopoly

*_Charters Granted to the East India Company;_ Macpherson, _India_, p. 428; Birdwood, _East India Company Charters_, pp. 1-2.

APPENDIX VII

DIVIDENDS PAID BY THE EAST INDIA COMPANY*

Year	Dividend % per year	Year	Dividend % per year	Year	Dividend % per year
1601–04....	95	1631–41...	3+	1755......	6
1606–07....	243	1641–57...	Never exceeded 12½	1766......	10
1607–08....	0	1676......	100	1769......	11
1608–09....	211	1708......	5 and 8	1770......	12
1609–10....	121	1709......	9	1771......	12½
1610–11....	218	1711......	10	1773......	6
1611–12....	211	1722......	8	1777......	7
1612.......	160	1732......	7	1778......	8
1612–17....	87½	1743......	8	1793......	10½
1617–31....	8				

DIVIDENDS PAID BY THE EAST INDIA COMPANY†

Years	Total Time year	Per Cent per year	Total Amount for Period	Capital Stock
1708–09..................	¼	5	£ 39,540	£3,200,000
1709.....................	½	8	126,528	....
1709–11..................	2	9	569,376	....
1711–16..................	5¼	10	1,660,680	....
1716–22..................	5½	10	1,756,744	....
1722–32..................	10	8	2,555,264	....
1732–43..................	11	7	2,459,442	....
1743–55..................	12½	8	3,194,080	....
1755–66..................	11	6	2,108,093	....
1766–68..................	2	10	638,816	....
1768–69..................	1	11	351,349	....
1769–70..................	1	12	383,290	....
1770–72..................	1½	12½	598,890	....
1772–76..................	4	6	766,579	....
1776–77..................	1½	7	335,378	....
1777–87..................	9½	8	2,427,501	....
1787–89..................	2½	8	800,000	4,000,000
1789–92..................	3	8	1,200,000	5,000,000
1792–93..................	½	10½	525,000	....
1793–1810................	17½	..	12,512,284	6,000,000
Total for period of 102 yrs...			£35,008,834	....

*See notes for appendix X. Based on Bruce, *Annals of the East India Company;* Macpherson, *India*, p. 430.

†Macgregor, *Commercial Statistics*, v. 4, pp. 508-09.

APPENDIX VIII

TONNAGE OF THE EAST INDIA COMPANY SAILING TO THE EAST (1601–1707)*

Year	No. of Ships Sent Out	Tonnage	Year	No. of Ships Sent Out	Tonnage
1601	5	1,530	1660–61	15	5,415
1604	6	1,740	1661–62	10	2,365
1606	3	1,250	1662–63	7	2,460
1608	2	660	1663–64	10	3,215
1609	1	260	1664–65	5	1,275
1610	6	2,542	1665–66	3	845
1611	5	2,469	1666–67	3	840
1612	4	1,633	1667–68	14	4,750
1613	5	2,350	1668–69	10	3,175
1614	13	4,063	1669–70	14	4,790
1615	9	4,363	1670–71	20	6,685
1616	5	2,950	1671–72	18	6,670
1617	10	5,096	1672–73	10	4,130
1618	8	2,736	1673–74	13	5,260
1619	12	7,644	1674–75	14	5,760
1620	5	1,930	1675–76	16	7,170
1621	10	4,306	1676–77†	12	5,350
1622	3	1,600	1677–78	13	6,720
1623	3	950	1678–79	8	4,260
1624	7	2,900	1679–80†	10	5,420
1625	7	4,230	1680–81†	11	5,430
1626	7	3,500	1681–82	23	9,160
1627	7	2,190	1682–83	19	7,700
1628	4	1,560	1683–84	28	12,980
1629	5	2,600	1684–85	14	5,300
1630	6	2,900	1685–86	27	9,783
1631	14	7,720	1686–87	10	4,020
1632	1	400	1687–88	14	5,195
1633	5	2,430	1688–89	4	2,245
1634	5	2,170		2 Private	
1635	4	2,260	1689–90	2	1,218
1636	2	1,300		1 Private	
1637	3	1,600	1690–91	6	2,325
1638	2	750		1 Private	
1639	5	2,490	1691–92	7	3,510
1640	5	2,500	1692–93	6	3,400
1641	6	3,250	1693–94	10	3,640
1642	4	1,950	1694–95	8	2,830
1643	6	2,200	1695–96	10	4,310
1644	4	1,910	1696–97	5	1,420
1645	4	1,920	1697–98	15	6,420
1646	6	2,380		4 Private	
1647	4	1,700	1698–99	13	5,025
1648	8	3,350	New Co.'s	6	2,338
1649	3	1,100	Private	1	300
1650	10	4,180	1699–1700	12	4,860
1651	4	1,400	New Co.'s	11	3,750
1652	4	1,450	Private	2	500
1653	2	390	1700–1	12	4,770
1654	3	1,050	New Co.'s	13	4,070
1655	1	260	1701–2	8	2,570
1656	3	1,250	New Co.'s	15	4,463
1657	None by the Co.		1702–3	17	6,043
1635–57	60 ships other than those of the Co. have been traced as having sailed to the East.		1703–4	15	5,195
			1704–5	15	4,720
			1705–6	9	2,660
1658–59	25	7,935	1706–7	9	3,020
	4 Private		1707–8	17	5,860
1659–60	7	2,140			

*Krishna, *Commercial Relations between India and England*, pp. 323-24.
†The tonnage differs in Macgregor, *Commercial Statistics*, v. 4, pp. 404-06.

APPENDIX IX

IMPORTS AND EXPORTS OF THE EAST INDIA COMPANY TO THE EAST*

Year	No. of Ships Sent Out	Export			Import £	Balance + Favor of Co. − Against Co.
		Money £	Goods £	Total £		
1601........	4	21,742	6,860	....	....	....
1603........	4	11,160	1,142	....	....	....
1606........	3	17,600	7,280	....	....	....
1607........	2	15,000	3,400	....	1601 to 1621	....
1608........	1	6,000	1,700	....	total equalled	....
1609........	3	28,500	21,300	....	2,004,600	....
1610........	4	19,200	10,081	....	....	....
1611........	4	17,675	10,000	....	....	....
1612........	1	1,250	650	....	....	....
1613........	5	18,810	12,446	....	....	....
1614........	9	13,942	23,000	....	....	....
1615........	8	26,660	26,065	....	....	....
1616........	7	52,087	16,506	....	....	....
1617........	9 }					
1618........	9 }	298,000	152,000	....	....	....
1619........	8 }					
1620........	10	62,490	28,508	....	}	....
1621........	4	12,900	6,523	....	} 1,255,444	....
1622........	5	61,600	6,430	....	}	....
1623........	7	68,720	17,345	....	}	....
1624........	..	....	....	62,000	120,000	....
1625........	..	....	....	80,000	103,000	....
1626........	..	....	....	90,710	360,000	....
1627........	..	....	....	64,700	....	....
1628........	..	....	....	61,000	571,000	....
1629........	..	....	....	200,000	104,587	....
1630........	..	....	....	334,171	....	....
1631........	..	....	....	160,700	170,000	....
1632........	..	....	....	22,454	70,000	....
1633........	..	....	....	80,386	303,000	....
1634........	..	....	....	95,000	58,000	....
1635........	..	....	....	162,780	....	....
1636........	..	....	....	40,342	200,000	....
1637........	..	....	....	31,719	49,309	....
1638........	..	....	....	22,000	....	....
1639........	..	....	....	42,427	218,701	....
1640........	..	....	....	50,000	40,800	....
1641........	..	....	....	95,000	127,507	....
1642........	..	....	....	82,928	....	....
1643........	..	....	....	92,130	173,000	....
1644........	..	....	....	50,000	....	....
1645........	..	....	....	60,000	....	....
1646........	..	....	....	60,000	2,229	....
1647........	..	....	....	80,000	100,000	....
1648........	..	....	....	116,000	80,000	....
1649........	..	....	....	70,000	....	....
1650........	..	....	....	102,000	50,000	....
1651........	..	....	....	70,000	90,000	....
1652........	..	....	....	30,000	40,000	....
1653........	..	....	....	481	....	....

*Figures in this table are found in Krishna, *Commercial Relations between India and England*, pp. 282-87, 296-97, and 323-24; Macpherson, *European Commerce with India*, pp. 419-20, and Macgregor, *Commercial Statistics*, v. 4, pp. 407-410.

IMPORTS AND EXPORTS OF THE EAST INDIA COMPANY TO THE EAST—*Continued*

Year	No. of Ships Sent Out	Export			Import £	Balance + Favor of Co. − Against Co.
		Money £	Goods £	Total £		
1654	..	....	......	7,372	......	......
1655	..	....	......	4,215	......	......
1656	..	....	......	16,622	......	......
1657	..	....	......	None	......	......
1658	..	242,304	......	305,750	......	......
1659	..	22,768	......	63,996	......	......
1660	..	151,077	......	188,033	......	......
1661	..	100,940	......	126,148	......	......
1662	..	91,224	......	138,330	......	......
1663	..	125,435	......	169,513	......	......
1664	..	24,130	......	55,010	......	......
1665	..	17,007	......	37,607	......	......
1666	..	1,000	......	3,967	......	......
1667	..	143,384	......	206,453	......	......
1668	..	132,167	......	202,919	......	......
1669	..	199,678	......	282,340	......	......
1670	..	207,648	......	346,309	......	......
1671	..	197,883	......	304,093	......	......
1672	..	....	......	182,612	......	......
1673	..	177,938	......	238,805	......	......
1674	..	325,517	......	440,551	......	......
1675	..	324,039	......	448,193	......	......
1676	..	189,290	......	288,249	......	......
1677	..	289,140	......	363,773	......	......
1678	..	340,884	......	387,725	......	......
1679	..	391,474	......	461,211	......	......
1680	..	524,197	......	596,657	......	......
1681	..	708,909	......	835,313	......	......
1682	21	....	......	515,216	......	......
1683	22	....	......	482,147	......	......
1684	14	....	......	520,341	......	......
1685	13	....	......	649,299	......	......
1686	6	....	......	298,958	......	......
1687	6	....	......	157,491	......	......
1688	2	....	......	30,239	......	......
1689	4	....	......	131,692	......	......
1690	6	....	......	125,101	......	......
1691	7	....	......	143,728	......	......
1692	5	....	......	171,812	......	......
1693	15	....	......	677,616	......	......
1694	9	....	......	395,391	......	......
1695	7	....	......	228,622	......	......
1696	4	....	......	115,570	......	......
1697	9	....	......	388,658	......	......
1698	14	....	......	590,914	......	......
1699	12	....	......	592,753	......	......
1700	7	....	......	452,716	......	......
1701	9	....	......	317,293	......	......
1702	12	....	......	220,223	......	......
1703	13	....	......	411,745	......	......
1704	17	....	......	349,711	......	......
1705	9	....	......	198,138	......	......
1706	9	....	......	333,245	......	......
1707	15	....	......	502,983	......	......
1708	10	....	......	550,358	......	......
1709	13	....	......	513,733	......	......

IMPORTS AND EXPORTS OF THE EAST INDIA COMPANY TO THE EAST—*Concluded*

Year	No. of Ships Sent Out	Export			Import £	Balance + Favor of Co. − Against Co.
		Money £	Goods £	Total £		
Total for Five-Year Periods 1601-1710						
1601-05	11	32,902	8,002	40,904	....	....
1605-10	6	67,100	33,680	100,780	....	....
1610-15	33	70,877	56,177	127,054	....	....
1615-20	44	376,747	194,571	471,318	....	....
1620-25	28	267,710	58,806	326,516	1,375,444	+1,048,936
1625-30	30	....	....	496,410	1,149,187	+ 652,777
1630-35	31	....	....	692,711	601,000	− 91,711
1635-40	16	....	....	299,268	468,010	+ 178,742
1640-45	25	....	....	380,058	341,307	− 38,751
1645-50	25	....	....	386,000	182,229	− 203,771
1650-55	23	....	....	209,853	180,000	− 129,853
1655-60	36	....	....	390,583	....	....
1660-65	47	492,806	184,318	677,124	....	....
1665-70	44	493,236	240,051	733,287	....	....
1670-75	75	708,786	703,584	1,512,370	....	....
1675-80	59	1,534,827	414,224	1,949,051	....	....
1680-85	90	....	....	2,798,413	....	....
1685-90	31	....	....	1,267,679	....	....
1690-95	42	....	....	1,513,648	....	....
1695-1700	46	....	....	1,916,417	....	....
1700-05	58	....	....	1,751,688	....	....
1705-10	56	....	....	2,098,457	....	....
From here on the figures are not totals for five-year periods but simply figures for the years given.† (Figures in thousands of £)						
1710	15	375	200	556	496	} + 421
1711	12	327	162	474	955	}
1715	12	422	60	476	1,159	+ 683
1720	20	454	121	564	1,397	+ 832
1725	12	466	79	537	1,519	+ 981
1730	13	539	136	661	1,589	+ 928
1735	16	487	185	654	1,997	+1,343
1740	19	489	257	721	1,795	+1,073
1745	22	481	217	677	2,480	+1,803
1750	16	816	305	1,091	2,221	+1,130
1755	15	625	245	846	2,106	+1,259
1760	21	91	520	564	2,570	+2,005
1765	23	317	538	812	2,789	+1,977
1770	31	305	520	782	3,688	+2,905
1775	19	10	510	487	3,638	+3,150
1780	20	15	386	616	3,402	+2,785
1785	43	724	529	1,253	5,259	+4,005
1790	25	532	928	1,461	6,035	+4,573
1795	76	38	1,260	1,298	8,098	+6,799
1800	49	601	1,702	2,304	10,323	+8,018
1805	49	699	1,897	2,597	8,791	+6,194
1810	53	....	1,876	1,876	9,572	+7,695

†Columns one and two are from Macpherson, *India*, pp. 419-20. Columns 3-5 are from Macgregor, *Commercial Statistics*, v. 4, pp. 407-08. The merchandise and bullion total will therefore not coincide exactly with the export total, as Macgregor's figures differ slightly from those of Macpherson.

APPENDIX X

THE FIRST TWENTY YEARS OF THE EAST INDIA COMPANY'S TRADE*

Year	Capital Stock of the Voyage £	No. of Ships	Cost of Equipping the Ships £	Amount of Mdse. Taken Out £	Amount of Bullion £	Profits Per Cent
1601	68,373	4	39,771	6,860	28,742 }	95
1604	60,450	4	48,140	1,142	11,160 }	
1606-07	53,500	3	28,620	7,280	17,600	234
1607-08	33,000	2	14,600	3,400	15,000	Wrecked
1608-09	13,700	1	6,000	1,700	6,000	211
1809–10	82,000	3	32,200	21,300	28,500	121
1610-11	71,581†	4	42,500	10,081	19,200	218
1611-12	76,375	4	48,700	10,000	17,675	211
1612	7,200	1	5,300	650	1,250	160
Joint Stock—						
1612-17	429,000	29	272,544 – Disbursed in 4 voyages.			87½
1613	......	8	......	12,446	18,810 }	120
1614	......	8	......	23,000	13,942 }	
1615	......	6	......	26,065	26,660	Very low
1616	......	7	......	16,506	52,087	......
Second Joint Stock—						
1617	1,629,040 of which 800,000 was distributed to 3 voyages.					
1617	200,000	9 }	350,000	152,000	298,000	......
1618	200,000	8 }				
1619	400,000	8 }				

*This table is based upon Bruce, *Annals of the East India Company*, v. 1, pp. 146-240; Macgregor, *Commercial Statistics*, v. 4, pp. 300-318; Macpherson, *India*, pp. 81-110; Hunter, *Br. India*, v. 1, pp. 291-307; Milburn, *Oriental Commerce*, v. 1, pp. v-xviii.

†Regarding the voyages of 1610-11. Bruce differs from Macpherson, Milburn, and Macgregor. The difference, however, arises from the manner in which they separated the voyages. If voyage 7 and 8 of Milburn, Macpherson, and Macgregor are combined they correspond with no. 7 of Bruce. Combine voyages 9, 10, and 11 of Macpherson, Milburn, and Macgregor and the result is number 8 of Bruce. Voyage number 12 of Milburn, Macgregor, and Macpherson is voyage 9 of Bruce. If Bruce is followed there were really only 9 voyages before the joint stock was formed in 1612 instead of 12 as ordinarily stated. Bruce's division is used because it is most complete and based upon cited documents. Bruce, Milburn, and Macpherson wrote at practically the same time. All agree that there were 26 ships in the voyages between 1601-12. Macgregor obviously copied from Macpherson, and Milburn and the version which they give is as follows:

Year	*No. of Voyage*	*Capital Stock*	*No. of Ships*	*Profit Per Cent*
1610	7	15,364	1	218
1611	8	55,947	3	211
1612	9	19,164	1	160
1612	10	46,092	2	148
1612	11	10,669	1	320
1612	12	7,142	1	133

APPENDIX XI

PROGRESS OF THE DUTCH TRADE*

(A) Year	Ships	Value in Florins	(A) Year	Ships	Value in Florins
1599–1613....	77	13,100,000	1669.........	19	4,026,481
1614.........	2	433,526	1670.........	19	5,024,150
1615.........	5	511,672	1671.........	18	5,186,414
1616.........	5	566,064	1672.........	15	4,023,998
1617.........	4	573,007	1673.........	7	1,688,316
1618.........	8	1,305,544	1674.........	9	1,836,015
1619.........	5	1,074,047	1675.........	14	3,549,518
1620.........	6	913,137	1676.........	15	4,127,657
1621.........	6	1,094,030	1677.........	15	3,575,483
1622.........	8	1,776,792	1678.........	11	2,459,739
1623.........	8	1,301,909	1679.........	12	3,889,605
1624.........	6	832,836	1680.........	11	3,386,577
1625.........	4	983,461	1681.........	13	5,110,897
1626.........	10	1,926,019	1682.........	8	2,987,190
1627.........	7	1,748,099	1683.........	11	4,909,309
1628.........	7	2,050,367	1684.........	15	5,080,391
1629.........	7	1,132,263	1685.........	14	4,193,729
1630.........	9	2,541,215	1686.........	16	5,568,644
1631.........	7	1,506,669	1687.........	16	5,630,940
1632.........	7	2,099,772	1688.........	15	4,305,812
1633.........	7	1,861,409	1689.........	15	3,092,896
1634.........	7	1,947,270	1690.........	17	3,839,469
1635.........	6	2,050,037	1691.........	8	2,400,104
1636.........	8	1,895,349	1692.........	12	4,246,879
1637.........	8	2,673,201	1693.........	15	3,336,236
1638.........	7	1,670,071	1694.........	12	2,988,927
1639.........	8	3,079,413	1695.........	15	5,154,468
1640.........	10	2,842,405	1696.........	12	3,532,244
1641.........	10	2,906,117	1697.........	19	5,410,517
1642.........	9	3,485,192	1698.........	19	5,373,256
1643.........	10	3,227,882	1699.........	17	5,321,290
1644.........	7	2,070,667	1700.........	18	5,298,741
1645.........	8	2,921,806	1701.........	20	6,293,703
1646.........	9	2,529,611	1702.........	21	6,725,962
1647.........	10	2,151,033	1703.........	18	6,177,447
1648.........	12	2,073,630	1704.........	21	5,382,196
1649.........	9	2,243,106	1705.........	18	4,603,338
1650.........	9	1,946,417	1706.........	17	4,719,600
1651.........	11	2,699,991	1707.........	15	4,248,532
1652.........	11	2,813,438	1708.........	18	5,219,729
1653.........	16	4,745,239	1709.........	18	5,477,439
1654.........	4	379,035	1710.........	21	5,732,998
1655.........	10	2,467,112	1711.........	20	5,311,869
1656.........	10	2,711,914	1712.........	21	6,111,822
1657.........	10	3,023,855	1713.........	17	4,684,643
1658.........	10	3,005,275	1714.........	21	5,260,128
1659.........	10	1,782,783	1715.........	27	7,730,000
1660.........	11	3,195,319	1716.........	28	6,825,290
1661.........	9	2,133,791	1717.........	28	7,299,512
1662.........	9	3,354,429	1718.........	24	7,175,000
1663.........	10	3,324,894	1719.........	30	8,352,000
1664.........	12	2,528,825	1720.........	26	7,600,000
1665.........	13	3,643,492	1721.........	34	10,235,000
1666.........	7	1,124,180	1722.........	26	....
1667.........	12	3,119,060	1723.........	29	8,800,000
1668.........	16	3,155,683	1724.........	31	....

*Krishna, *Commercial Relations between India and England*, pp. 289-91.

PROGRESS OF THE DUTCH TRADE—*Concluded*

(B) Years	Ships Sent Out	Crews	Specie Thousands Florins	Ships Returned	Proceeds of Sales Florins
1720	36	8,205	4,125	26	19,597,875
1721	40	8,000	6,825	34	14,985,073
1722	41	7,400	7,075	26	19,494,366
1723	38	7,785	6,887	29	16,247,506
1724	38	6,425	7,419	31	20,577,447
1725	35	6,250	7,412	36	19,385,441
1726	38	6,850	7,675	32	21,312,626
1727	40	6,400	8,092	36	18,564,987
1728	34	5,800	5,558	28	20,322,402
1729	34	6,390	4,525	25	18,100,117
Total for 10 years	374	69,505	65,593	303	188,587,840
Annual average	37½	6,950	6,559,300	30	18,858,784

(C) Years	Invoices Florins	Sales Florins	Ships
1750	7,372,177	19,024,209	22
1751	9,630,682	16,670,614	24
1752	7,883,361	23,133,580	20
1753	10,259,866	17,317,037	22
1754	8,859,297	19,840,766	22
1755	9,652,485	19,806,077	22
1756	8,421,419	19,890,066	25
1757	8,935,720	14,829,367	26
1758	6,506,717	18,934,386	22
1759	8,437,469	18,817,328	28
Total for 10 years	85,959,193	188,263,430	233
Annual average	8,595,919	18,826,343	23

APPENDIX XII

NUMBERS OF CHRISTIANS IN CHINA*

Year	Number of Priest	Estimated Numbers of Converts by Different Authorities	Number of Churches
1617	....	13,000	......
1627	....	13,000	......
1637	....	40,000	......
1650	....	150,000	......
1663	....	109,000	......
1664	....	254,980	......
1695	75 = 38 Jesuits	......	......
	9 Spanish Dominicans	......	......
	5 Spanish Augustinians	......	......
	7 French Jesuits	......	......
	12 Spanish Franciscans	......	......
	4 Italians	......	......
1700	....	500 adults baptized yearly in Peking	
1702	70 or more	......	......
1702	Another estimate 117 of which there were	......	......
	59 Jesuits	......	......
	29 Franciscans	......	......
	8 Dominicans	......	......
	15 Secular Priests	......	......
	6 Augustinians	......	......
1705	....	300,000	......
1724	....	300,000	300

*Latourette, *History of Christian Missions in China*, pp. 107, 128, 129, 158.

APPENDIX XIII

TRADE OF THE EAST INDIA COMPANY AT AMOY AND CHUSAN*

Year	Merchandise	Bullion	Total Import	Export	No. of Ships	Ton-nage
			Amoy			
1677....	T. 2,110	T. 4,778	T. 6,888	T. 13,499	1	...
1681....	£ 10,450	£ 12,500	£ 22,950	....	1	...
1682....	£ 14,599	£ 28,000	£ 42,599	No trade	4	760
1684....	....	....	....	....	1	...
1685....	....	....	....	....	1	170
1687....	....	£ 5,500 –	....	....	3	...
1694....	....	....	....	....	1	200
1698....	£ 2,500 –	£ 20,000 –	£ 65,000	....	2	650
1699....	....	....	£ 37,554	....	1	280
1700....	....	....	£ 38,126	....	1	250
1701....	....	....	£ 57,409	T. 32,473 –	2	445
1702....	T. 73,657	T. 150,000	T. 326,926	T. 309,157	3	1108
1704....	£ 3,770	£ 15,071	£ 35,345	T. 86,686	2	895
1735....	....	....	£ 29,964	....	1	460
			Chusan			
1700....	....	....	....	T. 87,196 –	2	560
1701....	....	....	£ 50,611	T. 82,198 –	2	525
1702....	....	....	£ 101,310	T. 230,000	3	688
1703....	....	....	£ 20,000 –	T. 178,448 –	4	390+
1704....	....	....	£ 16,345	T. 35,000	1	250
1707....	£ 2,781	£ 21,000	£ 23,781	....	1	250
1710....	....	....	£ 35,260	....	1	330
1736....	£ 2,068	£ 37,205	£ 39,273	T. 121,152	1	490

*Based on figures given in the back of Morse, *Chronicle*, v. 1.

APPENDIX XIV

EAST INDIA COMPANY'S TRADE AT CANTON*

Year	Imports in Mdse.	Imports in Coin	Total Imports	Exports	No. of Ships	Total Tonnage
1635†.......	....	....	....	....	1	.....
1637........	....	142,000 R8/8	142,000 R8/8	62,000 R8/8	4	.....
1644†.......	....	....	....	....	1	.....
1664†.......	....	....	9,573 R8/8	....	1	.....
1673†.......	....	....	....	....	1	.....
1683†.......	....	....	....	....	1	.....
1689†.......	£	£	£	Taels	1	730
1699........	£ 5,475	£ 26,611	£ 32,086	T. 45,928	1	250
1700........	....	....	....	38,080	1	350
1701........	....	....	....	46,876	2	380
1702........	....	....	....	55,000	1	270
1703........	....	30,000	30,000	....	1	350
1704........	4,966	46,484	51,450	127,000	4	1,460
1707........	2,680	43,000	45,680	....	1	350
1708........	....	....	36,290	....	1	220
1709........	2,635	31,000	33,635	....	1	330
1711........	....	....	80,512	....	2	650
1712........	....	....	82,492	....	2	700
1713........	....	....	34,322	....	1	350
1714........	....	....	19,916	....	1	250
1715........	....	....	52,069	....	1	450
1716........	....	....	89,167	54,000+	3	1,060
1717........	6,652	68,000	74,652	....	2	670
1718........	5,278	56,000	61,278	....	2	640
1719........	5,611	62,000	67,611	....	2	650
1720........	13,946	132,000	145,946	....	4	1,480
1721........	6,476	109,000	113,476	326,763	4	1,670
1722........	8,931	96,000	104,931	277,631	3	1,290
1723........	2,888+	34,000+	166,862	271,340	5	1,920
1724........	....	....	50,369	175,000	1	450
1725........	....	80,582	80,582	210,000	3	1,230
1726........	....	....	....	142,393	1	370
1727........	....	....	....	162,501	1	495
1728........	....	....	100,148	....	4	1,750
1729........	4,317	160,000	164,317	420,000	4	1,900
1730........	4,500	200,000	204,500	489,946	5	2,095
1731........	4,249	219,000	223,249	721,125	4	1,810
1732........	3,881	163,000	166,881	....	4	1,850
1733........	20,000	70,000	90,000	294,025	2	910
1734........	2,986	80,000	82,986	296,291	2	810
1735........	1,830	77,000	78,830	90,617+	2	955

*For the years from 1635-1771 figures are based on tables in the back of Morse, *Chronicle*, v. 1. For years 1775-95 figures are based on tables in the back and at the beginning of every chapter of Morse, *Chronicle*, v. 2, including pp. 11, 12, 29, 35, 40, 50, 61, 84, 95, 111, 119, 136, 152, 173, 180, 184, 193, 205, 256, 266.

†These ships were forced to leave without cargoes except the *Surat* in 1664 which obtained a partial one.

EAST INDIA COMPANY'S TRADE AT CANTON—*Concluded*

Year	Imports in Mdse.	Imports in Coin	Total Imports	Exports	No. of Ships	Total Tonnage
1736.......	11,200+	28,000+	119,194	....	3	1,425
1737.......	....	....	95,147+	31,488+	4	1,920
1738.......	3,829	162,000	165,829	....	5	2,040
1739.......	....	....	107,867+	....	5	2,470
1740.......	....	....	35,541+	....	2	990
1741.......	....	....	136,500+	....	6	2,934
1742.......	....	....	....	....	4	1,973
1743.......	....	....	70,392+	....	2	988
1744.......	....	....	30,480+	....	3	1,494
1745.......	....	....	104,509	....	3	1,494
1746.......	....	....	109,601+	....	6	2,988
1747.......	9,722	40,000	149,722+	....	9	4,482
1748.......	....	....	....	....	8	3–4,000
1749.......	3,069	58,000	91,069+	....	4–8	2–3,000
1750.......	....	....	64,000	....	7–10	4–5,000
1751.......	23,492	137,600	161,092	....	10	4–5,000
1753.......	....	....	....	....	6	2–3,000
				£ Sterling		
1762.......	....	....	121,435	243,097	..	.....
1763.......	....	....	65,835	299,230	..	.....
1764.......	....	....	81,156	372,118	..	.....
1765.......	....	....	428,951	521,434	..	.....
1766.......	....	....	390,081	507,106	..	.....
1767.......	....	....	55,225	431,350	..	.....
1768.......	....	....	118,917	585,638	..	.....
1769.......	....	....	345,743	514,852	..	.....
1770.......	....	....	339,632	447,783	..	.....
1771.......	....	....	512,317	678,846	..	.....
	Tls.	Tls.	Tls.	Tls.		
1775.......	....	....	....	....	5	.....
1776.......	419,921	....	419,921	....	8	.....
1777.......	....	....	....	....	9	.....
1778.......	384,756	....	384,756	....	7	.....
1779.......	....	....	1,022,694	1,022,694	5	.....
1780.......	474,179	....	474,179	....	12	9,239
1781.......	....	....	....	....	11	.....
1782.......	....	....	....	745,250	5	.....
1783.......	895,526	8,640	904,166	....	14	.....
1784.......	693,445	....	693,445	....	13	.....
1785.......	687,299	....	687,299	2,965,000	19	.....
1786.......	976,018	2,062,080	3,038,098	4,500,000	29	.....
1787.......	845,493	1,912,320	2,757,823	5,258,676	29	.....
1788.......	1,322,476	2,094,878	3,417,354	4,566,653	26	.....
1789.......	1,295,799	1,321,920	2,617,719	4,433,431	21	18,144
1790.......	1,832,873	2,106,041	3,938,914	4,668,136	25	......
1791.......	1,938,595	172,800	2,111,395	3,349,281	11	11,454
1792.......	2,038,139	518,400	2,546,539	3,535,407	16	12,271
1793.......	2,151,130	....	2,151,130	3,838,868	18	17,486
1794.......	2,171,897	....	2,171,897	4,704,488	21	20,333
1795.......	1,969,288	....	1,969,288	3,508,839	16	......

APPENDIX XV

VALUE OF THE EAST INDIA COMPANY'S IMPORT TRADE AT CANTON*

Year	Woollens from England Tls.	Total from England Tls.	Total Co. Impt. from India† Tls.	Total Goods Tls.	Bullion Tls.	Grand Total Tls.
1776	254,062	363,482	146,347	419,921	....	419,921
1778	351,513	384,756	....	384,756	....	384,756
1780	403,462	433,657	45,522	474,179	....	474,179
1783	708,629	769,281	126,245	895,526	8,640	904,166
1784	614,027	653,083	40,362	693,445	....	693,445
1785	577,368	687,299	....	687,299	....	687,299
1786	742,152	877,585	98,433	976,012	2,062,080	3,038,098
1787	619,049	741,823	103,670	845,493	1,912,320	2,757,823
1788	1,107,427	1,232,876	89,600	1,322,476	2,094,878	3,417,354
1789	....	1,130,874	164,925	1,295,799	1,321,920	2,617,719
1790	1,192,263	1,621,201	211,672	1,832,873	2,106,041	3,938,914
1791	1,451,795	1,851,491	87,104	1,938,595	172,800	2,111,395
1792	1,594,854	1,901,683	136,456	2,038,130	518,400	2,546,539
1793	1,788,309	2,063,030	88,100	2,151,130	....	2,151,130
1794	1,741,429	2,152,678	19,219	2,171,897	....	2,171,897
1795	1,634,796	1,879,945	89,343	1,969,288	....	1,969,288

*Morse, *Chronicle*, v. 2, pp. 6, 30, 50, 83, 111, 118, 135, 151, 172, 179, 184, 192, 205, 256, 265.
†Mostly raw cotton.

APPENDIX XVI
MERCHANDISE AND BULLION EXPORTED TO CHINA*

Year	Bullion £	Merchandise £	Total £	Woollens £ †
1708	32,387	1,571	33,958	....
1709	41,637	9,055	50,692	....
1710	71,770	8,170	79,940	....
1711	90,478	2,662	93,140	....
1712	30,694	3,545	34,239	....
1713	17,616	2,289	19,905	....
1714	47,597	4,492	52,089	....
1715	84,642	5,234	89,876	....
1716	62,577	9,898	72,475	....
1717	55,634	5,369	61,003	....
1718	58,291	6,993	65,284	....
1719	143,588	8,327	151,915	....
1720	96,439	7,278	103,717	....
1721	127,670	10,084	137,754	....
1722	115,505	8,030	123,535	....
1723	43,455	4,899	48,354	....
1724	69,230	1,136	70,366	....
1725	38,804	4,372	43,176	....
1726	38,659	3,608	42,267	....
1727	113,484	4,340	117,824	....
1728	136,453	5,693	142,146	....
1729	195,751	5,345	201,096	....
1730	193,810	4,860	198,670	....
1731	159,101	5,595	164,696	....
1732	....	1,154	1,154	....
1733	75,574	4,646	80,220	....
1734	99,916	6,032	105,948	....
1735	109,872	6,078	115,950	....
1736	133,289	9,303	142,592	....
1737	140,065	12,476	152,551	....
1738	70,441	10,586	81,027	....
1739	94,241	8,379	102,620	....
1740	88,126	11,787	99,913	....
1741	51,203	8,346	59,549	....
1742	39,024	7,460	46,484	....
1743	40,820	6,780	47,700	....
1744	32,133	8,758	40,991	....
1745	103,648	13,585	116,233	....
1746	133,064	13,742	146,806	....
1747	....	....	....	....
1748	95,012	14,012	109,024	....
1749	205,798	27,639	233,437	....
1750	152,017	21,438	173,455	....

*Macgregor, *Commercial Statistics*, v. 4, pp. 404-06.
†Macpherson, *India*, p. 418.

MERCHANDISE AND BULLION EXPORTED TO CHINA—*Concluded*

Year	Bullion £	Merchandise £	Total £	Woollens £†
1751	189,295	38,455	227,750	....
1752	266,539	41,590	308,119	....
1753	276,333	46,936	323,269	....
1754	218,751	29,236	247,987	....
1755	141,901	27,488	169,389	....
1756	244,868	42,193	287,061	....
1757	235,818	37,907	243,725	....
1758	139,679	40,440	180,119	....
1759	122,932	50,980	173,912	....
1760	53,081	60,019	113,100	....
1761	25,154	81,335	106,489	....
1762	28,126	59,218	87,344	....
1763	....	72,729	72,729	....
1764	307,410	70,281	377,691	....
1765	294,526	73,842	378,368	....
1766	946	54,718	55,654	....
1767	....	136,384	136,384	....
1768	162,137	154,467	316,604	....
1769	233,045	179,246	412,291	....
1770	293,210	152,798	456,008	....
1771	199,615	147,082	346,697	....
1772	....	132,553	....	....
1773	....	80,051	....	....
1774	....	92,810	....	....
1775	....	99,114	....	....
1776	88,574	107,848	196,422	....
1777	....	126,233	....	....
1778	....	92,745	....	....
1779	....	4,846	....	....
1780	....	182,066	....	....
1781	....	67,151	....	129,179
1782	....	106,126	....	94,992
1783	....	120,084	....	113,763
1784	....	177,480	....	146,741
1785	704,254	270,109	974,363	224,612
1786	694,962	245,529	940,491	202,023
1787	626,897	368,442	995,339	323,107
1788	469,408	401,199	870,607	335,392
1789	714,233	470,480	1,184,713	354,717
1790	....	541,174	541,174	431,385
1791	377,685	574,001	951,686	484,705
1792	....	680,219	....	587,421
1793	....	760,029	....	628,582
1794	....	744,140	....	642,405
1795	38,150	632,310	670,460	527,020

APPENDIX XVII

RAW SILK IMPORTED FROM CHINA TO ENGLAND*

Year	Pounds	Year	Pounds
1708	849	1757	149,283
1711	11	1758	18,103
1713	3,662	1759	65,142
1714	9,494	1760	75,693
1715	14,936	......	......
1716	7,006	......	......
1718	23,700	......	......
1720	512	1773	203,401
1723	8,964	1774	276,781
1724	29,705	1775	167,229
1725	13,003	1776	244,839
1726	2,184	1777	221,902
1729	4,550	1778	266,678
1731	11,272	1779	234,906
1732	47,481	1780	301,300
1733	12,333	1781	301,301
1739	2,677	1782	79,725
1742	2,361	1783	241,107
1744	3,545	1784	100,602
1745	47,667	1785	98,920
1746	2,116	1786	59,551
1747	1,903	1787	366,878
1748	12,408	1788	312,182
1749	5,301	1789	257,022
1751	61,041	1790	216,005
1752	119,555	1791	203,539
1753	83,124	1792	104,830
1754	124,378	1793	165,435
1755	124,245	1794	99,365
1756	82,291	1795	154,590

*From 1708-1760 the figures are from Krishna, *Commercial Relations between India and England*, pp. 310-11. From 1773-1795 the figures are from Milburn, *Oriental Commerce*, v. 2, p. 256.

APPENDIX XVIII

AMOUNT OF TEA IMPORTED INTO ENGLAND (1664–1710)*

Year		
1664	2 lbs. 2 ozs. Sold at £4 5*s*.	
1665	22¾ lbs. Sold at 50*s*. per lb.	
1669	143 lbs. 8 ozs.	
1670	79 lbs. 6 ozs.	
1671	266 lbs. 10 ozs.	
1673-74	55 lbs. 10 ozs. Bought by the Company from some English coffee-house	
1675-77	No imports	
1678	4,717 lbs.	
1679	197 lbs. from Bantam	Sold from 11*s*. 6*d*. to 12*s*. 4*d*. per lb. (1679–1686)
1680	143 lbs. from Surat	
1681	None	
1682	70 lbs. from India	
1683-84	None	
1685	12,070 lbs. from Madras and Surat	
1686	65 lbs.	
1687	4,995 lbs. from Surat	
1688	1,666 lbs. from Surat	
1689	25,300 lbs. from Amoy and Madras	
1690	41,471 lbs. from Surat	
1691	13,750 lbs. permission trade	
1692	18,379 lbs. from Madras and in the permission trade	
1693	711 lbs. from Madras and in the permission trade	
1694	352 lbs. from Madras and in the permission trade	
1695	132 lbs.	
1696	70 lbs.	
1697	22,290 lbs. 30*s*. per lb. selling price 126 lbs. from Holland	
1698	21,302 lbs.	
1699	13,201 lbs. 20 lbs. from Holland	
1700	90,947 lbs. 236 lbs. from Holland	Sold at 16*s*. (1700–1707)
1701	66,738 lbs.	
1702	37,052 lbs.	
1703	77,974 lbs.	
1704	63,141 lbs.	
1705	6,739 lbs. from East India and Holland	
1706	137,748 lbs.	
1707	32,209 lbs.	
1708	138,712 lbs.	Sold at 16*s*. 2*d*. per lb. (1708–1710)
1709	98,715 lbs.	
1710	127,298 lbs.	

*Milburn, *Oriental Commerce*, v. 2, pp. 531-34.

APPENDIX XIX

EAST INDIA COMPANY'S TEA TRADE

APPENDIX XX

AMOUNT OF TEA SHIPPED FROM CANTON IN FOREIGN SHIPS*

Year	English		European		American		European and American		Total	
	Ship	Thousands of lbs.	Ship	Thousands of lbs.	Ship	Thousands of lbs.	Ship	Thousands of lbs.	Ship	Thousands of lbs.
1767–8......	8	4,580	11	12,767	..	......	11	......	19	17,348
1768–9......	12	7,249	10	12,167	..	......	10	......	22	19,416
1769–70.....	17	11,294	9	10,592	..	......	9	......	26	21,886
1770–1......	13	9,198	10	12,891	..	......	10	......	23	22,089
1771–2......	20	13,118	No	account	..	......	..	......	20	13,118
1772–3......	13	8,869	11	13,652	..	......	11	......	24	22,521
1773–4......	8	3,885	12	13,838	..	......	12	......	20	17,723
1774–5......	4	2,159	15	15,652	..	......	15	......	19	17,812
1775–6......	5	3,402	12	12,841	..	......	12	......	17	16,243
1776–7......	8	5,673	13	16,112	..	......	13	......	21	21,785
1777–8......	9	6,392	15	13,302	..	......	15	......	24	19,695
1778–9......	7	4,372	11	11,302	..	......	11	......	18	15,674
1779–80.....	7	4,746	10	12,673	..	......	10	......	17	17,419
1780–1......	10	6,846	10	11,725	..	......	10	......	20	18,572
1781–2......	9	6,857	5	7,385	..	......	5	......	14	14,243
1782–3......	6	4,138	16	14,630	..	......	16	......	22	18,768
1783–4......	13	9,916	21	19,072	..	......	21	......	34	28,989
1784–5......	14	10,583	16	16,551	2	888	18	17,531	32	28,114
1785–6......	18	13,480	12	15,715	1	695	13	16,410	31	29,891
1786–7......	27	20,610	9	10,165	5	1,181	14	11,347	41	31,957
1787–8......	29	22,096	13	13,578	2	750	15	14,328	44	36,425
1788–9......	27	20,141	11	9,875	4	1,188	15	11,064	42	31,206
1789–90.....	21	17,991	7	7,174	14	3,093	21	10,267	42	28,258
1790–1......	25	23,369	7	2,291	3	743	10	3,034	35	25,404
1791–2......	11	13,185	9	4,431	3	1,863	12	6,294	23	19,480
1792–3......	16	16,005	13	7,864	6	1,538	19	9,403	35	25,408
1793–4......	18	20,728	5	3,462	7	1,974	12	5,436	30	26,165
1794–5......	21	23,733	7	4,138	7	1,438	14	5,577	35	29,311

*Milburn, *Oriental Commerce*, v. 2, p. 486.

APPENDIX XXI

PROFITS MADE BY THE EAST INDIA COMPANY

(a) *PROFITS MADE BY THE COMPANY ON THE EASTERN TRADE**

Year	Profit on the Total Trade £	Year	Profit on the Total Trade £	Profit on Export Trade from England
1765–66..........	2,484,187	1787–88..........	492,687	....
1775–76..........	3,088,346	1788–89..........	393,620	....
1776–77..........	778,861	1789–90..........	432,735	....
1777–78..........	223,168	1790–91..........	909,987	....
1778–79..........	79,261	1791–92..........	966,379	....
1779–80..........	65,837	1792–93..........	860,703	....
1780–84..........	1,847,920	1793–94..........	726,247	116,858
1784–85..........	479,992	1794–95..........	1,054,334	98,379
1785–86..........	587,247	1795–96..........	1,136,429	25,731
1786–87..........	533,763	....	....	....

(b) *PROFITS MADE BY THE COMPANY ON EXPORT TRADE TO CHINA*†

	1793–94 £	1794–95 £	1795–96 £	1796–97 £	1797–98 £
Prime Cost and Charges....	1,336,739	1,595,493	1,408,087	1,285,765	1,292,803
Customs................	41,284	27,322	25,802	20,341	18,589
Freight and Demurrage....	418,028	372,346	472,487	521,074	601,413
Charges on Mdse. 5% of Sales amount.....	125,729	143,072	148,636	133,417	128,895
Total Cost and Charges....	1,921,780	2,138,233	2,055,012	1,960,597	2,041,700
Amount of Sales..........	2,514,594	2,861,424	2,972,664	2,668,346	2,577,890
Profit of the Trade........	592,814	723,189	917,652	707,749	536,190

(c) *FACTORY EXPENSE FOR THE SAME YEARS*‡

	41,271	42,687	27,434	46,755	40,636

*Macgregor, *Commercial Statistics*, v. 4, p. 411. This is after prime cost, customs, freight, demurrage, and other charges have been subtracted from sales amount. It shows complete profit on years sales.

†Milburn, *Oriental Commerce*, v. 2, p. 477.

‡*Ibid.*, p. 477.

APPENDIX XXII
EXACTIONS ON TRADE

(a) *EMPEROR'S IMPORT DUTIES 1700**

	Tls.
Broadcloth per 10 cubits (141 inches)	0.50
Cloth Rashes per 10 cubits (141 inches)	0.50
Perpetts per 10 cubits (141 inches)	0.15
Says, Shaloons per 10 cubits (141 inches)	0.15
Cambletts per 10 cubits (141 inches)	1.00
Lead, per picul	0.30

(b) *EXPORT DUTIES IN 1704 ACCORDING TO LOCKYER*†

	Tls.
Raw silk (values Tls. 120 to 160)	1.800 per picul
Woven silks (value Tls. 250 to 350)	2.200 per picul
Musk (value Tls. 13)	0.200 per catty
China-root (value Tls. 1.50)	0.100 per picul
Rhubarb (value Tls. 10 to 18)	0.100 per picul
Copper (value Tls. 11 to 12)	0.400 per picul
Sugar (value Tls. 1.20 to 2.30)	0.100 per picul
Tea (value Tls. 25 to 50)	0.200 per picul
Tutenague (value Tls. 3.90)	0.300 per picul

(c) *ACTUAL LEVY IN 1704 ACCORDING TO LOCKYER*‡

The Hoppo was sent from Peking to tax the trade, and naturally he did not content himself with the modest amount of duty demanded by the 'Emperor's tariff.' Lockyer gives a specific example of the amount actually paid as duty on 1,000 piculs of copper costing 10,900 taels:

	Tls.
1,000 Pecull of Copper at 4m. Custom	400.00
The Hoppos have 24% on the Custom	96.00
Difference in Weights, the Emperor's being 18 per Mille larger than others	8.92
	504.92
The Emperor and Hoppos are to be paid in Sisee Silver, which makes Currant Silver at 93	542.92
Singphang has 2% Currant Silver, on the Emperor's Sisee	8.00
Lusees and other Servants 8 can. 4 ca. per Pecull	84.00
Weigher, 2 Cash per Pecull	2.00
Boat and Cooley Hire, 2 can. per Pecull	20.00
The Linguists have 1% on the Value from the Merchants you buy of	109.00
The Hoppos after all this have 3% more on the Value of the Goods from the Merchants you buy of	327.00
Total	1,092.92

(d) *PRICE, DUTIES, AND PROFITS 1798*§

	Market Price Tls.	Duties and Charges Tls.	Net Value Tls.	Company's Sale Price Tls.	Merchants' Profit + Loss − Tls.
Broadcloth: Worsters, Yd.	1.40	0.20	1.20	0.90	+0.30
Supers, Yd.	1.90	0.20	1.70	1.40	+0.30
Superfines, Yd.	2.50	0.60	2.30	2.10	+0.20
Camlets (average), Piece	40.00	10.00	30.00	27.50	+2.50
Lone Ells, Piece	9.00	1.30	7.70	6.70	+1.00
Lead, Picul	6.40	9.80	5.60	5.00	+0.60
Tin, Picul	13.20	2.50	10.70	15.00	−4.30

*Morse, *Chronicle*, v. 1, p. 93.
†*Ibid.*, p. 106; Lockyer, *Trade in India*, pp. 148-54.
‡Morse, *Chronicle*, v. 1, pp. 106-07; Lockyer, *Trade in India*, pp. 154-56.
§Morse, *Chronicle*, v. 2, p. 315.

EXACTIONS ON TRADE—*Concluded*

(e) *MEASURAGE FEE ABOUT 1800*¶

	Tls.
Basic measurage fee	1,387
Emperor's allowance deduced	277
Emperor's net duties	1,109
Add 7% to make it sycee	77
	1,187
10% of this amount to the Hoppo	118
	1,306
To the Collectors, etc., 2%	22
	1,328
Cumshaw	1,950
Total *Tls.*	3,278

(f) *DAILY CHARGES FOR UNLOADING A SHIP AT CANTON ABOUT 1800***

	Tls.
Hoppo	2.000
The Secretary	0.720
The Writer	0.720
The Linguist	0.720
The Whampoa officers' eating	0.300
Ditto, betel-nut, etc	0.300
The Weigher	1.110
For a boat	1.440
Hoppo's man to protect the goods	0.200
To the Three Hoppo-houses	0.720
Hoppo's officers' eating	3.000
Totals per day	11.230

(g) *WHAT THE CONSOO FUND WAS USED FOR IN 1793*††

	Tls.
Cong Ka, a sum annually presented to the Emperor originally established instead of clocks, watches, etc., but continued altho similar articles are again demanded	55,000
Quan Suie, a contribution to defray the expenses of the Army, which is demanded whenever revolt increases the expenses in this Department:	
for Fukien	50,000
for Setchuen	25,000
To discharge debts of Sinqua to Europeans	42,500
Clocks, watches, and pieces of mechanism purchased for the Emperor by order of the Hoppo	100,000
Total for 1793	272,500

¶Milburn, *Oriental Commerce*, v. 2, p. 492.
***Ibid.*, p. 493.
††Morse, *Chronicle*, v. 3, p. 62.

APPENDIX XXIII

MEASURING FEES AT DIFFERENT PERIODS*

Year	Place	Size of Ships Tons	Basic fee Tls.	Cumshaw Tls.	Total
1635	Macao	.....	.....	.....	1,400 R8/8
1644	Macao	.....	.....	.....	3,500 R8/8
1664	Macao	.....	.....	.....	2,926 R8/8
					Tls.
1687	Amoy	.....	750	361	1,111
1689	Macao	730	1,500	300	1,800
1699	Canton	250	480	89	569
1700	Chusan	310	.....	.....	400
1701	Chusan	250	.....	.....	300
1702	Amoy	425	1,250	856	2,106
	Canton?	270	1,300	1,900†	1,300
1704	Amoy	495	.....	.....	2,850
	Canton	350	650	217	867
1722	Canton	480	.....	.....	3,050
1727	Canton	495	1,320	1,950	3,270
1730	Canton	470	1,111	1,950	3,061
1735	Canton	460	1,323	1,950	3,273
1741	Canton	460	1,011	1,950	3,051
1750	Canton	499	1,444	1,950	3,394
1775	Canton	864	1,788	1,950	3,738
1780	Canton	758	1,611	1,950	3,561
1785	Canton	914	1,989	1,950	3,939
1790	Canton	1,252	2,378	1,950	4,328
1796	Canton	1,200	2,375	1,950	4,325

*Based on Tables in the back of Morse, *Chronicle*, v. 1 and 2.

†Original demands were T. 1,300 basic and T. 1,900 cumshaw but the total was eventually reduced to T. 1,300. See Morse, *Chronicle*, v. 1, p. 126.

APPENDIX XXIV

CARGOES OF SHIPS AT CANTON, 1722*

Cargo of the *Emilia* and *Lyell*, intended for England:

	Tls.
Raw silk, 200 piculs at 150	30,000
Woven silks, 10,500 pieces	53,700
Quicksilver, 200 piculs at 42	8,400
Tea (all head), Congo, 500 piculs at 38; Bohea, 2,000 piculs at 27; Peckoe, 250 piculs at 38; Bing, 250 piculs at 35; Singloe, 1,500 piculs at 19	119,750
Total	211,850

For the *Eyles*, intended for Bombay:

	Tls.
Quicksilver, 100 piculs at 42	4,200
Vermillion, 50 piculs at 42	2,100
Tutenague, 1,200 piculs at 6	7,200
Sugar, 2,500 piculs at 3	7,500
Sugar Candy, 500 piculs at 6	3,000
Camphor, 100 piculs at 25	2,500
Chinaroot, 250 piculs at 2	500
Alum, 1,000 piculs at 1.5	1,500
	28,500

For the *Walpole*, intended for Madras:

	Tls.
Alum, 350 piculs at 1.5	525
Tutenague, 2,500 piculs at 6	15,000
Sugar, 3,000 piculs at 3	9,000
Sugar Candy, 250 piculs at 6	1,500
Camphor, 20 piculs at 25	500
Chinaroot, 500 piculs at 2	1,000
Tea, Bohea, 1,000 piculs at 27	27,000
Gold, of 93 Touch, to be paid for in Silver of 94 Touch, 500 Shoes, which suppose at Tls. 9.75 each Shoe, at 100 Tale Sisee, or Tls. 106.37 Dollar Money per 10 Ta. Weight of said Gold, will amount to	51,855
	106,380

*Morse, *Chronicle*, v. 1, p. 172.

APPENDIX XXV
ENGLISH AND FOREIGN SHIPS AT CANTON*

Year	Company	Country	French	Dutch	Swedish	Danish	American	Others	Total
1716	3	..	6	..	..	..	..	11	20
1732	4	2	..	2	1	..	..	2	11
1733	5	..	3	4	..	..	..	..	12
1736	4	1	3	2	1	1	..	..	12
1737	4	1	2	3	1	1	..	..	12
1738	5	..	3	2	2	2	..	..	14
1739	5	2	3	3	1	1	..	..	15
1740	2	..	3	3	..	1	..	..	9
1741	4	1	2	2	4	1	..	..	14
1747	8	..	..	6	4	2	..	..	20
1750	7	..	4	4	2	2	..	..	19
1751	7	3	2	4	2	1	..	..	19
1775	5	8	4	5	2	2	..	..	26
1776	8	16	5	4	2	3	..	..	38
1777	9	9	7	4	2	2	..	..	33
1778	7	10	4	4	2	1	..	..	28
1779	5	8	..	4	2	3	..	1	23
1780	12	12	..	4	3	3	..	1	35
1781	11	6	..	..	2	3	..	..	22
1783	13	3	8	..	3	3	..	8	38
1784	13	8	4	4	..	4	1	..	34
1785	19	9	1	4	4	3	..	5	45
1786	29	24	1	5	1	2	5	3	70
1787	29	33	3	5	2	2	2	5	81
1788	26	24	1	4	2	2	4	3	66
1789	21	37	1	5	..	1	15	..	80
1790	25	21	2	3	..	1	6	1	59
1791	11	12	4	2	1	..	3	2	35
1792	16	23	2	3	1	1	6	5	57
1793	18	22	..	2	1	..	6	2	51
1794	21	23	..	4	..	1	7	2	58
1795	16	17	..	..	2	..	10	2	47

*Based upon Morse, *Chronicle*, v. 1, pp. 157, 212, 218, 247, 261, 264, 275, 282, 292, and v. 2, pp. 11, 12, 29, 35, 40, 50, 61, 84, 95, 111, 119, 136, 152, 173, 180, 184, 193, 205, 256, 266, 278, 294; Anderson, *Origin of Commerce*, v. 3, p. 262; Milburn, *Oriental Commerce*, v. 2, p. 486.

APPENDIX XXVI

SIZES OF SHIPS AND THE NUMBERS OF THEIR CREWS*

Year	Size of Ships Tons	Number in Crew on English Company Ship	Number of English Ships at Canton		Estimated Total Number of English at Canton	Total Number of Foreign Ships at Canton	Estimated Total Number of Foreigners at Canton
			Company	Country†			
1600	600	200	..	..	....	..	.....
	300	100	..	..	....	..	.....
	260	80	..	..	....	..	.....
	100	40	..	..	....	..	.....
1609	1000‡	...	..	..	....	..	.....
1677	300–600§	...	..	..	....	..	.....
1700	500 largest	...	..	..	....	..	.....
1709–10	180	36	..	..	....	..	.....
	200	40	..	..	....	..	.....
	250	50	..	..	....	..	.....
	300	60	..	..	....	..	.....
	440	88	..	..	....	..	.....
	450	90	..	..	....	..	.....
	500	100	..	..	....	..	.....
1716¶	300 rep. ship	60	3	..	240	20	1,300
1732**	470 rep. ship	94	4	2	652	11	1,134
1733	440 rep. ship	...	5	..	....	12	.....
1736	470 rep. ship	...	4	1	....	12	.....
1737	480	...	4	1	....	12	.....
1738	490	...	5	..	....	14	.....
1739	495	...	5	2	....	15	.....
1740††	495	100	2	..	200	9	970
	French	127	..	..	....	..	.....
1741‡‡	495 rep. ship	100	4	1	500	14	1,680
	French	150	..	..	....	..	.....
1747§§	English 498	100	8	..	800	20	2,000
	French and Dutch 700	150	..	..	....	..	.....

*This table is based upon figures found in a number of books. Bruce, *Annals of the East India Company*, v. 1, p. 129; Macpherson, *India*, pp. 12, 74, 81, 87, 133, 144; Krishna, *Commercial Relations between India and England*, p. 325; Chatterton, *The Old East Indiamen*, pp. 182-86, 166-70, 230-32; Martin, *China*, v. 2, p. 146; Gutzlaff, *China History*, v. 2, p. 333; Anderson, *Origin of Commerce*, v. 3, p. 262; Morse, *Chronicle*, v. 1, pp. 154, 157, 212, 218, 247, 261-62, 264, 275, 282, 292, and v. 2, pp. 11, 12, 29, 35, 40, 50, 61, 84, 95, 111, 119, 136, 152, 173, 180, 184, 193, 205, 256, 266, 278, 294, 311, 322, 348.

†"The Country" ships were somewhat smaller than the Company ships after about 1790.

‡First ship built by the Company. The largest ever built in England up until that time.

§These were English Company ships and most of them ran around 300 tons.

¶These figures include ships at Canton and Macao. This is an exceptional year.

**Figures are not estimates but are actual numbers on shipboard, average crew for 2 Country ships = 140; for 2 Dutch ships = 108; for 1 Ostend = 140; 1 Swedish = 96; 1 Spanish = 30.

††Figures are not estimates but are actual numbers on shipboard with the exception of the English. Average crew for 3 Dutch ships = 85; for 1 Danish = 135.

‡‡Figures are not estimates but are actual numbers on shipboard. Average men for 1 Country ship = 100; for 2 Dutch = 110; for 1 Danish = 150; for 4 Swedish = 128.

§§Between 1740-1760 practically all of the Company ships were between 498-499 tons and probably averaged about 100 men per ship; Morse, *Chronicle*, v. 1, p. 150 and tables. See also Chatterton, *op. cit.*, pp. 182-86.

SIZES OF SHIPS AND THE NUMBERS OF THEIR CREWS—*Concluded*

Year	Size of Ships Tons	Number in Crew on English Company Ship	Number of English Ships at Canton		Estimated Total Number of English at Canton	Total Number of Foreign Ships at Canton	Estimated Total Number of Foreigners at Canton
			Company	Country†			
1750	499	100	7	..	700	19	1,900
1751¶¶	499	100	7	3	1000	19	2,289
About 1775***	400–500	70	..	..	....	..	.....
	560–600	85	..	..	....	..	.....
	600–650	90	..	..	....	..	.....
	650–700	95	..	..	....	..	.....
	499	100	..	..	....	..	.....
	750–800	101	..	..	....	..	.....
	900	110	..	..	....	..	.....
	1000	120	..	..	....	..	.....
	1100	125	..	..	....	..	.....
	1200	130	..	..	....	..	.....
1775	761	...	5	8	1300	26	2,600
1776	758	...	8	16	2400	38	3,800
1777	804	...	9	9	1800	33	3,300
1778	723	...	7	10	1700	28	2,800
1779	758	...	5	8	1300	23	2,300
1780	786	...	12	12	2400	35	3,500
1781	758	...	11	6	1700	22	2,200
1783	758	...	13	3	1600	38	3,800
1784	755	...	13	8	2100	34	3,400
1785	758	...	19	9	2800	45	4,500
1786	755	...	29	24	5300	70	7,000
1787	870	...	29	33	6200	81	8,100
1788	809	...	26	24	5000	66	6,600
1789†††	816	...	21	37	5800	80	8,000
1790	800	...	25	21	4600	59	5,900
1791	1021	...	11	12	2530	35	3,850
1792	804	...	16	23	4290	57	6,270
1793	1175	...	18	22	4400	51	5,610
1794	1050	...	21	23	4840	58	6,380
1795	787	...	16	17	3630	47	5,170
1796‡‡‡	1200	...	23	17	4800	54	6,480
1797	1200	...	18	22	4800	57	6,840
1798	884	...	16	16	3840	51	6,120
1799	1200	...	15	15	3600	52	6,240
1800	1200	...	19	21	4800	70	8,400

¶¶These figures with the exception of the English are based on an actual count, Morse, *Chronicle*, v. 1, p. 292. The average crew of 2 French ships = 140; of 4 Dutch = 110; of 2 Swedish = 137; of 1 Danish = 204.

***Based on Chatterton, *op. cit.*, pp. 230-32. Each ship had about 50-55 special titled men as listed on p. 230 while the number of foremast men differed with the size of the ship. Ships above 750 tons had the crew required by the East India Company. 100 men per ship is used as an average from 1740-95.

†††After 1789 the company began to order most of its ships to be built at 1200 tons. From 1790 to 1795 the average crew is taken as 110.

‡‡‡After 1796 most of the Company's ships were of 1200 tons burden. From 1796 to 1800 the average crew is taken as 120.

BIBLIOGRAPHY OF MATERIALS ACTUALLY USED

1. PRIMARY SOURCES

A. General Comment upon Source Materials

The sources for the study of Anglo-Chinese relations are exceedingly extensive and varied. The majority of these primary materials are found in English, but valuable suggestive and amplifying records are to be found in Portuguese, Dutch, French, Spanish, Russian, and Chinese. Because the great majority of these latter materials have been either more or less completely treated in English, or to a large extent translated or otherwise incorporated into British documents it seems unnecessary in this work to give especial attention to them. The English sources may be divided into the following groups:

Charters and Grants of Privilege made by the King to the East India Company and other groups.

The China Factory Record, found in manuscript form in the India Office under *China Materials*, Vols. 1-291. The essential part of this material is published in Eames, *The English in China*, and Morse, *Chronicles of the East India Company Trading to China*. (See *infra* for full titles).

Chinese Memorials, Edicts, and Communications, found in: *The Chinese Repository;* Martin, *China;* Morse, *Chronicle;* and Williams, *Middle Kingdom*. (*Infra*.)

Chinese Repository, a magazine published at Canton by E. C. Bridgman and S. Wells Williams between 1831-51. It contains articles by contemporary observers and translations of edicts, laws, correspondence, etc.

Court Record of the East India Company, found in manuscript form in the India Office under titles *Court Book* and *Home Miscellaneous*. Published partly in *Calendar of State Papers; Calendar of Court Minutes*, and other groups of documents. (See *infra* for full titles).

Diplomatic Correspondence, found published in *British and foreign State Papers; Calendar of State Papers; Correspondence Relating to China* (1834 and 1840); and Morse, *Chronicle*. (*Infra*.)

Hakluyt Society Publications, entitled *Voyages, Travels, and Discoveries of the English Nation*. Various volumes.

Indian Factory Records. The manuscripts are found in the India Office under *Factory Records*. These are published in part in Foster, *The English Factories in India*. (*Infra*.)

Letters exchanged between the Court of Directors and their agents in the East. The manuscripts are found in the India Office in the *Letter Book*, and *Letters Received from Bengal*. Some of the letters are published in Bruce, *Annals of the East India Company; Court Minutes; Calendar of State Papers;* Morse, *Chronicle; English Factories in India* (Cf. *infra*), and in Sir George Birdwood and W. Foster, *The First Letter Book of the East India Company* (1600-1619).

Marine Records of the East India Company, found in the India Office in manuscript form in *Marine Records, Miscellaneous; Marine Journals*, and other *Miscellaneous* records.

MOREAU, CAESAR, *East India Company's Records*. London, 1825.

Parliamentary Papers and Materials, including the *Parliamentary Histories; Commons Debates; Lords Debates;* Hansard, *Parliamentary Debates; Commons Journal; Lords Journal; Parliamentary History* (Cf. *infra*), and the reports of various committees of investigation appointed by the House of Commons.

Petitions and Memorials relating to the East India Company, found in all publications cited in twelve above, also in Bruce, *Annals of the East India Company; Calendar of State Papers* (*Infra*), and in various collections and individual publications.

Penal Code of China, translated by Sir George T. Staunton under the title *Ta Tsing Leu Lee*. London: Cadell and Davies, 1810.

Statutes of Great Britain, found in *Statutes at Large* and *Statutes of the Realm*. (*Infra*.)

Treaties, found in Hertslet, *Treaties between Great Britain and China* (*Infra*), or in his *Commercial Treaties* or in various other collections.

The following source materials in foreign languages are worth mentioning:

Archives diplomatiques.

MARTENS, *Nouveau recueil général des traités*.

Documents Remittidas da India (Portuguese).

Conselho Ultramarinho (Portuguese). Both in India Office.

Hague Transcripts. Series I and II, in the India Office.

B. Documentary Materials Consulted

BOWMAN, FLORENCE L. and ROPER, ESTHER J., *Traders in East and West*. London: Sheldon, 1924. Contains a number of extracts from original sources.

BIRDWOOD, SIR GEORGE C. M., *Papers of the East India Company*. Apparently published for the *Journal of Indian Art*. No date or place of publication is given, but it was obviously published after 1860. Contains pictures and facsimile copies of charters and papers of the East India Company.

British and Foreign State Papers (1833-1843). London: Harrison and Sons, various dates.

Calendar of the Court Minutes of the East India Company. 2 vols. 1635-43 and 2 vols. 1660-67. Edited by Ethel Bruce Sainsbury. Oxford: Clarendon press, 1907-ff. Referred to in footnotes as *Court Minutes*.

Calendar of State Papers, Colonial Series; East Indies, for years 1513-1616, 1617-21, 1622-24, 1625-29, and *East Indies and Persia* for years 1630-34. Edited by W. Noel Sainsbury. London: Eyre and Spottiswoode, various dates. Referred to in footnotes as *State Papers, Colonial*.

COBBETT, WILLIAM, *Parliamentary History* (1660-1803). London: Longmans and T. C. Hansard, various dates. Referred to in footnotes as *Parliamentary History*.

Commons Debates (1660-1743). London: R. Chandler, 1742-44.

Correspondence Relating to China, 1840. Blue Book.

Charters Granted to the East-India Company from 1601: also the Treaties and Grants made with, or obtained from, the Princes and Powers in India, from the year 1756 to 1772. London, about 1774.

Chinese Repository. 20 vols. Edited by E. C. Bridgman and S. Wells Williams. Canton, 1831-51. It was originally published in magazine form, and contains articles by contemporary observers and translations of edicts, laws, correspondence, etc.

English Factories in India, The (1618-69). 13 vols. Edited by William Foster. Oxford: Clarendon press, 1906-27. Referred to in footnotes as *Factories in India*.

GREY, ANCHITELL, *Debates of the House of Commons* (1667-97). 10 vols. London: O. Henry and R. Cave, 1763.

Hakluyt Society publications. *Voyages, Travels, and Discoveries of the English Nation*. London, various dates.

HANSARD, T. C., *Parliamentary Debates* (1803-1843). London: Longmans and T. C. Hansard, various dates.

HERTSLET, GODFREY E. P., *Treaties between Great Britain and China;* and between China and Foreign Powers; and orders in Council, Rules, Regulations, Acts of Parliament, Decrees, etc., affecting British Interests in China. 2 vols. London: Harris and Sons, 1908.

Journal of the House of Commons.

Journal of the House of Lords.

Lords Debates (1660-1743). London: E. Timberland, 1742-43.

MORSE, HOSEA BALLOU, *Chronicles of the East India Company Trading to China.* 5 vols. Cambridge U. S.; Oxford University press, 1926-29. The most recent and reliable source of material for the study of early Anglo-Chinese relations in publication. Referred to in footnotes as Morse, *Chronicle.*

MCCULLOCH, JOHN RAMSAY, *Select Collection of Early English Tracts.* London: Lord Averstone, 1859. Contains a valuable collection of tracts attacking the East India Company, and discussing economic problems of the 18th century.

Parliamentary History of England (1066-1660). 23 vols. London: William Sanby, 1751-71.

Petition and Remonstrance of the Governour and Company of Merchants of London trading to the East Indies, exhibited to the Right Honourable, the Lords and Commons, in the High Court of Parliament Assembled. London: Nicholas Bourne, 1641.

Report of the Select Committee of the Court of Directors of the East India Company upon the subject of the Cotton Manufacture of this Country, with appendices. London, 1793.

Statutes at Large. Edited by George K. Richards. London: Eyre and Spottiswoode, various dates.

Statutes of the Realm.

STEVENS, HENRY (Editor), *Dawn of the British Trade in the East Indies* as recorded in the Court Minutes of the East India Company (1599-1603). London: Henry Stevens, 1886.

WALTHOPE, J. (Editor), *Collection of Papers Relating to the East Indian Trade,* wherein are shown the disadvantages to a nation by confining a trade to a corporation with Joint-Stock. London: J. Walthope, 1730. Contains valuable examples of 18th century attacks upon the East India Company.

C. *Writings of Contemporary Observers in England and the Far East*

ALLEN, NATHAN, *The Opium Trade.* Lowell, Mass: James P. Walker, 1853. Has a strong bias against the opium trade. Is especially good for period after 1800, having descriptions and tables.

ANDERSON, AENEAS, *Narrative of the British Embassy to China.* London J. Debrett, 1795. A reliable and interesting account by a member of the Macartney Embassy. Particularly good for obtaining dates.

CHILD, SIR JOSIAH, *A Treatise Concerning the East-India Trade.* London: Robert Boulter, 1681. An able defense of the Company.

CLIVE, LORD ROBERT, *A Letter to the Proprietors of the East India Stock.* London: J. Nourse, 1764. A defense of his activities in India.

————, *Commercio-Political Essay on the Nature of the Balance of Foreign Trade* as it respects a Commercial Intercourse between Great Britain and France and Between Great-Britain and other Nations. London: Stockdale, 1791. An interesting exposition of 18th century political-economic thought.

————, *Complete View of the Chinese Empire,* London: Cawthorn, 1798. This appears to be a revised and reduced reproduction of Staunton's account of the Macartney Embassy.

————, *Considerations on the Dangers and Impolicy of Laying Open the Trade with India and China.* London: Longmans, 1813. An excellent argument in favor of continuing the Company's monopoly.

COCKS, RICHARD, *Diary* (1615-22). 2 vols. Published by the Hakluyt Society, London, 1883. The best source for the Company's trading experience in Japan and the early interest in the China trade.

CRAWFORD, J., *An Inquiry into Some of the Principle Monopolies of the East India Company.* London, 1830. An argument against the Company's monopoly.

DEFOE, DANIEL, *A Tour thro the Whole Island of Great Britain.* 2 vols. London, 1927. A good account of mid 18th century life and conditions in England.

GASKELL, PAUL, *The Manufacturing Population of England.* London: Baldwin and Cradock, 1833. An excellent account of the lives of workers during the early stages of the Industrial Revolution.

GRAY, *Chinese Empire.* See below: Tcheng, Ki Tong.

HAMILTON, ALEXANDER, *A New Account of the East Indies.* 2 vols. Edinburgh: John Mosman, 1727. Especially valuable as the account of a man who traded to China for many years.

HUC, E. R., *The Chinese Empire.* 2 vols. London: Longman, Brown, Green, and Longmans, 1855. An interesting account of a journey through China by a French missionary.

LOCKYER, CHARLES, *An Account of the Trade in India.* London: Samuel Crouch, 1711. A valuable contemporary account of trading conditions in China.

MILBURN, WILLIAM, *Oriental Commerce.* 2 vols. London: Block, Parry and Co., 1813. One of the most valuable and reliable accounts of the ports, produce, manufactures, and trade of the Orient obtainable for the period. The book is deduced from authentic documents, and founded on the practical experience of years of service for the East India Company and seven voyages to India and China. Has valuable statistics.

MORRISON, JOHN ROBERT, *A Chinese Commercial Guide.* Canton, first edition 1834. A valuable guide to conditions of trade at the time of the Opium War, and contains valuable documents.

MUNDY, PETER, *Travels of.* 2 vols. London: Hakluyt Society, 1919. Parts I and II of volume III of the second series. An especially valuable source in that Peter Mundy accompanied the Weddell expedition to Canton in 1637. It is amplified by documents from the India Office records.

OSBECK, PEHR, *A Voyage to China and the East Indies.* 2 vols. Translated by J. P. Forster. London: Benjamin White, 1771. An interesting account of conditions at Canton, and the attitude of the Chinese populace toward foreigners about 1750.

PAPILLION, THOMAS, *The East India Trade,* the most profitable trade of the Kingdom, and best secured and improved in a Co. of Joint-Stock. London, 1677. An able defense of the Company by one of its important members.

PARKER, EDWARD H., *China, her History, Diplomacy, and Commerce, from the Earliest Times to the Present Day.* London: John Murray, 1917. "Masses of diligent research packed into small compass," illuminated by the personal experience and observation of a careful student. Referred to in the footnotes as Parker, *China History.*

PHIPPS, JOHN, *China and the Eastern Trade.* Calcutta: Thacker and Co., 1835. Has reliable statistics and is filled with extracts from other contemporary observers.

PRICE, R., *Essay on the Population of England from the Revolution to the Present Time.* London: T. Cadell, 1780. The author presents evidence to show that England's population was on the decline when in reality it was on the rapid increase. An interesting comment on 18th century psychology.

ROBBINS, HELEN H., *Our First Ambassador to China.* London: John Murray, 1908. Valuable because it reproduces in full the *Journal* of Lord Macartney.

STAUNTON, SIR GEORGE LEONARD, *Authentic Account of an Embassy from the King of Great Britain to the Emperor of China.* London: W. Bulmer and Co., 1798. A most valuable account of the Macartney Embassy, written by its secretary. Has more descriptive details than documentary material. Has some valuable statistics in appendix.

STAUNTON, SIR GEORGE THOMAS, *Miscellaneous Notices Relating to China,* anp our Commercial Intercourse with that Country including a few translations from the Chinese Language. 2 vols. Edinburgh; 1822 and 1850. Referred to as Staunton, *Miscellaneous Notices.* Is very valuable for the period between 1812 and 1840. Was written by a man who knew the Chinese language and who served as a member of the Select Committee at Canton for many years.

TCHENG, GENERAL KI TONG and GRAY, JOHN HENRY, *The Chinese Empire Past and Present.* New York: Rand, McNally Co., 1900. A very interesting and valuable account of Chinese manners, customs, government, etc., by contemporary observers. Referred to in the footnotes as Gray, *Chinese Empire.*

2. SECONDARY MATERIALS

A. Books Relating to Foreign Relations in the Far East

ABBOTT, WILBER CORTEZ, *The Expansion of Europe* (1415-1789). 2 vols. New York: Henry Holt, 1924. A standard work on the expansion of Europe.

ANDERSON, ADAM, *Historical and Chronological deduction of the Origin of Commerce.* 4 vols. London: J. Walter, 1787. A standard work for all phases of English commercial development. Has valuable statistics.

AUBER, PETER, *China, an outline of its Government, Law, and Policy:* and of the British and Foreign Embassies to and intercourse with that Empire. London: Parbury, Allen Co., 1834. A chronological narrative of English intercourse with China by the secretary of the Court of Directors. It is based upon personal knowledge and the author had access to the documents. It is one of the two most complete connected accounts obtainable. Is generally accurate.

BAU, MINGCHIEN JOSHUA, *Foreign Relations of China.* New York: Fleming H. Revell Co., 1921. A valuable work by an American-trained Chinese.

BRUCE, JOHN, *Annals of the Honorable East India Company* (1600-1708). 3 vols. London: Cox, Son, and Baylist, 1810. The best obtainable account of the East India Company from 1600 to 1708. It is written by the keeper of the Kings State Papers and Historiographer of the Company. He had access to all of the documents and used them extensively.

CAMPBELL, GEORGE, *Modern India;* a Sketch of the System of Civil Government. London: John Murray, 1852. An especially valuable discussion of India in the 19th century showing the factors that influenced its relations with China.

CAWSTON, GEORGE and KEANE, A. H., *Chartered Companies* (1296-1858). London: Edward Arnold, 1896. A valuable treatment of early chartered companies with a good chapter on the East India Company.

CHATTERTON, E. KEBLE, *The Old East Indiamen.* London, n.d. The best account of the early ships and shipping of the East India Company.

CORDIER, HENRI, *Histoire des relations de la Chine avec les puissances occidentales* (1860-1900). 3 vols. Paris: Félix Alcan, 1901. Deals mainly with events after 1860 but has some valuable material upon the earlier periods.

CORNER, JULIA, *History of China and India.* London: Dean and Co., 1846. An ordinary brief discussion of the history of China and India.

DAVIS, JOHN FRANCIS, *China: A General Description of that Empire and its Inhabitants.* 2 vols. London: John Murray, 1857. Written by a one time supercargo and one of the Superintendents of British Trade after the abolition of the Company's monopoly. He defends the Company but his facts are generally reliable.

DENNETT, TYLER, *Americans in Eastern Asia.* New York: Macmillan, 1922. The standard work on Chino-American relations.

DOUGLAS, ROBERT K., *Europe and the Far East.* Cambridge: University press, 1904. A valuable account of relations between the Far East and Europe with excellent chapters upon the period covered in this work.

DUTT, ROMESH, *The Economic History of India Under Early English Rule* (1757-1837). London: Kegan, Paul, Trench, Trübner, 1906. An excellent discussion of the economic forces in India which had their reaction upon the Indo-China trade.

EAMES, JAMES BROMLEY, *The English in China* (1600-1843). London: Pitman and Son, 1909. Based upon a study of the East India Company's records. Is probably a more valuable and complete account of the East India Company's relations with China than is Auber.

EITEL, E. J., *Europe in China: the History of Hongkong to the Year 1882.* Hongkong: Kelly and Walsh, 1895. Morse considers this as "history written to support the utmost pretentions of the Hongkong residents."

FOSTER, JOHN W., *American Diplomacy in the Orient.* New York: Houghton, Mifflin, 1903. A good book for the later period of American relations, but has numerous errors in the early chapters.

FRAZER, R. W., *British India.* New York: G. P. Putnam, 1901. Valuable and readable account of the rise of English power in India and the Far East.

GUTZLAFF, REV. CHARLES, *China Opened, or a Display . . . of the Chinese Empire.* 2 vols. London: Smith Elder Co., 1838. A valuable work by a German missionary, but requires checking in many details. Personal observation and documentary evidence are blended. Referred to in footnotes as Gutzlaff, *China Opened.* By the same author see *A Sketch of Chinese History.* (*Infra.*)

HARRIS, NORMAN D., *Europe and the East.* New York: Houghton, Mifflin, 1926. Contains little information of value relative to the period discussed in this volume.

HUNTER, W. C., *The Fan-Kwae at Canton before Treaty Days, 1825-44.* London: Kegan, Paul, Trench, 1882. "Recollections of an eye-witness, one of the few having then any knowledge of the Chinese language."

HUNTER, SIR WILLIAM WILSON, *History of British India.* 2 vols. London: Longmans, 1899. A very complete and interesting account of the rise and expansion of English trade and power in the East by a competent and thorough student. A standard work.

ILBERT, SIR COURTENAY, *The Government of India.* London: Humphrey Milford, 1915. Perhaps the best historical account of the development of British rule and government in India.

IRELAND, ALLEYNE, *China, and the Powers.* Boston: Laurens Maynard, 1902. A special study of the problem without outstanding merits.

KAYE, JOHN WILLIAM, *The Administration of the East India Company;* a History of Indian Progress. London: Richard Bentley, 1853. A good discussion of the Company's rule in India showing its relationship to policies pursued in China.

KRISHNA, BAL, *Commercial Relations between India and England* (1601-1757). London: George Routledge, Sons, 1924. Has a good account of the development of English trade with India, and has invaluable trade figures based upon authentic documents. Figures are scattered throughout the book and the appendix is filled with tables.

LATOURETTE, KENNETH SCOTT, *History of Early Relations between the United States and China* (1784-1844). New Haven: Yale University, 1917. The best account of early Chino-American relations. It is based upon an extensive study of American documentary materials. Referred to in the footnotes as Latourette, *Early American Relations.*

LAVISSE, ERNEST et RAMBAUD, ALFRED, *Histoire générale.* Paris: Armand Colin, 1891-1901. Volumes V and VIII have valuable material relating to the subject of this work.

MACGREGOR, JOHN, *Commercial Statistics.* 5 vols. London: Whittaker and Co., 1850. Vols. 4 and 5 have valuable accounts of the East India Company's relations with the East, but the author has borrowed extensively from other sources without giving references. This is also the best statistical work available.

MACPHERSON, DAVID, *History of European Commerce with India.* London: Longmans, 1812. The best connected account of the early relations of all nations with China, India, and the Spice Islands. It is based upon valuable original sources, and has many statistics. Referred to in footnotes as Macpherson, *India.*

MACPHERSON, DAVID, *Annals of Commerce, Manufactures, Fisheries, and Navigation.* 4 vols. London: Nichols and Sons, 1805. A readable statistical and chronological account of the development of commerce. Referred to in footnotes as Macpherson, *Annals.*

MARTIN, R. MONTGOMERY, *China, Political, Commercial, and Social.* 2 vols. London: James Madden, 1847. Martin was in a position to get at the records and he gives a great mass of valuable material, but it is tinged with a bias toward China and toward opium while many of his dates are wrong. The volumes are filled with inaccuracies.

MATHESON, JAMES, *The Present Position and Prospects of the British Trade with China.* London: Smith, Elder Co., 1836.

MORSE, HOSEA BALLOU, *Trade and Administration of China.* New York: Longmans, Green and Co., 1921. Referred to in notes as Morse, *Trade and Administration.*

MORSE, HOSEA BALLOU, *International Relations of the Chinese Empire.* 3 vols. London: Longmans, 1910-18. Referred to in notes as Morse, *International Relations.* These two books are standard works upon the trade and foreign relations of China. They represent a carefully compiled mass of information, and are better for the 19th century than for earlier dates. Note also *The Gilds of China by the same author. (Infra.)*

OSBORN, SHERARD, *Past and Future of British Relations in China.* Edinburgh, 1860. A very prejudiced and unnoteworthy account of Anglo-Chinese relations during the first half of the 19th century.

OWEN, DAVID E., *Imperialism and Nationalism in the Far East.* New York: Henry Holt Co., 1929. Brief but interesting and readable; deals mainly with 19th and 20th century developments.

PITKIN, TIMOTHY, *Statistical View of the Commerce of the United States.* New Haven: Durrie and Peck, 1835. Has excellent statistical tables showing American trade with China.

REMER, CHARLES FREDERICK, *The Foreign Trade of China.* Shanghai, 1926. A good account of 19th century relations, but has little material on the 18th.

ROBINSON, F. P., *The Trade of the East India Company from 1700-1813.* Cambridge, 1912. A reliable account of the trade of the East India Company with an especially good chapter on China.

SARGENT, ARTHUR JOHN, *Anglo-Chinese Commerce and Diplomacy.* Oxford, 1907. The best short connected account covering the whole of Anglo-Chinese relations. It has only a few chapters dealing with relations before 1840.

SEE, CHONG SU, *Foreign Trade of China.* New York, 1919. A fairly good work for the 19th century relations, but has little material of value prior to that time.

SMITH, C. A. MIDDLETON, *The British in China and the Far Eastern Trade.* London: Constable and Co., 1920. Of little value for the period under examination but has some interesting biographical sketches.

SMITH, VINCENT A., *The Oxford History of India.* Oxford: Clarendon press, 1928. A very compact factual history of India with considerable emphasis upon the development of British rule.

———, *Universal History, Modern.* London: C. Bathurst, 1781. v. 7, *Tartary, China and Japan.* v. 8, *East Indes.* v. 9, *East Indes and the Ottoman Empire.* An interesting early account compiled from writings of contemporary observers. Often inaccurate.

WOODWARD, WILLIAM HARRISON, *A Short History of the Expansion of the British Empire* (1500-1870). Cambridge: University press. 1899.

WILLIAMSON, JAMES A., *A Short History of British Expansion.* New York: Macmillan, 1922. The last two books both contain sound, well-written chapters dealing with the expansion of England into the Far East.

B. Books dealing with Chinese History, Government, Law, and Culture

BASHFORD, JAMES W., *China, an Interpretation.* New York: Abingdon press, 1919. A sympathetic interpretation of Chinese life and culture by a Methodist missionary resident for many years in China.

BOULGER, D. C., *History of China.* 2 vols. London: W. Thacker Co., 1898. A reliable and valuable account of China's political history.

BARD, ÉMILE, *Chinese Life in Town and Country.* New York: G. P. Putnam's Sons, 1905. Interesting comments upon Chinese culture by a Frenchman.

BROOMHALL, MARSHALL, *The Chinese Empire, a general Missionary Survey.* Chicago: Fleming H. Revell Co., 1907. A good survey of protestant missions in the 19th century, but has little material upon the earlier centuries.

Catholic Encyclopædia. See articles under China, Missions, Rites Controversy, Ricci, Schaal, Verbiest, and Bulls.

DENBY, CHARLES, *China and Her People.* 2 vols. Boston: L. C. Page, 1906.

GILBERT, RODNEY, *What's Wrong in China?* New York: Frederick A. Stokes, 1926. A very prejudiced and biased picture of Chinese life and character by an American newspaper man.

GILES, H. A., *China and the Chinese.* New York: Columbia University press, 1912. Interesting lectures about Chinese things by one of the greatest authorities upon Chinese Civilization.

GORST, HAROLD E., *China.* London: Sands and Co., 1899.

GOODNOW, FRANK J., *China, an Analysis.* Baltimore, 1926. An interesting and illuminating discussion of the various phases of Chinese life by a competent American observer.

GOWEN, HERBERT H. and HALL, JOSEF W., *An Outline History of China.* New York: D. Appleton, 1927. One of the best and latest short histories of China by men versed in the Chinese language and thoroughly acquainted with things Chinese through personal experience.

GUNDRY, R. S., *China and Her Neighbors.* London: Chapman and Hall, 1893. Has an illuminating chapter on the relations between Tibet and India, but otherwise is only of ordinary interest.

GUTZLAFF, REV. CHARLES, *A Sketch of Chinese History, Ancient and Modern;* a Retrospect of the Foreign Intercourse and Trade with China. 2 vols. London: Smith, Elder Co., 1834. One of the best early histories of China by a German missionary. Based upon personal experience and documentary evidence. Referred to in the footnotes as Gutzlaff, *Chinese History.*

GUTZLAFF, REV. CHARLES, *Life of Taou-Kwang,* late Emperor of China. London: Smith, Elder Co., 1853. An interesting but none too reliable biography of the colorless Emperor, in which most of the space is devoted to a discussion of events in China for the fifty years preceding the date of publication. Note also *China Opened (Supra)*, by the same author.

HSIEH, PAO CHAO, *The Government of China* (1644-1911). Baltimore: John Hopkins press, 1925. By far the best account of the government of China during the Manchu period. The author has used both the Chinese and foreign sources and secondary works.

JERNIGAN, T. R., *China in Law and Commerce.* New York: Macmillan, 1905. A clear compilation from the best secondary and a number of original sources.

KRAUSSE, ALEXIS, *China in Decay.* London: Chapman and Hall, 1900 (third edition). A slightly biased work by a recognized authority on Chinese affairs during the 19th century.

LATOURETTE, KENNETH SCOTT, *The Development of China.* New York: Houghton, Mifflin, 1924. A reliable short analysis by one of the outstanding modern authorities on China. Enriched by personal observation and experience.

LATOURETTE, KENNETH SCOTT, *A History of Christian Missions in China.* New York: Macmillan, 1929. The very latest and most reliable single volume on missionaries in China. It is a carefully compiled and documented work. Referred to in the footnotes as Latourette, *Missions.*

LEONG, V. K. and TAO, L. K., *Village and Town Life in China.* New York: Macmillan, n.d. A valuable account of life in the basic units of Chinese society as interpreted by the Chinese themselves.

LEE, MABEL PING-HUA, *The Economic History of China,* with special reference to agriculture. New York: Columbia University, 1921. A valuable book by a Chinese woman student in America. Based upon original Chinese sources. About half of the work is devoted to translated extracts. One of the best books available on the history of Chinese agriculture.

MACGOWAN, JOHN, *A History of China from the Earliest Times down to the Present.* London: Kegan, Paul, Trench, Trübner and Co., 1897. Is a condensed imperial history of China based upon a minute study of the Chinese edition of the *Standard History of China.*

MARTIN, W. A. P., *The Awakening of China.* New York: Doubleday, Page Co., 1907. A mediocre work by the former president of the Chinese Imperial University.

MORSE, H. B., *The Gilds of China.* New York: Longmans, 1909. The standard work upon the gilds of China, with an especially worthwhile chapter upon the Canton Co-hong.

PARKER, EDWARD HARPER, *China Past and Present.* London: Chapman and Hall, 1903, and

PARKER, EDWARD HARPER, *China, her History, Diplomacy, and Commerce.* London: John Murray, 1917. Two excellent works by an English professor of Chinese who lived a great many years in China. Many facts are packed into a small space.

ROSS, E. A., *The Changing Chinese.* New York: Century, 1914. One of the best sociological interpretations of China by an eminent American sociologist. Based upon a year's intensive study and observation in China.

STEIGER, G. N., BEYER, H. O., and BENITEZ, CONRADO, *A History of the Orient.* Boston: Ginn and Co., 1926. An especially well written and unified account of the whole of Far Eastern History. Is, however, very simple and brief.

TREAT, PAYSON J., *The Far East,* a political and diplomatic history. New York: Harpers, 1928. A late book by a leading American authority. Has especially good chapters on the government under the Manchus and on the early trade relations.

VINACKE, HAROLD M., *A History of the Far East in Modern Times.* New York: Knopf, 1928. An especially good treatment of China since the opening of the 19th century.

WEALE, PUTNAM (Betram Lenox Simpson), *The Fight for the Republic in China.* New York: Dodd, Mead & Co., 1917.

WEALE, PUTNAM, *The Vanished Empire.* London: Macmillan, 1926. The latter is the best of this English publicist's numerous works on China. Both suffer in accuracy because of the breezy style.

WILLIAMS, EDWARD THOMAS, *A Short History of China.* New York: Harpers, 1928. Perhaps the most brilliant and inclusive single volume published on China in recent years by a competent student of Chinese literature and language. Referred to in footnotes as E. T. Williams, *China.*

WILLIAMS, S. WELLS, *The Middle Kingdom.* 2 vols. New York: Scribners, 1883. For many years, perhaps still, the standard analysis of Chinese culture. Referred to in footnotes as Williams, *Middle Kingdom.*

WILLIAMS, S. WELLS, *A History of China.* New York: Scribners, 1897. A short history with main emphasis upon the 19th century. Referred to in the footnotes as Williams, *History of China.*

C. Books Relating to English Political and Economic History

BOWDEN, WITT W., *Industrial Society in England toward the Close of the 18th Century.* New York: Macmillan, 1925. A reliable book as far as facts are concerned but out of date in the interpretation of the Industrial Revolution.

CHEYNEY, EDWARD P., *An Introduction to the Industrial and Social History of England.* New York: Macmillan, 1927. A standard brief treatment of English economic history.

CHALMERS, GEORGE, *Considerations on the Commerce, Bullion and Coin, Circulation and Exchanges;* with a view to our present circumstances. London, 1811. An excellent contemporary exposition of the commercial and financial problems of England, with many statistics.

CHAPMAN, S., *The Lancashire Cotton Industry.* Manchester: University press, 1904. An excellent study of the organization of the new machine industry.

CRAIK, GEORGE L., *History of British Commerce from the Earliest Times.* 3 vols. London: Charles Knight, 1844. Contains many figures on British trade but they are badly scattered.

CUNNINGHAM, WILLIAM, *The Growth of English Industry and Commerce during the Early and Middle Ages.* Cambridge: University press, 1905.

CUNNINGHAM, WILLIAM, *The Growth of English Industry and Commerce: Modern times.* 2 parts. Cambridge, 1907. The last two are standard works on English economic development, based upon enormous and painstaking researches. Valuable statistical tables are to be found in the appendix of part 2.

DIETZ, F. C., *The Industrial Revolution.* New York: Henry Holt, 1927. The latest interpretation of the Industrial Revolution. Very brief.

DIETZ, F. C., *A Political and Social History of England.* New York. Macmillan, 1927. An excellent economic interpretation of English political life.

ELLISON, THOMAS, *The Cotton Trade of Great Britain.* London: Effengham Wilson, 1886. The best statistical account of the development of the cotton industry.

HEWINS, WILLIAM A. S., *English Trade and Finance in the 17th Century.* London: Methuen, 1892. Perhaps the best treatment of the financial side of early chartered companies. Has several good chapters on the East India Company.

INNES, ARTHUR D., *England Under the Tudors.* London: Methuen, 1926. A standard work on the Tudor period.

LARSON, LAURENCE M., *History of England and the British Commonwealth.* New York: Henry Holt, 1924. An interesting political history enriched with cultural features.

LEVI, LEON, *History of British Commerce.* London: John Murray, 1872. A reliable account of the development of English commerce, with many statistics in the appendix.

LIPSON, E., *The History of Woollen and Worsted Industries.* London: A. and C. Black, 1921. One of the best accounts of the woollen industry.

LOWE, JOSEPH, *The Present State of England in regard to Agriculture, Trade, and Finance.* New York: E. Bliss and E. White, 1833. A reliable account of late 18th and early 19th century England.

MALTHUS, THOMAS R., *An Essay upon the Principles of Population.* 3 vols. London: John Murray, 1817.

MAITLAND, F. W., *Constitutional History of England.* Cambridge: University press, 1911. A standard work by a leading English constitutional lawyer.

MANTOUX, PAUL M., *The Industrial Revolution.* New York: Harcourt, Brace and Co., about 1927. A translation from the brilliant French original. Somewhat out of date in viewpoint, but still one of the most reliable interpretations of the Industrial Revolution supported by a mass of facts.

MOFFITT, LOUIS WILFRID, *England on the Eve of the Industrial Revolution.* London: P. S. King, 1925. A good account of industrial and agricultural organization in Lancashire about 1750.

SCHMOLLER, GUSTAV, *The Mercantile System.* New York: Macmillan, 1896. A translation from the original German of the founder of modern economic history.

SMART, WILLIAM, *Economic Annals of the 19th Century* (1801-1831). 2 vols. London: Macmillan, 1917. An excellent treatment of economic history as shown in the Parliamentary debates.

TASWELL-LANGMEAD, THOMAS PITT, *English Constitutional History.* New York: Houghton, Mifflin Co., 1881. For years the standard text book on English constitutional history. Exceptionally clear and readable.

TOYNBEE, ARNOLD, *Lectures on the Industrial Revolution.* New York: Longmans, 1908. Brilliant lectures by one of the earlier students of the Industrial Revolution.

TRAILL, H. D. and MANN, J.S., *Social England.* 6 vols. New York: G. P. Putnam, 1894. An excellent history of England from its social and economic side, with good chapters on commercial expansion.

TREVELYAN, G. M., *History of England.* London: Longmans, 1926.

TREVELYAN, G. M., *British History in the 19th Century.* London: Longmans, 1922. Brilliant and sparkling interpretations of English political history.

UNWIN, HUME, and TAYLOR, *Samuel Oldgnow and the Arkwrights.* New York: Longmans, 1924. Documentary account of the rise of early industrialists showing their attitudes towards trade and the influence of commercial crises upon them.

URE, ANDREW, *Cotton Manufacture of Great Britain.* 2 vols. London: H. G. Bohen, 1861. A valuable but prejudiced account by a great manufacturer.

USHER, ABBOTT P., *The Industrial History of England.* Boston: Houghton, Mifflin Co., 1920. An excellent short account with a good chapter on the East India Company and the cotton trade.

D. General Works—Good for Background Material

BOWLEY, A. L., *A Short Account of England's Foreign Trade in the Nineteenth Century.* New York: Scribners, 1893. One of the most reliable works on English trade during the century.

Cambridge Modern History. Vol. XI. Cambridge: University press, 1909.

DUTCHER, GEORGE M., *The Political Awakening of the East.* New York: Abingdon press, 1925. Treats the Mohammedan and Asiatic world generally, with an excellent chapter on China.

ELDRIDGE, FRANK R., *Trading with Asia.* New York: D. Appleton, 1926. A fairly good account of trading methods in recent times, but has little reliable material dealing with the earlier period.

Encyclopaedia Britannica. Under topics, China, Opium, and Tea.

GIBBONS, HERBERT ADAMS, *Introduction to World Politics.* New York: Century Co., 1922.

GIBBONS, HERBERT ADAMS, *The New Map of Asia.* New York: Century Co., 1919. Accounts which are correct in general, but which often err in detail due to the journalistic style and lack of extensive preparation.

GOOCH, G. P. and WARD, A. W., *Cambridge History of British Foreign Policy* (1783-1919). Cambridge: University press, 1922-23. Brief but reliable account dealing with China. Has a good bibliography.

GOWEN, HERBERT H., *A Short History of Asia.* Boston: Little, Brown, and Co., 1927. A reliable but brief account of Oriental History.

HORNBECK, STANLEY K., *Contemporary Politics in the Far East.* New York: D. Appleton, 1926. Has interesting material on the government of China and upon early 20th century developments.

International Encyclopaedia. Under subjects, China, Opium, and Tea.

KING-HALL, STEPHEN, *Western Civilization and the Far East.* London: Methuen, 1925. A brilliant account of recent developments showing their cultural causes and significances.

KIRKALDY, A. W., *British Shipping.* New York: E. P. Dutton, 1914. Has a good account of the development of shipping in the 19th century with a few chapters devoted to earlier centuries.

MOON, PARKER THOMAS, *Imperialism and World Politics.* New York: Macmillan, 1926. Perhaps the best recent exposition on imperialism with an excellent chapter on China.

NORTON, HENRY KITTRIDGE, *China and the Powers.* New York: John Day, 1927. An excellent recent work which reaches back into the cultural past for the roots of China's modern disorder.

PACKARD, LAURENCE BRADFORD, *The Commercial Revolution.* New York: Henry Holt Co., 1927. The latest interpretation of the Commercial Revolution and of Colbert's Mercantilism.

STEPHEN, LESLIE and LEE, SIDNEY (Editors), *Dictionary of National Biography.* New York: Macmillan, various dates. The standard work on English biography.

WILLOUGHBY, W. W., *Foreign Rights and Interests in China.* Baltimore: John Hopkins press, 1920. The best legal account of the foreign claims in China and their origin.

WILLOUGHBY, W. W., *Constitutional Government in China*, Washington, 1922. A discussion of the first attempt at constitutional government in China, with an explanation of its failure which looks into the features of former Chinese political organization.

3. PERIODICALS AND MAGAZINES

Annual Register. London: W. Otridge and Son. Modern publication by Longmans, Green Co., various dates. Helpful information is to be found scattered throughout the various yearly numbers.

Critical Review of Annals of Literature. London: A. Hamilton, v. 8, 1793, and v. 10, 1794. The volumes referred to have reviews of contemporary pamphlets defending and denouncing the East India Company.

Edinburgh Review. Edinburgh, 1810. Article in August number dealing with the Chinese Criminal Code.

New London Magazine. Vol. II. 1786. London: Alex. Hogg, 1786. "A Short and Accurate Sketch of the Settlements and Trade of the English in the East Indies, taken from the celebrated Abbé Raynal's History of the Europeans in the East and West-Indies." By G. Drake. pp. 240, 285, 366, 427, 455, 525, 573, 636.

4. BIBLIOGRAPHICAL MATERIAL

The books in this list all have valuable bibliographical material. Most of them have been mentioned previously so their titles will be abbreviated.

ABBOTT, *The Expansion of Europe.* In chapter form at end of book.

Cambridge Modern History, v. 11, Bibliography of chap. 28.

CORDIER, H., *Bibliotheca sinica; dictionnaire bibliographique des ouvrages relatifs à l'empire chinois.* 2nd ed., 5 vols. Paris, 1904-24.

CUNNINGHAM, *Growth of English Commerce and Industry: Modern Times.* At the end of part 2.

Encyclopaedia Britannica. After article on China.

GOOCH and WARD, *Cambridge History of British Foreign Policy.*

GOWEN and HALL, *An Outline History of China.* In the back.

GOWEN, *A Short History of Asia.* By chapters in the back.

HAYES, *Political and Social History of Modern Europe.* In vol. 2 at ends of chapters.

HAZEN, *Europe since 1815.* By chapters in the back.

KRAUSSE, *China in Decay.* Good bibliography in the back.

KRISHNA, *Commercial Relations between India and England.* In front.
LATOURETTE, *Development of China.* Classified bibliography in back.
Ibid., History of Christian Missions in China. In the back.
Ibid., History of the Early Relations between U. S. and China. In the back.
MORSE, *International Relations.* In the back of each volume are exceptionally good bibliographies.
ROBINSON, *Trade of the East India Company.* In the back.
SARGENT, *Anglo-Chinese Commerce and Diplomacy.* Exceptionally good bibliography in the back.
SCHAPIRO, *Modern and Contemporary Europe.* By chapters in the back.
SEE, *The Foreign Trade of China.* Exceptionally good bibliography in the back.
TREAT, *The Far East.* Splendid bibliography in the back.
WILLIAMS, E. T., *A Short History of China.* Excellent bibliographies given at the end of each chapter.
WYLIE, A., *Notes on Chinese Literature.* Shanghai, 1902.

INDEX